Jumpstart Your Music Career

Simon Cann

Course Technology PTR

A part of Cengage Learning

COURSE TECHNOLOGY
CENGAGE Learning·

Australia • Brazil • Japan • Korea • Mexico • Singapore • Spain • United Kingdom • United States

COURSE TECHNOLOGY
CENGAGE Learning

Jumpstart Your Music Career
Simon Cann

Publisher and General Manager, Course Technology PTR: Stacy L. Hiquet

Associate Director of Marketing: Sarah Panella

Manager of Editorial Services: Heather Talbot

Marketing Manager: Mark Hughes

Acquisitions Editor: Orren Merton

Project Editor/Copy Editor: Cathleen D. Small

Interior Layout Tech: MPS Limited, a Macmillan Company

Cover Designer: Luke Fletcher

Indexer: Kelly Talbot Editing Services

Proofreader: Kelly Talbot Editing Services

For product information and technology assistance, contact us at
Cengage Learning Customer & Sales Support, 1-800-354-9706

For permission to use material from this text or product, submit all requests online at **www.cengage.com/permissions**
Further permissions questions can be emailed to
permissionrequest@cengage.com

Library of Congress Control Number: 2011933239

ISBN-13: 978-1-4354-5952-6

ISBN-10: 1-4354-5952-0

Course Technology, a part of Cengage Learning
20 Channel Center Street
Boston, MA 02210
USA

Cengage Learning is a leading provider of customized learning solutions with office locations around the globe, including Singapore, the United Kingdom, Australia, Mexico, Brazil, and Japan. Locate your local office at: **international.cengage.com/region**

Cengage Learning products are represented in Canada by Nelson Education, Ltd.

For your lifelong learning solutions, visit **courseptr.com**

Visit our corporate website at **cengage.com**

Printed in the United States of America
1 2 3 4 5 6 7 13 12 11

Acknowledgments

This is the second edition of this book. I would like to thank everyone who bought the earlier edition of this book (published under the title *Building a Successful 21st Century Music Career*). Without your support, there would be no second edition.

I would also like to single out a few other people for special thanks:

- Orren Merton for commissioning this book and being an all-around good egg on the acquisitions editor front.

- Cathleen Small for her editorial work and guidance through the production.

- Mark Hughes for getting the book noticed.

- Stacy Hiquet and the rest of the Course Technology PTR family for all their great work.

- Richard Moody for all the many conversations we had over the years about building communities. I look forward to catching up with you for lunch sometime in December, Richard.

About the Author

Simon Cann is a musician and writer based in London. He is the author of a number of music-related and business-related books.

He worked for more than 15 years as a management consultant, where the clients he advised included global companies in the music, entertainment, and broadcasting industries, as well as companies in the financial services, aeronautical, pharmaceutical, and chemical sectors.

His music-related books include *How to Make a Noise*, *How to Make a Noise: iPad Synthesizers Edition*, *Becoming a Synthesizer Wizard: From Presets to Power User*, *Sample This!*, and *Rocking Your Music Business*. His business-related books feature the experiences of international entrepreneurs who have built successful companies in the hottest business locations around the world.

Get Connected

You can read more about Simon at his website: simoncann.com.

Check out Simon's music-related books at his Noise Sculpture website: noisesculpture.com.

If you do the Twitter thing, then follow Simon: twitter.com/simonpcann.

If you want to talk about this book, please drop by the Noise Sculpture Facebook page and say hi: facebook.com/noisesculpture.

Contents

PART II
THE FAN BASE   21

Chapter 2
Building and Keeping Your Fan Base   23

Chapter 3
Your Presence on the Web   65

PART III
THE PRODUCT   93

Chapter 4
Creating Products: Generating Income   95

Chapter 5
The Logistics of Creating and Developing Products   115

PART IV
THE NASTY COMMERCIAL BITS   149

Chapter 6
Economics 101   151

Chapter 9
Developing Your Own Career Plan

243

Getting Started

1 First Principles

It has never been so easy to have a career in music.

- Barriers to entry have never been lower. Gear is cheaper than it has ever been and can produce higher quality results, the need for musical skills are low (although skill can help, but technology can do more), and the cost of distribution is close to zero.

- The access to fans—and the ways to find fans—have never been easier.

- The options to generate income (and to transmit money into your bank account) have never been more plentiful.

So why isn't everyone who makes music a multimillionaire?

There is probably a range of reasons for everyone who has "failed" to make a living making music. For instance, they may be awful, they may have gotten ripped off, or they may have had difficulty standing out from the crowd.

I can't stop you being awful and having no talent. I can't stop you from failing. However, I *can* suggest a few reasons why many people do not have the career in music that they want—and while it may sound glib, those reasons are quite simple:

- A failure to connect with and nurture a fan base.

- A failure to take responsibility. If you don't have a better idea of how your career should be run than anyone else has, then you won't be successful. Taking responsibility for making the decisions and living with the consequences is tough, but it's a crucial part of being successful.

- No strategy to achieve the objective. Too many people hope or wish—they don't sit down and plan each and every step that is necessary to take them from their present position to the place they want to be.

- Once started on the path, people often don't stick to their objective. In other words, they give up too easily, which isn't surprising when they don't have a strategy that will get them to where they want to be. And of course, very often, life gets in the way.

Now please don't misconstrue the point I'm trying to make here. I'm not suggesting that it is easy to be successful, that you don't need to work hard (you do, very), that anyone who isn't successful is a personal failure, or that you can be a multimillionaire within a few days. However, I'm stating that it is possible to earn a living by making music, provided you set about that goal with a businesslike approach and have reasonable ambitions.

The purpose of this book is to set out ways that you can proactively start, develop, and manage your own music career so that you can earn your living by making music—whether as a musician playing pop, rock, soul, R&B, classical, or any other style of music; as a songwriter; or as a composer.

In short, this is a "how to" book: I am assuming that you have the musical talent—or if you don't have the talent yet, that you are actively improving your skills.

Do You Really Want a Career in Music?

I was watching one of those reality TV talent shows where all-comers have the chance of winning a £1,000,000 record deal. The show had reached the initial public auditions (which are mostly stuffed with the deluded and the talentless).

One guy who turned up for an audition was interviewed outside the venue, where he proudly showed off his car. He obviously had spent a lot of time working on his car (or "pimping his ride," to use the vernacular that I'm sure would appeal to this guy). This interview led me to an obvious question: What is this guy's passion? Music or his car?

I suspect neither. I suspect his passion is for chasing women, and he sees his car and music as being two ways to achieve his aim.

Now, please do not misconstrue the point I am trying to make. I'm not suggesting that chasing women (and/or men) is wrong. I am simply asking what the priority is in this guy's life: women, cars, or music? My suspicion is music comes third on his list.

I think there are two easy tests for this guy to check out his commitment to a music career:

- Test 1: Compare how much money he has spent on his car to how much money he has spent on his music career.

- Test 2: Compare how much time he has invested in his car to how much time he has invested in his music career.

From the sound of his audition, he has never had a singing lesson in his life. I would also guess that he has never spent any of his cash getting inside a recording studio with a hot producer to lay down some tracks.

If I'm right, and music is third on this guy's list, then music is not a priority for him. Music is either a priority that comes at the top of the list, or it's not a priority. If it's not a priority, then a career in music is probably never going to happen.

So what matters to you—your music career or something else?

Are you passionate about music? Are you committed to your music career? Or is music something that comes way down on the list after work, study, home, family, friends, and your other hobbies?

And when you actually get around to music, what are you doing then? Are you spending your time setting up your computer so that it runs your newest piece of software without a hitch? (And when it doesn't work, are you spending countless hours talking to several software developers, trying to get to the root of the problems and then testing new fixes?) Or, are you getting out there and actually furthering your career?

If music is something you do for fun, that's great. However, don't pretend you want it to be a career if it's just something you do for fun. Please carry on enjoying your music—you may even find you make some money from an activity that brings you pleasure. However, please do not kid yourself that you are trying to pursue a career in music if you aren't prepared to make the commitment to sustain your livelihood.

If you are certain you want a career in music, you'll need to deal with all areas of the business if you are to succeed. Realistically, you cannot spend every waking hour making music: Time spent not making music is time you will need to spend on business matters. If you are going to have a career in music, what you are actually deciding is to set up a business, where the product of that business is music and you are the chief executive officer. If you're not ready for the realities of setting up a business, then you're not ready to have a career in music.

I would not expect you to have the same passion for the business aspects as you do for the music. However, you will need to have a similar level of commitment. If you can't commit to doing the business side or ensuring that there is someone to attend to the business side on your behalf, then your musical career will fail.

After this rather harsh introduction, I am going to ask what may seem an odd question: Do you really want a career in music? Take a moment and think about what it means and how you can achieve it. Now, are you really sure you want it?

If you are sure, then answer me a few questions:

- What are you passionate about? Do you have a passion to be a writer or a performer? Are you interested in the fame and the adulation, or are you just chasing the money and women/men?

- Can you live with the lack of security and especially the perilous state in which your finances are likely to be?

- Do you have a husband/wife/significant other? Do you have kids? What are their attitudes about this? Are they happy with the risks you want to take? How will your relationship with these people be affected by a career in music?

If you're still convinced that you want a career in music after you've thought about some of these issues, great. If you're not convinced, then get a proper job. It will give you far more financial security and probably a much larger income, as well as a pension and healthcare coverage (if you're lucky). If you're not 100 percent committed, then why would anyone else want to help you with your career (or risk their career on working with you)?

So, if you're sure that you want a career in music, when does it begin?

That's an easy question: Your music career begins whenever you decide it should begin.

You don't need permission to start your career. Heck, no one is going to give you permission. You don't need endorsement by a manager or a record company. You don't need to wait for someone to give you a contract. You just need to decide that your career has started and then take responsibility for making it happen.

So if it hasn't already started, then your career in music begins today. And once you have made your decision to start your career, the hard work begins.

This book is a guide to the hard work: the practicalities of how you take the decision that you want a career in music and make it happen.

Even if your music career has already begun, this book is still for you. It is aimed at everyone who wants to earn a living making music: musicians, including singers (of course); aspiring musicians; TV talent show contestants; songwriters; beat creators; and music students.

Fundamentals

So what do you need to do to have a music career?

The reality is quite straightforward (see Figure 1.1). All you need is an audience—in other words, someone to buy your records—and you're set.

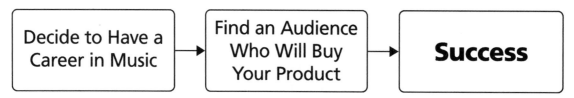

Figure 1.1   The key to success is blindingly straightforward: All you need is an audience who will buy your music. No audience = no career.

You really do need to get your head around the simplicity of what you need to survive. All you need is a source of income, and then you will have a career. If you like formulas, then let me express it in simple terms: no audience = no income = no career.

You don't need a record company, you don't need a publishing contract, and you don't need a manager—all you need is an audience. At the end of the day, the audience, the fans, or whatever you want to call them are the only people who matter, because they will be funding your career. Without an audience, you will not have any income, and you will have no career.

This book is about the hard work needed to make your music career happen. It is about the hard work that you need to undertake to acquire and keep an audience, and all you need to do that is a strategy.

An Introduction to the Business Strategy for the Musician

Business strategy? For the musician? This sounds boring, and it sounds like work.

However, you have a choice here (yes, another choice): Do you want a career in music, or do you want to find a job and become a wage slave?

If you want a career in music, then you'll have to understand the business aspects. When you're starting out, you will be dealing with the business aspects directly. As you progress and bring in other people to help you with your career, it is important to understand the business side of things so that you can keep control and ensure you don't get ripped off (especially when you are dealing with "experts").

Once you have decided to have a career in music, then you need to dedicate the necessary time and energy (that is, all of your time and all of your energy) to making your career happen. I will go into this in more detail throughout the book, but let me give you a brief introduction to the process you need to follow to have a successful music career:

■ The first step is to create a product. When I say "product," I mean something that can be delivered in some form to an audience and that can generate income. This product could be a song (or a collection of songs) packaged as a live performance, as a CD/download, or as a video.

■ When you have your product, then you need to start finding your audience. These are the people who will buy (or consume) your product.

■ You then need to start generating an income from your audience. In other words, you need to create products your audience wants to either buy or consume in a manner that generates income.

■ Once you have established your audience that is consuming your product, you need to keep your audience. It is so much easier to sell to an existing fan than to find a new fan to sell to. As well as keeping your audience, you should look to expand it. An expanded audience will give you:

 ● More people to buy your new products

 ● A new source of people to buy your existing products

- Once you have more people to buy your new products, you need to fire up the factory and develop new/updated products so that your audience can keep buying and remain as fans. Without new products, you will lose the relationship with your audience.

- When you have an audience, then you need to interact with them. The easiest way to contact them directly will probably be by email, but don't rule out snail mail and the phone (especially cell/mobile phones with which you can send SMS/text messages to a list of people). However, there are many other ways to stay in touch, in particular through Twitter, Facebook, YouTube, and other social media conduits, which are becoming an increasingly important element of the strategy of musicians.

Figure 1.2 shows a simple way to start thinking about your business strategy.

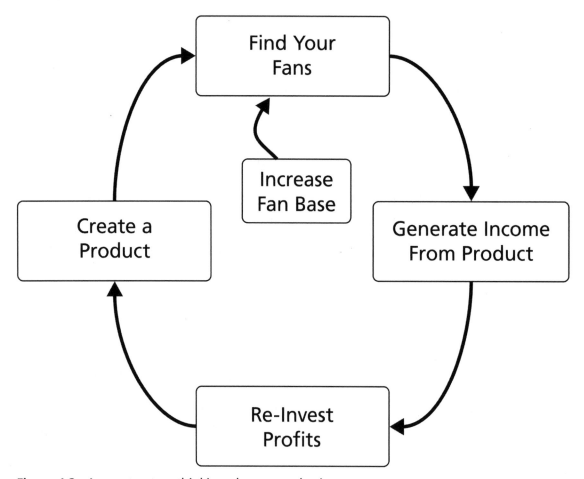

Figure 1.2 A way to start thinking about your business strategy.

One decision you will have to make is where you intend your income to come from. For instance, you could decide that you are purely a live musician, and so your income will be generated solely from live performances. (In other words, you will get your income from the tickets purchased by punters at the gig door.)

Surviving on live gigs alone is likely to be tough, so you might decide you want to sell CDs too, but only CD albums because CD singles smack of a sellout, and you don't want to mess with downloads. You may also feel comfortable with some merchandising: T-shirts and souvenir programs, perhaps. Then again, you may want to go all the way and generate income from as many (legal) sources as possible, such as all merchandising options (including, perhaps, dolls that look like you), sponsorship deals, and endorsements.

What you decide to do is up to you. For the purpose of this book, I will assume that you will consider any income-generating source, but at least initially, the range of sources is likely to be restricted. (For instance, if the band only started last week, then you're unlikely to be able to secure an endorsement with a major clothing label…but please don't let me discourage you if you've got something great to offer.)

I would actually go a step further and suggest that you have a range of different income sources—some of which require action by you (for instance, live performances), and others of which do not (such as download sales). By generating income from a range of sources, you will:

- First, increase the amount you can earn.

- Second, and perhaps more importantly, immunize yourself against one specific market dying.

Why Adopt a Business Strategy?

Now that we've had a brief look at the main thrust of the strategy, let me give you some of the logic behind this strategy and some of the reasons why you should consider it.

- First, this strategy will help you become profitable (and stay profitable). At its most basic, being profitable means you can generate an income to live on. If there are no profits, then there is no money to buy stuff like food…

- This strategy will make you more desirable. If you have a solid business that can generate income, then people will want to work with you. This will mean that instead of approaching industry types, such as managers, record companies, and booking agents, saying "We think we're going to be huge," you can approach them with proof of how much money you can already generate. Once you start demonstrating how much you can earn for your business partners, you will be in a better negotiating position.

- Your career will last much longer. Instead of being a packaged commodity that is hot today and cold tomorrow (and immediately dropped by a label or other partners), by looking after your fan base, you can expect to continue to make money from your music throughout your working life. You will not be on the shelf at the age of 30 (and left with the prospect of having to find a proper job to support the husband/wife and kids).

- You can cut out the middleman. For instance, if you have your own fan base and you know they will all turn up to your gig, then why do you need a promoter for your gig? As you will read later on, if your promoter can bring more people to a gig, that's great; however, if you have already reached all of your fans (and potential fans), then do you need someone else taking a cut?

Your Guarantee of Success

In the strategy I have outlined, there is one guarantee of success: your audience.

You don't need talent, you don't need connections, but you *do* need an audience. Without somebody being there to buy or consume your product, you will not have income. Without an income, you cannot put food on the table or keep a roof over your head.

I will repeat this point: The only guarantee of success is your audience.

When you have an audience, your talent does not matter. You may have a voice that makes dogs howl and only be able to play your instrument with one finger (and then not in time—not that the concept of 4/4 time is understood by your drummer). Your shortcomings don't matter, provided that your audience loves you.

If you have an audience, you will have income and you will have power. Your income means that people will be interested in you. (If nothing else, they will work out what commission they can generate based on your income.) Your income also means that you will have power to negotiate—you will be able to walk away from deals because you already have your own income.

However, I caution you against being too talentless. Although your audience may love you today, will they love you tomorrow? In six months' time, will they realize that you are a talentless bunch of no-hopers whose songs all sound the same? If you want a long career, you can't be a novelty act—you need a credible product that will continue selling.

Defining Success

One thing I want to talk about before we go any further is success and what success actually means. There is something of a clichéd view about what success means in the music industry. Many people associate success with multi-platinum albums, huge tours, vast income, many huge properties, substance abuse, and a lot of sexual intercourse. In particular, many people think a career in music equates to riches behind their wildest dreams. This may happen for one or two people; for instance, with assets of around £495 million (around $825 million), Paul McCartney hasn't done too badly for himself.

However, in any field of human endeavor, some people make a lot of money, but most people do not. Outside of music, those who do not make the huge dollars will still usually earn enough to live a comfortable existence.

I do not wish to discourage you if you have an ambition for a multimillion-dollar income. In fact, I would positively encourage you. If you can follow the principles in this book and become a multimillionaire, then please tell me and please tell everyone else. I'm sure the kudos will increase sales of this book. However, I do want you to think a bit about what you want to achieve with a career in the music industry (beyond frequent, guilt-free sexual intercourse) and exactly how much money you need (rather than want).

The nature of success is hard to define and is personal for everyone. I'm sure we've all known of, or have heard about, miserable millionaires and joyful paupers. In thinking about your career, I encourage you to consider your reasonable expectations from a career in music—don't just think about how much the top stars earned last year (see Figure 1.3). Once you have your expectations, then you can start planning your career and ensure that those expectations will be included in your plan.

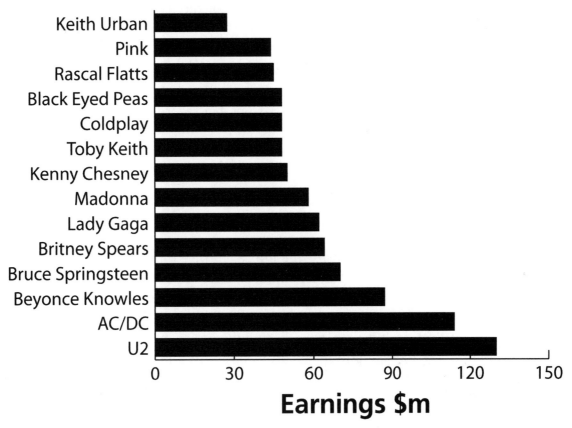

Figure 1.3 Earnings of mega-millions will always hit the headlines. (The figures in this graph come from *Forbes* magazine and show earning during 2010.) But how much do you really need to earn to consider yourself successful?

Here are some of the expectations you may want to consider:

■ A career in music that spans the rest of your working life (or until you want to end your career in music).

■ The freedom to make the type of music you want to make without compromise.

- Sufficient income to provide for your family and loved ones, and for you all to be able to live in comfort.

- The ability to control your life and make the decisions you want to make (for instance, to be able to spend time with your kids when you want to and when they need you).

- Sufficient income to save for your retirement so you will still be able to buy food when the music stops.

- A flow of income from your music after you have ceased to be active in the industry. That is income from music, not from savings.

As I said, the nature of success is personal. However, for me, a career in which you can earn a living doing what you want to do seems pretty much perfect.

Why the Emphasis on Being Proactive? I Just Wanna Play Music!

If you would prefer to sit around and wait for some big record-company executive to call you and offer you a deal, please feel free to stop reading now and put down this book. However, if you don't take control of your music career and make it happen, then it is almost certain never to come about.

There are many other compelling reasons for following the approach I'm advocating here.

Own the Relationship

The first and most significant reason for the approach that I am advocating is that it puts the relationship between you, the artist, and the fan at its heart. No one else but you, the artist, can have a relationship with your fans. No one else but you can create and maintain this relationship. You wouldn't expect to get married and then ask someone else to have a relationship with your husband/wife, so why is it acceptable for musicians to ignore the most important relationship in their professional lives?

If you ignore this relationship or leave it to someone else, then eventually your fan base (and remember, your fan base equals your income) will walk away feeling as if they have had cash stolen out of their pockets.

Economies of Small

We're used to talking about the economies of scale. And it's true; there are many economies to be gained at scale. However, what people think less about is the economies of small—in other words, the things that small organizations can achieve that big organizations cannot.

Once organizations get above a certain size, their overheads grow disproportionately—they have to pay for property, there are staff employed in administration, there are pension costs, and so on. In short, once a company reaches a certain size, it needs to generate a certain level of income just to stay alive.

By contrast, the small organization—and your music career will be a small organization—has much lower overhead. This means you can:

■ Generate a smaller income, but

■ Achieve a higher profit.

In short, you can make a living where it would not be economically viable for others—in particular, it would not be viable for others with higher overheads because of the deals they have entered into.

Control

Another reason for following the ideas in this book is that you keep control (see Figure 1.4).

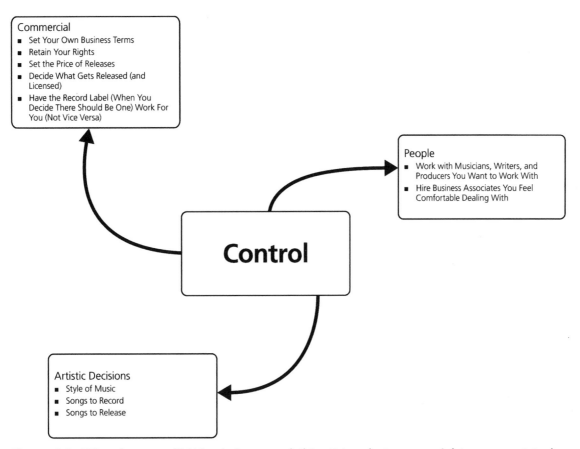

Commercial
■ Set Your Own Business Terms
■ Retain Your Rights
■ Set the Price of Releases
■ Decide What Gets Released (and Licensed)
■ Have the Record Label (When You Decide There Should Be One) Work For You (Not Vice Versa)

People
■ Work with Musicians, Writers, and Producers You Want to Work With
■ Hire Business Associates You Feel Comfortable Dealing With

Control

Artistic Decisions
■ Style of Music
■ Songs to Record
■ Songs to Release

Figure 1.4 What is control? Why is it a good thing? In what areas might you want to have control?

Control is one of those vague terms that musicians usually waffle over without really having any idea of what it means, so let me list some of the areas where you get to have control:

- **Artistic control.** You can write the songs you want, you can record the songs you want to record, and then you can release the songs you want to release.

- **Deals.** You are in control of every deal. You don't need to sign away any rights. You won't hear your song used in a TV advertisement for hemorrhoid cream (unless, of course, you want to and you are being financially rewarded).

- **People.** You can deal with the people you want to deal with (and when you want to deal with them). If there is a producer whom you have always wanted to work with, if you have control you can hire that person (provided he wants to work with you). Equally, if there is anyone with whom you wish to collaborate, you can—provided she is willing.

In short, control means you decide every who, what, where, when, and how in connection with your career. In particular, you decide when your career begins and how it is run.

The other great benefit of having control is that the chances of you getting ripped off are reduced. If you have control over all aspects of your business, then there will be far fewer opportunities for shady characters to take a slice of your income.

The Commercial Imperative

Talking about the commercial aspects of the music business is not very rock and roll. But remember, what *is* very rock and roll is ending up heartbroken and busted with no money.

There are certain basic human necessities: food and shelter, to name two. In the capitalist world, you need money to procure food and shelter. I therefore presume you are happy with the basic concept that you need to generate money from your musical endeavors if you are going to eat and pay for a roof over your head.

However, we need to go further than just accepting that you need money to buy food. If you're not going to pay attention to the business end of the business, then how are you going to know if/when you're being ripped off?

You also need to ensure that you (and your partners) are financially credible individuals—in other words, you're not blacklisted with credit agencies or bankrupt. If you lack credibility, then you will find it hard to deal with the banks, which in this wired-up world could be quite a challenge. You will find it hard to use cash or barter if you're trying to sell your music to someone on the other side of the world.

Adopting the Strategies Set Out in This Book

Beyond owning the relationship with your audience, there is no one way or magical formula to ensure a successful music career, so this book sets out lots of separate ideas. It is up to you how you put these pieces together. How you do so will depend on what you want to achieve and your particular circumstances. You will see that the final part of this book (Part V, "Putting the Theory into Practice") is dedicated to looking at different ways that you can manage your career.

This flexibility is good news: It gives you many more chances to forge a successful career. However, the range of options also means that you have greater freedom to make mistakes. Although it might be unlikely that you will get anything wrong as such, you are far more likely to do things in the wrong order. We all know that you shouldn't learn to walk before you can crawl, and this principle applies equally here. For instance, you shouldn't release a DVD if you don't have an audience ready to buy it.

As we progress through the book, you will see that there are certain recurring themes. Often I will look at these themes from different angles so you can see how one idea can be applied in several different ways or in different situations.

There are, however, certain principles that are not negotiable. The principles I see as being set in stone are:

- Cut the expenses of doing business as far as you can (and in particular, cut your expenses).

- Cut out the middleman (or middle-woman) as far as possible, but do not ignore people who can make you more profitable.

- Make a living by generating income over a longer period. Don't look to make a million immediately and then walk away (if you want that, then buy lottery tickets); instead, aim to generate income over your whole career.

This is unashamedly a book about business: My intention is that you will create an ethical, sustainable business. As part of this goal, I focus on how to foster organic growth of your business. I do look at some of the more "hard sell" tactics you can use, but over the longer term, I don't believe these tactics create a sustainable business, so I have given less importance to them.

Getting the Most from This Book

There are many opportunities for a musician to carve his or her own career. This book is not a guess about the future—it is about how you can make money and survive now.

The book discusses a range of music business and general business principles. It brings forward a range of tried and tested working practices and combines them with the new opportunities and thinking that are available in the twenty-first century. The combination of tried and tested with new thinking will help you to be successful.

While reading this book, I suggest you keep a pen, a highlighter, and a supply of those little yellow sticky notes close by and mark any areas that are of interest to you. These notes should make it easier to refer back to this book when you are drawing up your own strategy. I also suggest that you re-read this book (perhaps after 12 months) when you want to review or revise your strategy. You may find that ideas that didn't work earlier are now worth considering.

Before you start reading, let me offer you a few thoughts about the information in this book. If you are of an impatient nature, then skip over the rest of this chapter and start reading Chapter 2, "Building and Keeping Your Fan Base." However, if you skip ahead, please do come back and read some of these words of caution at a later date.

Each chapter in this book is intended to be freestanding. You don't need to read it from start to end, although you will find the content does flow more logically if you do. There are five parts, and you may find this book easier to digest if you take the chapters in each part together.

Each of the five parts has its own distinct focus.

- **Part I, "Getting Started."** This part introduces the main themes and ideas that are then applied throughout the book.

- **Part II, "The Fan Base."** This part looks at your most important asset (your fan base) and considers how to nurture these people for your and their mutual benefit.

- **Part III, "The Product."** This part considers the things you do that make money and discusses how to do these so that (a) your fans are happy and (b) you make money.

- **Part IV, "The Nasty Commercial Bits."** This part looks at the whole money issue—in particular, what money you can make and where it comes from.

- **Part V, "Putting the Theory into Practice."** This final part takes all of the ideas discussed in the book and shows how you can mix and match the concepts to create your own successful music career.

You will see that I have cross-referenced between chapters. I have also overlapped the content where this aids the understanding (or where the need for emphasis justifies the repetition).

There are a few other points I would like you to think about before you proceed.

Changing Times

It's always good to throw in a cliché as early as possible, so let me throw you my first...

We are now living in a time when the only constant is change, and as the world around us develops, this book will go out of date. This book was written in the middle of 2011, and all examples quoted were current and relevant at that time. For instance, there is currently a declining market for CDs. I don't know where the CD market will be in one year's time, let alone five or ten years.

My hunch is the CD market will continue to decline as the download market exerts its dominance. However, my hunch about the future is irrelevant: Because most projections about the future turn out to be wrong, this book deals solely with the here and now. In reading this book and applying the principles, you need to consider changes that may have taken place since the book was written.

To give you an example of something that may change, look at the cost of CD reproduction. When CDs first came out, the reproduction costs were comparatively high. Today, the reproduction costs have fallen. My guess is the costs will continue to fall; however, that is a guess. If you are going to produce your own CD, you need to find the costs that will apply to you. The price you will pay will depend on many factors, including the number of CDs to be produced, the printing (on the CD and the booklet), and the location of the reproduction plant (you will find that costs in different countries and different cities within a country vary enormously).

Regional Variations

I'm a Brit, and some of the data and examples quoted in this book come from UK sources. Where I'm quoting UK sources, the principles can be applied globally. However, there will be times when I quote UK data in order to highlight regional variations, and in these situations I will note that I am highlighting the variation.

To give you an example of regional variations, think about touring. Mainland United Kingdom is a few hundred miles in each direction (roughly 400 miles wide and 600 miles high). Within that area there is a population of 60 million people. By contrast, Australia has a population of around 20 million people but is roughly 3,000 miles wide and 2,000 miles high. The implications for physically reaching an audience if you are touring make the UK a far more efficient location.

However, if you look at gasoline (petrol) costs and compare the UK and the US, then the US is a much better place if you're using road transportation.

I know my American friends think that you all pay a lot for gas, but what you pay is nothing compared to what we pay in Europe. At the moment (subject to regional variations within both countries), the price of gasoline in the U.S. is around $4.26 per gallon (which is nearly twice the level it was five years ago). By contrast, the price for a liter of petrol in the UK is around £1.40.

Converting liters to U.S. gallons (1 liter = 0.2642 gallons) and pounds to dollars (at the rate of $1 = £0.60), petrol in the UK is equivalent to nearly $8.83 per gallon—in other words, more than two times the price. This has implications for touring in the UK and Europe (where fuel costs are similar).

I am not going to look at all possible regional variations, because that would really get to be tiresome. Instead, I suggest that you make sure you understand how each factor discussed in this book can be affected by your local market conditions.

I should also point out that laws vary by country (and state). Please ensure that you make yourself aware of any legal requirements that apply to you.

What This Book Does Not Cover

This book is about how to develop and maintain a successful career in music. I have assumed a certain level of understanding/knowledge, and that you have the common sense to figure out how to make certain things happen. So for instance, this book does not explain:

- How to write a song

- How to sing in tune

- How to find gigs (although I will talk about ways to use gigs to increase the size of your fan base)

- How to get a CD pressed and the legal requirements associated with releasing a commercial recording

- How to commission artwork for a poster and the necessary copyrights you should obtain in order to use the artwork.

Things You Don't Understand

We shouldn't go any further without a word of caution: Be wary of things you don't understand.

For instance, I don't understand eBay. This is not a matter that I'm stupid—I can write a book, so I figure I must have a certain level of intelligence—however, I have never bought or sold anything on eBay; therefore, I don't have the understanding that comes with experience in conducting a transaction on eBay. My perception, which is probably wrong and prejudiced, is that eBay is a place where other people sell their unwanted tat. I've got enough tat of my own without being taken in by my ignorance of the whole eBay process.

Now, I'm not suggesting you shouldn't do anything that you haven't done before. But rather, I'm suggesting that you recognize the things you don't know (such as eBay for me), acknowledge this piece of learning that you still have to do, and proceed with caution (see Figure 1.5). If you're going to do something new, research it first. Once you've researched it, try it in a small-scale way. Once you have some experience, refine what you're doing in light of that experience, and then go for it in a big way.

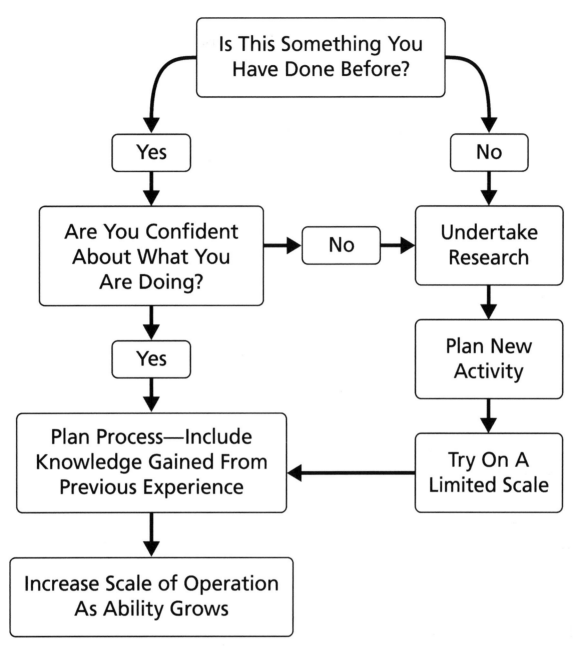

Figure 1.5 If you have never done something before, start small and learn. Even if you have done something before, always be sure to keep improving what you are doing as you gain experience.

Whatever you do, please don't risk your whole career and financial stability on something that only *sounds* like a good idea.

Scalability

It is common sense that you should start small. In that way you will be less likely to make disastrous financial mistakes. However, you should always be sufficiently flexible to grow. Sometimes your system may be able to grow with you, and sometimes you may have to completely change what you are doing.

For instance, you might start off by sending out T-shirts by hand. If you are sending 10 or 20 T-shirts a week, that is quite feasible. However, if you suddenly have to send out 10,000 T-shirts, then you may have difficulties (although having an order for 10,000 T-shirts does sound like a nice problem to have).

You should also remember that you don't have to employ only one solution for any problem. For instance, you can sell T-shirts at gigs but engage someone else (such as a fulfillment service, which I will discuss later) to send out your internet/mail orders.

Products and Services

Throughout this book, I make reference to various products and services. The mentions I make are not endorsements. I only mention these to illustrate the range of products/ services that are available. As always, you should undertake your own due diligence and only choose a product/service once you understand what you are taking on.

Onward…

This chapter has introduced some of the main ideas that are discussed in this book. The remainder of the book fleshes out those ideas and looks at how you can implement them in a practical manner.

So if you're ready, let's move on to Part II, "The Fan Base," and talk about the most important part of your career.

The Fan Base

2 Building and Keeping Your Fan Base

At all times, you need to remember one thing: your fan base = your source of income. In other words, you need your fan base in order to have a career.

It goes without saying that in order to sustain your career, you need to sustain your relationship with your fan base, and that relationship should be deep and broad. You should be interacting with your fan base in many different ways, and equally, you should be looking to derive income from your fan base from a range of different products.

This chapter looks at how to build—and sustain—a community around you in order to have a successful music career.

Before we jump in, one quick point. You can't necessarily pigeonhole every activity under a specific heading—sometimes, indeed often, one action will have several results. Let me give you an example: Say you create a video and post it on YouTube. This could achieve several ends:

- First, it could generate income for you.

- Second, it may generate income for someone else who embeds it on his or her site and sells advertising around it.

- Third, it is a potentially excellent piece of marketing.

- Fourth, it might be a catalyst to help you communicate and interact with your fan base.

You get the idea… Accordingly, there is some overlap between the topics discussed in this part and the next, and please don't think that just because something has one purpose, it can't have a benefit in other areas.

Exploiting with Integrity

The key route to sustained success is through marshaling a large fan base and using the attention and the spending power of the fan base. Any artist with a large fan base can:

- Generate income by selling products to the fan base.

- Generate income by directing the fan base's interest. (This sounds cryptic—in straightforward terms, what I mean here is selling advertising.)

- Negotiate with third parties (such as major record companies) from a position of strength (due to the spending power of the fan base it can bring with it).

There will never be a situation in which you as an artist do not need a fan base (of some sort).

The fan base is also the best sales force and ambassador for any artist, as well as being a harsh critic when an act fouls up. If an artist abuses the trust of his fan base, then the relationship with his fan base is over. This could even mean the end of the artist's career.

And while we're talking about the possible end of an artist's career, before we go any further, I want to quickly talk about the use of the word "exploit" (and its variants).

You may be quite uncomfortable with the use of the word—I am sure you don't want to do anything as ruthless as exploiting your fellow human beings. It's good to be uncomfortable with this concept; it shows you are a caring human being who hasn't lost your integrity.

As you know, the word "exploit" has two main interpretations:

- To benefit unjustly or unfairly from a situation.

- To make full use of and derive benefit from.

I am using the term in the second interpretation; in other words, I'm talking about how you can make full use of your fan base and derive a benefit from that use. The benefit you will derive will be more than just financial.

I could use a different term. However, I have chosen to use the word "exploit" to remind you that there is the possibility for you to overstep a line. To my mind, the key in exploiting the fan base is to remember that you are in a relationship, that each party in the relationship needs to benefit, and that the benefit needs to be roughly equal for each side. As Figure 2.1 shows, each party expects something from the relationship—that's why I talk about exploiting with integrity.

What Can Your Fan Base Do for You?

For an artist, the fan base is everything. Among other things, a fan base will bring you:

- Income

- Power and influence

- Credibility

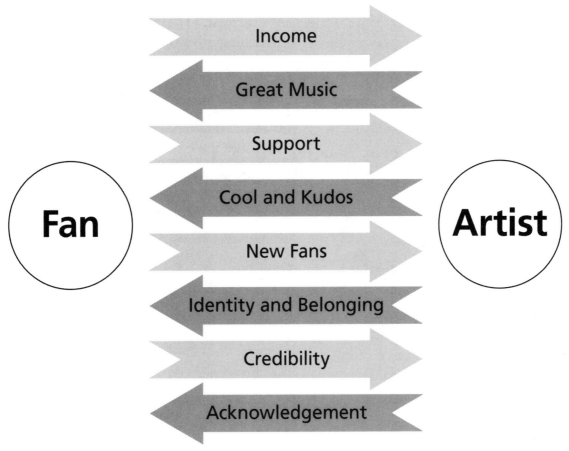

Figure 2.1 Both fans and artists expect something from their relationship with each other.

- Support at gigs
- New fans
- Radio/TV coverage/chart position

In short, nothing else really matters apart from the fan base.

Let's look at these benefits in turn.

Income

The central chunk of your income (see Figure 2.2) to support your career will come from your fan base. They will do the things that bring you money, such as buy CDs/ DVDs/downloads and merchandise, as well as come to your gigs.

There are other potential sources of income out there (for instance, from television or sponsorship). These other sources are particularly significant if you don't have a fan base or if you don't have a significant fan base. However, without a fan base, you are beholden to other people (such as music supervisors) to decide to use your work (and so generate income).

Figure 2.2 It's all about money. You need it; other people have it. You need to find a way to encourage them to give it to you.

Even if you already make your income from other sources (for instance, you may already compose music for video games), there is no reason not to start to develop your own fan base. It will give you several advantages:

- You will be able to sell your services more easily, provided you can demonstrate to potential employers that they will sell more of their product by using your services. (You need to use a "hire me, and I bring a following" type of argument.)

- You will be able to capitalize on your reputation for creating music when you start selling your product. So, for instance, if you release your music, you will be able to market it with the line "from the creator of the music for [whatever your game was]."

- Far more importantly, you will develop an independent source (or sources) of income. You will be reliant on your own efforts for the income you generate, rather than relying on your paycheck as an employee.

In short, the fan base is the source of income for a musician. Although there are other sources of income, as a general rule of thumb, no fan base equates to no money. An unhappy fan base or one that feels exploited (in the bad sense of the word) will lead to a severe reduction in income.

I will discuss the many sources of income later in the book.

Credibility

If you're in the music business (whether as a manager, a record company, a gig promoter, a journalist, or whoever), who are you going to take more seriously—an artist who performs a gig in a bar every month or so, or an artist who has sold 1,000,000 CDs? Having a fan base converts potential into fact. In other words, once you have a fan base, you are a credible person (or group of people) to deal with.

Record companies only want to sign you for what can be sold. If no one is going to buy your recordings, then you won't get signed. If you already have an audience, then you are a proven quantity. This principle applies for any business relationship you may have.

Power and Influence

A step forward from having credibility is having power and influence. Credibility will get you through the door and bring you to the negotiating table. Power and influence mean that you can cut the deals that you want to cut on your terms.

When you speak on behalf of your fans (or, more to the point, when you speak on behalf of their wallets), you can start to shape your business.

Support at Gigs

Imagine a gig at which no one turns up. Imagine a gig at which people turn up but stay in their seats and clap very politely after each song (or don't even clap).

Now imagine a gig at which the audience turns up, sings along with the songs, shouts out for their favorites, goes wild at the end of each song, demands an encore, and then crowds around the stage door after the show is over.

Which would you prefer? I think Figure 2.3 has the answer.

Figure 2.3 They turn up to your gig, they sing along with the songs, they shout out for the favorites, they go wild at the end of each song, and they give you money for this. Gotta love your fan base.

New Fans

One of the best ways to grow your fan base is through word of mouth. Your fan base will work as a combination of your sales force and your ambassador.

Your fans will reach more potential fans than you ever can. More to the point, potential new fans are more likely to listen to the opinion of a trusted friend than they are to listen to the words of an advertisement that appears to be trying to sell a dodgy product.

Radio/TV Coverage/Chart Position

One way to get radio and TV coverage is for people to call and ask for your song to be played. A good fan base will do this for you, creating a lot of buzz about your newest releases without incurring any costs for you.

Another way to get publicity is to get on the charts. If nothing else, this will get you heard on the chart shows.

The band Marillion took a novel approach to get their single "You're Gone" onto the charts. They asked their fans to buy the single during a specific week (and encouraged fans to buy more than one copy). The fans did, and the single entered the charts at number 7, Marillion's highest chart placing for nearly 20 years.

This created quite a buzz about the single. First, Marillion were back on the charts for the first time in many years. Second, there was the story of how the band marshaled their fans to get their chart placing.

Your Fans' Expectations: What Can You Do for Your Fan Base?

We've looked at some of the things a fan base can do for you. Let's now look at the other side of the coin: What can you do for your fans?

Remember that we're trying to create a relationship with the fan base. We want a loyal fan base who will purchase our product (and not just once) and who will act as our ambassadors to increase the size of our product-buying fan base.

We want to exploit (in a good way) the resource that is the fan base. To do this, you need to have a deep understanding of what your fans expect in return for what they give you. Think of a marriage in which each partner brings something different to the relationship. The same principle can be applied to the relationship (or hopefully marriage) between artist and fan.

One thing that might help to focus your mind on the fan base is to think of these individuals as your clients who purchase your services. Most service providers will have a contract with their clients, setting out the rights and responsibilities, as well as the legitimate expectations of both parties and the measures of success. Although you will never have such a formal relationship with your clients (your fan base), take a moment or two to think about the terms that could be included in a contract with your fans.

What legitimate/reasonable expectations could your fan base have? These are many and varied and will depend on the nature of your act. However, there are likely to be some common themes, which probably include:

- **Great music, whether live or recorded.** There is never any excuse for giving a poor performance or releasing a bad track.

- **New products to buy.** Fans want new things to buy. One CD every 10 years isn't going to be good enough. They want regular recordings (without compromising the quality of your output). They want live DVDs. They want T-shirts so they can show the rest of the world that they love your music and share your values.

- **Regular products to consume.** As well as things to buy, fans will also expect to see activity on your part. For instance, they will want to read interviews by you and see videos of your performances, and they will expect you to tell them when (and where) these interviews/videos and so on are available.

- **A relationship.** Fans want to have a relationship with the artists they follow. They want to feel that they can "touch" (in a metaphorical sense, and sometimes in a real sense) the acts they follow. In short, they want contact with real human beings. This can be achieved in many ways:
  - Often, just reading or seeing an interview will give a fan a sense of the human beings who make the music that moves them.
  - Technology affords many opportunities to interact. For instance, you can send your fan base an occasional email. However, there are many better options for keeping in touch through social media. (For instance, Twitter and Facebook give you the opportunity to keep in touch and to interact on a regular basis while also building a sense of community.)

- **Acknowledgement and respect.** Fans expect to be thanked for their efforts. Fans expect to be thanked in CD notes, when they hear you interviewed, and at gigs for turning up and for their warm reception. In fact, any time they hear you communicate, fans expect to be acknowledged. If ever you mention that your fans are less than intelligent or have poor taste in music and so on, it is probably the end of your career.

- **Cool and kudos.** Fans do not want to be associated with artists who have (in their view) dangerous beliefs (and I'm not just talking about edgy views). More than that, they want you to take a lead on certain issues. What constitutes dangerous issues and the issues for which you should take a lead is very subjective in both cases and will very much depend on the audience you are targeting.

For instance, if you are targeting a teenage male audience, they may be unlikely to want to hear about politics, but they may want to hear about girls, and indeed, they may be impressed by tales of your "conquests." By contrast, if you are targeting the housewife market (housewife being used as a generic description, not in a pejorative sense), then your audience may expect you to align yourself with worthy causes, such as breast cancer research, in addition to creating great music.

In short, your individual fans want to feel better about themselves, and they want other people to feel good about them and respect them, due to the fan's relationship with you. You don't necessarily need to make people look cool by their association with you, but it certainly doesn't do any harm.

That being said, there are limits to what a fan can expect, and I think the vast majority of fans will respect these limits. (You will only rarely come across a stalker.) For instance, I don't think that your fan base needs to know where you live (beyond your city of residence), and your family's privacy (especially that of any children) should always be of the highest priority.

Communicating with Your Fan Base

Communication should be an integral part of your web presence, so I will come back to this issue in the next chapter. However, for the moment, I want to look at your fans' expectations about communication. In particular, I want to talk about how you can communicate and the nature of that communication.

Over the last few years, with the rise of social media, there has been a radical shift in the way artists and their audience can communicate. It is now possible for an artist to communicate directly with her fans, for fans to communicate directly with artists, and for a dialogue to be undertaken.

Although the options to communicate through social media are great, they don't necessarily make all of the old ways of communicating obsolete. (Remember, not everyone is on Facebook, even if it feels as if they are.) However, what social media has done is brought into sharp focus something that should have been obvious: Communication is a two-way process—it is not something that you "do" to your grateful fan base.

Whichever ways you choose to communicate, there is one key point to remember: Communication is not what you say; it is what the other person (that is, your fans) understands.

Communicate the Way Your Fans Communicate

It would be simple to, say, open a Twitter account and open a Facebook account (or an account with another current hot social network) and leave things at that.

However, as I've already mentioned, not everyone has access to the social networks. Equally, you might choose to communicate through one, while your fan base uses another network. It's very easy to see Facebook as the answer—and at the time of this writing (mid 2011), Facebook is all-pervasive—however, there are other options. Many people regard Orkut (orkut.com; see Figure 2.4), Google's social network, as a failed social network. In reality, this "failure" has more than 50 million users and is hugely popular in India and Brazil.

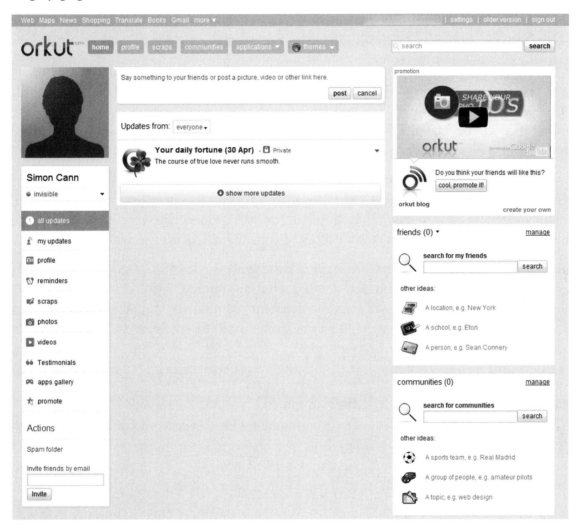

Figure 2.4   Google Orkut.

You may be relaxed about ignoring 50 million people—and indeed, if these people aren't interested in your music, you should ignore them—but if a large proportion of your fans are using a certain way to communicate, you should join them.

Making Communication a Two-Way Dialogue

You cannot make communication a fully two-way dialogue unless you communicate individually with each fan on a one-on-one basis. However, with new social media—in particular, Twitter and Facebook—you can get close to that. But not everyone is happy communicating that way, and not everyone has access to these services, so you need to make your communications *feel* like a two-way dialogue.

Perhaps the most sensible way to make communication a two-way dialogue is to respond to questions that come to you, and it is easy to respond to questions through the social networks. However, it's even easier to miss a question thrown through the social networks.

You should make sure you have systems in place (in other words, people given specific responsibility for tracking any conversations about you) so that you pick up on any discussions about you and can join in.

By equal measure, just because a question is asked in a specific manner, that doesn't mean you have to answer in the same manner (although it does make a lot of sense to). Let me give you an example: Say you had to cancel a gig. Hopefully, you would have communicated the reasons for this, but let's say someone tweets asking for more information.

Now, of course you can respond on Twitter to such a question, but I'm guessing that giving an answer that explains the issue fully in 140 characters or fewer might be tough. A better option *could* be to record a brief video answering the question, which you could then upload onto YouTube (putting a link to the video on Twitter).

You should, of course, anticipate certain questions. If the lead singer quits your band, then people are going to want to know why, what he is doing next, whether the band is going to split, whether there will be a replacement, whether the replacement will be as good as the previous incumbent, and so on. You should be ready to answer these sorts of questions before the news becomes public. Better still, you should anticipate these questions and answer them as part of making the announcement.

How Should You Communicate?

Technology offers many new ways to communicate. However, some of the older methods are still good choices. Very often, how you choose to communicate will depend on the message you need to impart and the nature of how your fan base likes to receive messages. Also, simplicity will often drive your chosen tools.

To cut to the conclusion of this discussion, I recommend that you communicate in different forms. Each member of your audience will want to receive communications in a different manner. There is the potential to miss sections of your audience by communicating solely in one manner.

Let's look at your main choices.

The Social Networks

Today, the obvious way to communicate and interact with your fan base is through the social networks. At the time of this writing, the two powerhouse social networks are:

- Twitter (twitter.com)
- Facebook (facebook.com)

Twitter allows you to send messages of up to 140 characters. Want to know what that limit looks like? OK, this paragraph has 140 characters.

As you can see, Twitter messages are really short. You can therefore afford to send messages frequently, and there is no expectation of detail. Facebook does not have an express limit, but it encourages short messages (more like a paragraph than like Twitter's sentence).

With both services you can send messages, link to other material (for instance, photos or videos), and read messages from other people. You can access the services through an internet browser, but the real power comes when you access the service through a mobile device (to you and me, that's a phone, such as an iPhone, an Android-based phone, or another smartphone; see Figure 2.5). Once you're mobile, then you can give a real-time commentary about what you're doing, and you can respond immediately to any communications to you.

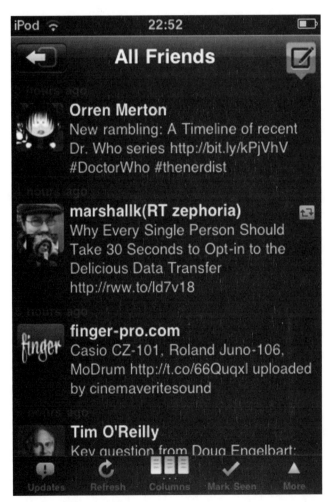

Figure 2.5 TweetDeck, a combined Twitter and Facebook client that runs on a range of platforms, including iPhone/iPod Touch (shown), iPad, Android, Mac, PC, and internet browser. A client such as TweetDeck allows you to send and read messages, track your mentions, and send/receive direct messages (all from your phone, tablet, laptop, or desktop).

Video

Conventional thinking holds that video is expensive and requires professional input. Common sense says that is rubbish, and that video is a great way of communicating.

In many ways, video is the ideal way to communicate with your fan base, since you can quite literally talk directly to your audience.

There are many really good but very cheap video cameras readily available. Sure, you can use the camera on your phone, but why do that when for a few hundred bucks you can get really good results. For instance, the Zoom Q3HD (see Figure 2.6) is a really handy video camera.

Figure 2.6 The Zoom Q3HD video camera.

So why the Zoom?

In short, it's a straightforward, easy camera, and it's very cheap (currently £189/$299). The quality is good—video quality is HD 1080, and the microphones are great (which you need for recording audio)—and you can also perform basic edits.

With this camera or a similar model, you can record a quick video—maybe a short message or a quick song (for instance, a live performance or an acoustic version of a track)—you can edit the recording to cut off the start and end, and you can upload the video to YouTube. This can be completed within minutes and does not require the involvement of video/audio professionals, nor do you need a studio, so you could, for instance, record a video while you are on the road.

Now, of course, you would get better results by handing the project over to professionals and using gear that costs thousands of dollars, but then you would lose the direct and immediate communication with your fan base (as well as having to wait weeks for other people to complete their work).

SMS/Text Message to Cell/Mobile Phones

In many ways, SMS (text) messages have lost their immediacy due to Twitter (and to an extent, to the other social networks). As well as being "of the moment," there are certain practical advantages to Twitter (and the other social networks):

- **Cost.** This is the biggest advantage. Twitter does not charge to send messages or receive messages.

- **Viral spread.** Messages can be passed on to a user's group of contacts. So, for instance, in Twitter, all a user has to do is hit the re-tweet button in her client, and your message will be shared with her contacts.

- **Platform independence.** You don't need a cell phone to join Twitter; you could, for instance, access your Twitter stream on a desktop computer.

However, SMS messages still have many advantages over Twitter. For instance:

- People tend to read every SMS message they receive, but they may not apply the same diligence to their Twitter stream, where messages can get lost in the deluge.

- Not everybody is on Twitter.

- You can choose who should receive your message when you send an SMS—if you are relying on Twitter, that presupposes that the person to whom the message is being sent is following you.

SMS (text) messages are great if you have a message that is short and urgent, and where the information only has value for a very limited time. For instance, if you have spare tickets for a gig, then you might want to send an SMS message to let fans know about the opportunity (and you would probably want to tweet the information and disseminate through other social networks).

By contrast, if you want to send out a long newsletter with photos, then an SMS/Twitter message is unlikely to be appropriate, irrespective of the nature of your audience.

From a practical perspective, SMS messaging is often easier to manage when you have a smaller list of recipients.

Email

Email is a great way of communicating:

- It's simple.

- It's fast.

- You can send one message to many people.

- You can send a short message or a long message.

- Often people pay more attention to email messages (or take them more seriously—they are less likely to be overlooked than a tweet, for instance).

- You can send attachments (such as photos or a form to fill in to apply for tickets).

- You can include links to internet sites (for instance, "Click here to see pictures of our gig last night").

However, email is not a panacea and does present many challenges. In addition, with the rise of social media, it has something of an "old" feel about it. Email definitely has a place—and personally, I like it as a tool—but always think whether it would be better to communicate through the social networks before you send out a mass email campaign.

From a logistical perspective, one of the first challenges with email is keeping addresses up to date. People frequently change their email addresses—they change schools or colleges, they get new jobs, they change internet service providers, or they close an email address because it has been receiving too much spam. To ensure that your message gets through, you need to find a way to ensure that your list of email addresses is kept up to date.

Spam (that is, unsolicited commercial email) is a huge problem for all of us. It clogs our email boxes, and for legitimate mass-email senders (such as a musician trying to keep in touch with his fan base), it presents the problem of how to send multiple emails without them looking like spam. One thing you can do to prevent your emails from looking like spam is to simplify the message. Many spam messages include graphics as attachments (which may be a cover for viruses). If you send a message in plain text (perhaps you could link to graphics on your website), you will find you are less likely to have your message stopped.

There is another reason not to attach graphics: People don't like them, especially if they have a dial-up internet connection (in other words, not a broadband/ADSL/DSL connection). If you send an unsolicited email that takes 10 minutes to download, you will not be popular.

I've already mentioned graphics in the context of spam. Let me now add a few thoughts about the presentation of your email in general. As an electronic medium, you have great flexibility over how you present your email. You can use colors, graphics, different-size fonts, pop-ups, and any number of devices to grab the reader's attention.

Don't.

If your message isn't strong enough to stand on its own, then rewrite the message (or wait until you have something important to say). The beauty of email is that you have the reader's undivided attention; you don't need to stand out from the crowd. Adding lots of flashing lights is just going to distract the reader and annoy her. Now, please don't misconstrue what I'm suggesting here—I'm not implying that you shouldn't make your message look as attractive as possible. I'm simply suggesting that you should get the message right first and then add in the design elements.

You can do a few things to help the reader:

- Put in a sensible subject line so the reader can identify that the email is from you and what it's about.

- Write in short paragraphs. Long paragraphs are always difficult to read—it is even harder to read long paragraphs when the text is displayed on a computer screen.

- If the message is longer than a few paragraphs, add headings to break up the text and to show where one subject ends and another one starts.

- Make it short. Get to the point quickly and then go away. People are busy and don't want to listen to your self-indulgent drivel. If you've got more to say, then refer the reader to your website (or anywhere else where further information might be available). On the whole, people like short emails but are happy to spend hours browsing websites and "finding" information for themselves.

Mail

I've talked a lot about technological options, but please don't forget the more traditional mail services. Although they are not "free" like email and the social networks or cheap like SMS messages, they are in many ways more personal and more effective. Many people still like receiving letters (that aren't bills) and enjoy receiving tangible goods through the mail.

The real advantage of the mail is that you can send things. For instance, you can send a newsletter, posters, or a DVD. There are several downsides to this, though. First, the goods that you are sending cost money. Second, postage costs—it isn't free. Third, it takes time to address and stuff envelopes (which again may incur costs if you have to hire someone to complete this task).

What Should You Communicate?

The purpose of communication is several-fold, but primarily you are trying to:

■ Promote something that you are selling.

■ Foster the relationship between you and your fan base.

Just communicating for the heck of it means you are generating noise. However, any communication must be seen within the context of the medium you are using to communicate. If you are dropping an email just to say hi, then you are probably wasting your fans' time, but if you tweet to say that you've just woken up and the sun is shining, then some people may be interested. But do be cautious—irrespective of the medium, too many "pointless" messages (as perceived by the individual followers), and you'll start to alienate people.

As a general principle, you should communicate when you've got something to say. You've got something to say when there is something happening in the future that will interest your fan base: If you have just spent six months in the studio and your new single will be out next month, then that is something to say.

Equally, when you communicate, you should communicate the significance of your news (if that is appropriate for the medium). For instance, if you say, "We signed a record deal," who cares? However, if you say, "We signed a deal, so the new album will be in shops next week," then that puts the news in a context that really means something to fans.

When you come to look at the details you need to communicate, there are two approaches. You can give all of the details, or you can give none of the details and just communicate the headline news. Let me explain the difference with a practical example. Suppose you are announcing a gig. The pertinent details here are:

■ The date of the gig and the time it starts

■ The location of the gig

■ The cost of tickets and where they are available

■ Any special restrictions (for instance, if you're playing in a club at which people must be 18 or 21 to be admitted)

This is the bare minimum of information that you must communicate. There's much more you could say, such as whether you're playing any special songs, whether there will be an opening act, and so on.

Now let's say you decided to communicate details of this gig by email. You could either send out an email with all of the details (which would be quite long by the time you've explained all the purchase options), or you could send out an email that says, "We're playing a gig in London on November 25th" and include a link to a website for further details.

The advantage of referring people back to your website is that you can give much more information than you could easily give in an email. For instance, you can include a link to a map of the gig's location. Also, you could include links to purchase tickets, thereby encouraging people to buy them.

Another advantage of this approach is that if you make any changes (for instance, if there is a mistake in the published date of the gig), then you can change the web page very easily. Obviously, if you make a change like that, I would expect you to drop a brief email to say, "Whoops…we made a mistake on our website, and the correct date is now shown."

By contrast, if you included the wrong date in an email, even if you send a correcting email, there is always the chance that someone will look at the wrong email and end up being disappointed (or embarrassed/angry if he turns up at the venue on the wrong night).

Mind Your Language

Even if the whole basis of your act is that you swear like troopers, when communicating directly with fans (in other words, when tweeting, sending SMS messages, emails, letters, and so on), I recommend that you remove as much profanity as possible.

I recommend this for several practical reasons:

- First, many people, particularly corporations, use profanity filters to block emails that may contain bad language. You may craft the most literate and amusing email, but it will be to no avail if it gets caught in a nasty spam filter.

- The other reason for caution in your language is that you don't know where your communication is going to end up. Emails can get sent to the wrong people, letters and emails can be opened by other members of a family, tweets get re-tweeted, and so on.

You should also use the fans' language when writing as much as possible. That is to say, you should use terms that they use in a manner that they would understand. You should refine your language in a similar manner, although I caution against using the vernacular if it is going to sound false. We've all heard middle-aged people trying to get "hip with the kids." It never works and it isn't pretty, so don't do it!

As a final point (and the irony of this comment is not lost on me), remember that not everyone speaks English as a first language. We're dealing with music here, so it's not necessary to use your most flowery prose. (Save that for your lyrics, if you really must.) The simpler and more straightforward you can keep your communications, the better.

The Mechanics of Bulk Communication

The practicalities of how you communicate need some thought, so I'll address that in the next few sections.

Mechanics of Social-Network Communication

The content of the social networks is almost exclusively communication of one form or another.

Virtually all of the social networks allow you to communicate in a range of ways, usually including through a web browser or through a dedicated client on your phone or tablet. (Look back to Figure 2.5 for an example of a combined Twitter/Facebook client.) Pretty much the only prerequisite for being able to send a message over the social networks is an internet connection, and that is not always necessary if you are delaying the sending of a message (perhaps to ensure that an announcement is not made until, for instance, tickets are available) or if your network accepts SMS messages.

To be able to communicate with people across the social networks, they must know that you have a presence on a specific network—they can then follow you, like you, or do whatever is necessary to ensure that your messages hit their inbox or come into their information flow. Accordingly, you should ensure that:

- Your presence on specific social networks is flagged on your website, on your marketing materials, and so on.

- You are actually present where you say you are. If it looks like you use social media only when you've got something to sell, then people are less likely to follow you/try to interact with you, and you'll lose the benefit of being able to communicate through these mediums.

Mechanics of Bulk SMS/Text Communication

There are several ways you can send one SMS message to many people:

- Most mobile phones will allow you to send one message to several people. However, this is not really practical when you're sending a message to more than a few people.

- To make life easier, many mobile phones allow you to connect your computer so that you can type your message and manage your mailing list. If your phone has this feature, it will make sending SMS messages much easier; however, it's still not really practical when you start getting into reasonable numbers.

- Perhaps the most practical option is one of the many internet services that allow you to send SMS messages. You type a message (you can use your favorite word processor to check the typing), and then you load the message and a list of the phone numbers to which you want to send the message. You hit a button, and the messages are all sent for you. These services are not particularly cheap. (They tend to cost in the region of 5 to 10 cents per person per message.) However, they are much more convenient than using your cell phone to do all this.

Mechanics of Bulk Email Communication

A regular email program (such as Microsoft Outlook or Mozilla Thunderbird) or an online mail service, such as Gmail or Yahoo! Mail, will allow you to send emails to more than one recipient. However, this is practical only up to a certain size of mailing list, and beyond a certain point, internet service providers are likely to throttle the amount of email you can send per hour (to prevent spam).

There are specialized mailing programs. These are useful but ultimately limited, since they will be running on one computer, which may not be accessible if you aren't in "the office" (and if you're carrying your email list on a laptop, then there's a different issue of data security).

In my opinion, a better option for sending out bulk emails is to use a specialized service, such as Campaign Monitor (see Figure 2.7; campaignmonitor.com) or MailChimp (mailchimp.com).

The advantage of using a specialized service, such as Campaign Monitor or Mail-Chimp, is that you bring power, know-how, and infrastructure online at the flick of a switch. There are, of course, downsides—the most immediate being the cost—but when used sensibly, these services offer excellent value and a range of services.

The main functions you can expect this type of service to offer are:

- Integration with your website so that individuals can join (or leave) your mailing list without leaving your website. In addition, these changes can be effected immediately.

- Subscription management—in other words, administering the process by which people join and leave your mailing list and maintaining a database of all your contacts.

- Sending an email to multiple contacts. When you're sending an email to a few hundred people, this may not seem like a big deal. When you're sending an email to thousands or tens of thousands of people, it is quite a tough logistical issue, and you can expect the company to also handle bounced/failed emails (which again present a challenge when you're sending in large quantities).

In other words, these services offer pretty much everything you need to manage your mailing list.

One other significant advantage of this approach is accessibility: You can access your mailing list (and so contact your following) from anywhere you have access to the internet. This gives you geographic flexibility and is another form of data protection. (If the house burns down, then you'll still be able to get to your email list—it won't matter that your hard drive melted.)

Mechanics of Sending Out Letters in Bulk

Do I really need to spell this out for you? You send the same package to everyone on the list. It is a very tedious, manual process, so you may want to outsource the work.

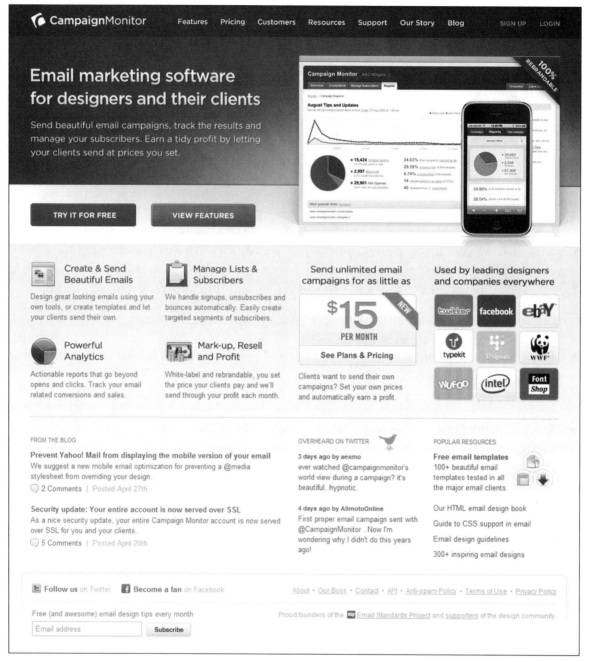

Figure 2.7   The Campaign Monitor website, which gives an indication of some of the company's services.

So Will You Exploit with Integrity?

I want to reiterate my point about exploiting with integrity.

Think about when you go into a restaurant. You eat a meal, and you are then charged for that meal. The charge is greater than the cost of the ingredients. The charge is greater than the cost of the ingredients plus a share of the cost of running the restaurant (including property and staff costs, as well as taxes). Provided it was a good meal, you are happy to pay the bill and will probably even add a tip (through generosity, because you feel it is deserved, or just because you feel bad about not leaving a tip).

So does the restaurant exploit you?

Good exploit? Yes, probably. They give you something you can't get at home—a meal without hassle (perhaps better than you could cook yourself), ambience, choice of food, wine maybe. The reasons are many and varied.

Bad exploit? Probably not.

If you like the meal, you will probably return to the restaurant and will probably recommend it to your friends. And here we are reaching the heart of the point I am trying to make. The factor that is going to grow your fan base the fastest is word of mouth— trusted friends telling each other about your music and recommending it because they like what you do. In today's connected social-media world, word of mouth can spread the message in an instant. Remember, if word of mouth is going to work, then you need to give people something to talk about.

Building and Keeping the Fan Base in Practical Terms

Let's move on and look in a bit more detail at the mechanics of building and keeping your fan base.

I've said this before, but I'll say it again because it's important: Any career in music will only succeed if there is someone to buy the product. The people who will buy the product are the fans. You need to cherish and nurture your fans (as people) if you are to survive and have a career in music.

The Conversion Process

There is a process by which you develop interest into income. There are several stages to this process:

1. Generate some sort of interest so that people come to you.

2. Develop the interest so that the individual becomes someone you could regard as a fan.

3. Persuade the fan to (a) keep coming back, and (b) perhaps spend money.

4. Ensure that the fan is happy about spending money and keeps visiting your money-making activities on a regular basis.

Figure 2.8 shows that conversion process and illustrates how a new fan can then bring in more fans by word of mouth.

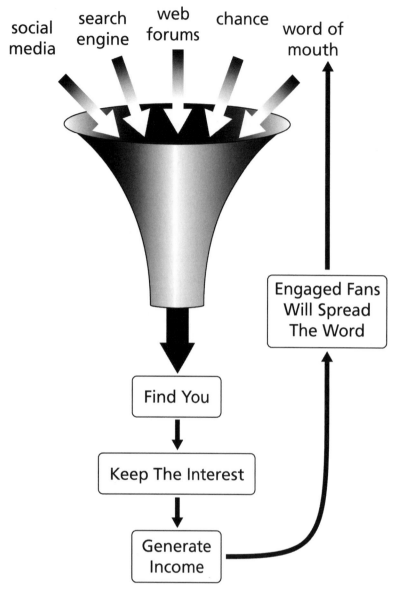

Figure 2.8 Once you have drawn in your potential fans, it is crucial that you keep their interest and create a situation where they want to spend money (on you).

As soon as you start making some noise (figuratively), you will get interest. Your key challenge is to convert that interest into a fan base and to convert that fan base into an income stream. It would be a rather foolish act to try to raise your public profile without being able to capitalize on the interest.

In this section, I want to look at how you can proactively manage that conversion process.

Generating Interest so That People Come to You

People are likely to come to you through one of two routes:

- **Personal recommendation.** Direct word of mouth from someone who could already be regarded as a fan.

- **Chance.** People may come across you by chance if they hear a track on the radio, see an interview with you in a magazine, find a reference to you from one of their social-media contacts, or come across you while browsing the internet (and in this category, I'm including finding you on the video-sharing sites, such as YouTube).

If you are really lucky—really, really lucky—then people will hear some of your music, will love it, and will want to buy it. That's great: It provides you with income, as long as the new potential fan can find out where to buy the product. Your challenge then is to make sure that person becomes a true fan and keeps consuming your output/spending money on your products.

However, you may not always be that lucky. Many people won't hear your music or will want to hear more before they decide whether they like you. Whenever somebody wants to know more about an artist, the most logical place to look for information is a website. This could be your own website or on YouTube (or something similar). As I'll talk about later in this part of the book, realistically, if you don't have a web presence, then it is very difficult for potential fans to decide whether they like you. And if they can't find a way to like you, then you won't be able to convert them into a source of income.

Developing Interest into a Fan

It may feel great when you look at your website statistics to see that thousands of people have been hitting your site, but however good this may feel, it means nothing. It means nothing because you don't know who these people are, and they are not spending money on you.

To take a significant step forward, you will need to get these people to tell you how you can contact them. Once you can contact them, then you can enter into a relationship with them and start talking about what you're doing. If they stay interested, then they'll check out what you're up to, and you can start generating income.

There are a number of ways that people will allow you to contact them:

- By giving you their email address (usually by joining your mailing list)

- Through social media (by liking or following you, or something similar)

- Through some sort of internet forum

It's much easier—and far less risky from their perspective—for people to follow you through the social-media channels. For instance, you only have to click the Follow button on Twitter to follow someone. If you don't like what they are saying, or if they bore you, then you can click the Unfollow button, and that's it—end of relationship.

In this case, the follower has the power—she determines whether the relationship continues. Once the relationship has ended, there is no easy way for you to contact that person, and indeed, she can block you and report inappropriate activity on your part if she wants.

This is very different from the situation with email, where data (the email address) is being disclosed to you. Although there is legislation in much of the world about how data is treated, and theoretically email addresses should be deleted if the owner so requests, we all know that this doesn't always happen. While I am sure you would have honorable intentions about how data is treated, and you may back these intentions with actions, that doesn't stop people from being cautious about giving out their details.

If you are going to try to capture email data—and because direct email is such a powerful communication medium, I suggest you do—then be aware that most people first will want to see how they can unsubscribe, and second will want some sort of reassurance in the form of a privacy policy before they give out their email address. And even then, many people will remain skeptical. Your privacy policy may be explicit (in the form of "Click here to see our privacy policy") or implicit, with a note to the effect that "We hate spam as much as you do and will *never* share your email address with anyone."

So what else might persuade someone to give you his email address (or other contact details)?

If you ask nicely, then I'm sure some people will be happy to give you their email address. However, I would be a bit suspicious of anyone who asked for my email address and didn't give me a reason why. If you ask nicely and explain what you're going to do with the email address, then I think you'll get much better results.

For instance, if you say something to the effect of, "Please let us have your email address so we can keep in touch with you and let you know about our gigs and releases," then you may get more favorable results.

Many people aren't going to want to give you an email address unless they feel they are really getting something in return. For these people, you need to be more subtle in your approach. Instead of simply asking for an email address, you can give access to a password-protected area of your website, perhaps by encouraging people to sign up for a virtual "backstage pass" or something else suitably musical (but perhaps slightly less corny).

You will also find that there are some people who simply will not give you their email address or any other personal details. On the whole, these people are less likely to become fans with whom you can develop a relationship. However, you may still be able to reach these people in other ways (such as through social media).

Deriving Income from Your Fans

So now you've got the potential fans interested. They may even think of themselves as being fans. So how do you get them to spend money?

You don't. It just happens.

Now before I get more cryptic, let's look at the two ways income will flow from your fan base to you.

- The first way is if your fan base buys things, if you sell—directly or through a retail outlet—goods such as CDs, downloads, DVDs, T-shirts, gig tickets, and so on.

- The second way is through advertising.

Let's look at these in turn.

Spending Money Directly

There's no need to beg fans to spend money on you.

Your role is to provide the right product for your fans to buy. Let them know what they can buy, and—provided they want to—they will buy. Remember, we're exploiting fans in a good way, not a bad way. You're a musician, not a secondhand car dealer.

Sometimes the buying happens quickly, and sometimes it happens slowly. Sometimes you don't realize it has happened. If your songs are available from iTunes, then you won't know the identity of the purchaser. Even if the only place where any of your products can be purchased is your website, you may not know that you have converted someone into a purchase—a friend could have bought his ticket for a gig or given him a CD as a present.

Advertising

The thought of advertising may be quite uncomfortable for you.

However, it is a reality of commerce today and is one of the reasons why so many of the services that support our online lives are "free."

Rightly or wrongly, many people are of the view that music should be free. They hear music on the radio, and from their perspective it is free (even if it's not because someone else is paying—usually an advertiser). Once the principle of music-for-free has been established by the radio (and other outlets), people then have a hard time figuring out why they should, for instance, pay for a download. After all, it's digital, so there's no cost, right?

And for people who don't want to pay you for your music, you can still earn money through advertising.

Beyond that, the more you look, the more you will see that there is advertising put up against a lot of content. Someone somewhere is often making money on the basis of your work, so why shouldn't the person making the money be you?

Advertising also has some other real benefits:

- New acts can generate income at a much earlier stage in their career by giving away their music and earning advertising revenue.

- Fans can discover and consume new music for free, but the artist can still receive some income.

- Acts can use their music for publicity purposes and generate income.

Perhaps the most obvious example of a situation where you can generate income from advertising is YouTube (see Figure 2.9). If you join the YouTube Partner Program (which does require a certain level of content/traffic before you are allowed in), then you can share the advertising revenues.

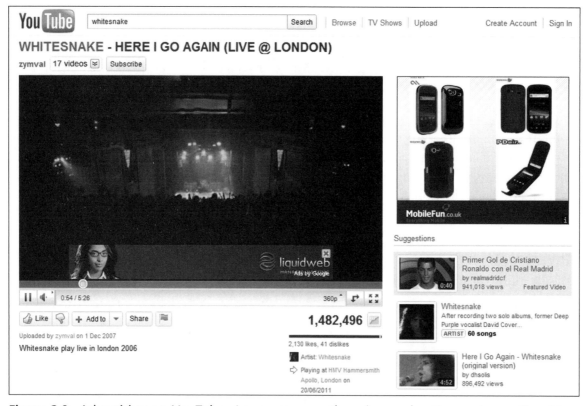

Figure 2.9 Advertising on YouTube. As you can see, there is an advertisement over the video and another to the right of the video. Someone is making money—if you created the video, why shouldn't you be making money?

To make serious money with advertising, your content needs to be consumed a lot so that a lot of advertisements can be displayed. More consumption equates to more opportunities to show advertisements. From an income perspective, there is little difference between having your content consumed on many occasions by a smaller number of people and having it consumed by a large number of people once or twice.

While YouTube is a great example of how you can generate advertising revenue, as your fan base expands, you will find many other ways to generate advertising-related income. This could include carrying advertisements, endorsements, and so on.

Keeping Fans Happy

Let's assume everything has gone according to plan, you are building your fan base, and your fans are consuming content and are happy to spend money with you.

Great! Congratulations.

You now know how hard it can be to start building a fan base. That hard work should never cease; you will always want new fans. However, there is one thing easier than trying to find a new fan and converting that person into someone who will generate income—keeping your existing fans.

Existing fans know and like you. Existing fans will have spent money with you and will be happy to spend more money with you. Whenever you release a new product, you can be sure that many of your existing fans will buy it at the earliest opportunity (or will provide opportunities to generate advertising-related income). For these reasons, existing fans should be your highest priority.

In many ways, you don't need to do anything out of the ordinary to keep these existing fans happy. However, you *should* keep them happy, and there are two simple things that you can do to ensure this:

- **Come up with new products.** Come up with new tracks, new videos, new CDs, new DVDs, new posters, new merchandise, and so on. You get the idea. Fans want to know that you are thinking of them and working to create new stuff for them.

- **Interact with your fans.** When you interact with your fans, they feel as if you care, and in addition to buying your product, they will continue to work as your sales force and ambassadors.

The other thing you need to do is not upset your fans. This issue is discussed later in this chapter, in the "Losing Fans" section.

Finding Potential Fans and Building the Fan Base

Later, I will look at more of the options for publicity. For the moment, I want to look at the main places where you can get in touch directly with potential fans.

I've talked a bit about growing the fan base. Because it is such an important factor in your career, I want to look at some specific ways you can find your fans and grow your fan base. This really is one area where you have to be very proactive—if you're not prepared to be proactive here, then you are unlikely to have a career.

There are two things to remember when looking at the number of your fans:

- The numbers will not grow in a linear manner. Some weeks you will pick up many new fans, and others you will pick up only a few fans. You will probably find that you pick up more new fans when you make a noise (or shortly thereafter) and fewer new fans during your quiet periods. However, this will not always be the case.

- When you are relying on word of mouth, the increase in numbers can be startling. At some times you may even see exponential growth in the number of your fans (where one person tells two people, those two people each tell two people, making four new people, then those four people each tell two people, making eight people, and those eight people each tell two people, and so on—see Figures 2.10 and 2.11). However, exponential growth is ultimately unsustainable (you will eventually run out of people to tell) and doesn't reflect human nature, where you will usually find one person telling lots of people and many people not passing on the word. More realistically, the longer you keep a fan, the more people he will introduce to you.

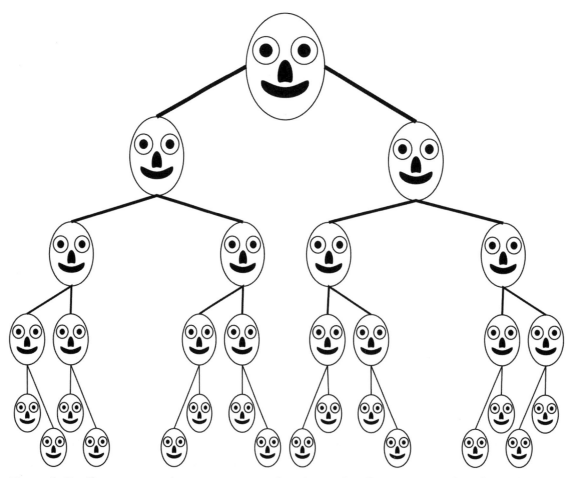

Figure 2.10 If you can reach out to two people, who each talk to two people, who each tell two people about you (and so on), then your number of contacts will grow rapidly.

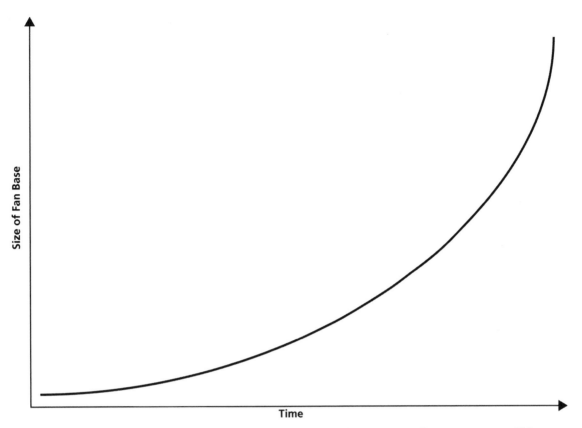

Figure 2.11 As Figure 2.10 shows, your total number of contacts will grow more swiftly as you have more people finding new contacts for you.

To connect with a potential audience, you need to find the place where people who could make up your audience go (whether physically or metaphorically). You then need to go there. This destination could include:

- Social networks

- Websites

- Magazines/fanzines

- Radio shows, TV shows, internet sites

- Gig venues

To a certain extent, finding fans is a numbers game—the more people you approach, the more people you are likely to find. However, you should perhaps be a bit discriminating. For instance, if you're a thrash metal band, maybe your grandmother's friends would not be the best source of new fans. Then again, your grandmother's friends may have their own grandchildren who would like your music. You never know…

Anyway, the following sections discuss a few of the places to start looking for fans. Remember, these people are of no use to you until you know how to contact them, so get ready to start collecting email addresses.

Family and Friends

The obvious place to start your quest for new fans is with your family and friends. Your friends may be happy to come and support you at gigs, but they are unlikely to want to buy every piece of merchandise you have. In fact, many will expect you to give them stuff for free in exchange for their support. However, your friends will have friends (and those friends will have friends). Use word of mouth, and you will start to grow your numbers.

Social Networks

Social networks are, of course, a place to find new fans. There are many ways to find fans this way—for instance, many networks have affinity groups (people interested in similar topics). Equally, you can find people who like music that might be similar to yours. (On most networks, people tell you what they like and don't; they will give you a great start.) By beginning a dialogue with people who like music similar to yours, you can find potential new fans.

But perhaps the best way to find new fans through the social networks is simply by being there—create great music, let your fans spread the word (even if you only have a small number of fans), and be ready to interact with new people as they come along.

Website

I've mentioned your website several times and will discuss it in greater detail in the next chapter.

Gigs

Gigs are an excellent place to find new people, but gig venues (which may be dark, sweaty rooms) are often not great places to collect contact details. However, because gigs present such a great opportunity to reach new people, you should try.

It may not be practical to get people to join your email mailing list at a gig. However, you may persuade them to join your social-media network. (For instance, if they have a phone with them, they may be able to follow you on Twitter—you might even tweet from stage to encourage them to sign up.)

It's easy to see a gig but then to forget to go to the band's website and sign up for the mailing list, so you should do whatever you can to encourage people to follow up. As one example, if you take pictures at a gig, you can put them on one of the photo-sharing sites (such as Flickr; flickr.com). If you tell people their picture will be up tomorrow morning, that will encourage them to take a look and hopefully will also provide a conduit to searching out more information about you.

A great way to grow a fan base with gigs is to swap gigs with another act: You play a hometown gig, and they act as support, and they play a hometown gig with you acting as support. Of course, it helps if you are from different geographic locations (even different sides of the same city). If the other act is as well organized as you, it will also have its own contacts (in a combination of an email list, social media contacts, and so on), so each act can engage its own fan base and direct its fans to the other act's web presence.

Press, Broadcasting, and Blogs

Press and broadcasting covers a very wide range of media, including radio (terrestrial, satellite, and internet), television (in all its forms and variants, such as video podcasting, and we should include video-sharing sites too), and newspapers and magazines (real and online).

You would be crazy to ignore these outlets. However, as a means to increase your fan base (and increase numbers on your mailing list), the mainstream press and broadcasting are fairly blunt instruments. Think about radio, for instance. Very often you don't know whose song is being played. Even if someone hears you and likes what they hear, you have to hope that your name is given out clearly and that the listener then writes down the name and searches you out on the internet. This may happen (especially if your record is played several times on the radio); however, you are more likely to find that this is a tough way to create a fan base.

Before I move on from the media, I want to mention blogs and fanzines briefly. It is easy to look disparagingly at fanzines because they are often "amateur" productions. However, fanzines are often very closely aligned to their target audience, so if you find one that covers your niche, you will find a very quick way to access a large potential audience. This audience is likely to be very engaged with and very passionate about their music.

Added to this, fanzines are usually run by people with a genuine passion for music, who are more interested in finding something cool and including it in their magazine than they are in chasing the commercial imperative.

When you tour (if you tour), it is well worth taking the time to meet as many fanzine editors as possible, because they will introduce you to many fans.

There is a similar principle with blogs. Although the audience for any one blog may seem small, blogs offer several advantages, the main one being that you are connecting to a community of people with a very specific interest. This highly targeted nature of blogs makes them well worth seeking out as a means of finding new fans.

Losing Fans

There are bad things in this world. One bad thing is losing fans, as Figure 2.12 shows.

Figure 2.12 Take a look at these formulas. Provided you can increase your fan base faster than you lose your fans, you can increase your earnings from your fans. However, if you lose fans at a higher rate than you gain fans, then you are likely to see your income start to fall.

You usually will lose fans for one of two reasons:

- **Boredom.** It could be that your act has grown stale, or it could be that the fans' tastes have changed.

- **Active dislike.** If you do something really stupid, it is quite possible to change devoted fans into a well-motivated group of upset individuals who could do serious damage to your career.

All lost fans usually are lost forever. The former group (that is, the bored fans) may come back to you at a later stage, but this is unlikely. However, those who have chosen to actively dislike you are almost always lost forever, as well as being vocal in their criticism of you. Clearly, this vocal criticism will not help in your efforts to expand your remaining fan base.

We'll look at the boredom factor later in the book. For the moment, I want to talk about some of the things that will alienate your fan base and cause the people who have provided your income to actively dislike you.

Bad Things You Can Do with Your Contacts

There are several bad things you can do with email (and SMS) contacts. The first time you use your mailing list to do one of the following things is when you will instantly lose fans (and find out how quickly they tell their friends about your appalling behavior—you really will see the social networks in action):

- Sell your mailing list, especially if you sell it to an organization that supports, for instance, the clubbing to death of baby seals. In this case, you would lose fans for two reasons: first for selling the list, and second for being associated with something that most of your fans are likely to regard as very uncool.

- Spam your mailing list, which in this context means bombarding your mailing list with unsolicited emails. You should also be careful if you have several email addresses for one person (assuming you can notice this), because people tend to get annoyed if you send an email more than once (even if it's their fault that you have multiple email addresses on file for them).

- Use the mailing list to advertise products that are not your own. For instance, if you start sending advertisements for power tools, then your fan base is likely to become disgruntled.

This, of course, is not the end of the list, and as you would expect, there are a lot of other ways you can upset people (especially through social media).

Remember, we live in a high-tech world, and most people are pretty tech savvy. They instinctively realize when they're being ripped off or used. Some people have disposable email addresses to check where spam and the like originates, so if you start abusing the trust people have put in you by giving you their email address, then you are likely to be found out and exposed very quickly.

I also suspect that if any of your fans think you have undertaken any of these activities (even if you have not), the results will be equally disastrous.

Bad Things You Can Do with Your Website

I will talk about website design in the next chapter, but before we get there, I want to mention a few things that will alienate your fans (and your possible fans).

Associate links (for instance, to Amazon) on your website are fine within reason. If you have a link so that someone can purchase one of your products at Amazon, it will not be a problem. If you are linking to a related product (for instance, if you are a Celtic band placing links to books about the origins and history of Celtic music), I'm sure no one will object. However, if your site is linking to all sorts of (apparently) unrelated products, and it just looks like a bad imitation of Amazon, then people are likely to distrust your motives and feel alienated.

I talked about advertising earlier in this chapter. It is a really tricky issue, and one where you must know your audience.

Some sites carry advertisements placed around their content. You may be able to get away with this form of advertising, but to my mind this is a truly naff thing to do and is likely to turn people off. You really must have a good reason to convince your fan base that advertisements are justified. This, along with other forms of rampant commercialism, is likely to alienate many people.

Other Bad Things You Might Do

You can also alienate your fan base through your actions (and sometimes inactions). For instance:

- If you are accused (or convicted) of a crime, your image will be tarnished. Whether the tarnishing will turn off fans depends on the crime, the level of reporting, and the nature of your fan base. For instance, most crimes of violence are likely to be unpopular with your fan base (unless you're a gangsta rapper, in which case your fans may be somewhat more likely to accept criminal behavior on your part). On the other hand, drugs may not be a problem unless you have a squeaky-clean image or a young fan base.

- Selling out, as in giving up on your principles in return for money, will cast you in a bad light with your fans. Try not to do it or allow the perception that you have sold out to arise.

- Fans want to interact on a human level. If you are from the "treat 'em mean to keep 'em keen" school, then you may have difficulty with long-term relationships (with your fans and your partners).

There are many other ways you can upset your fans. Before you take any actions, take a moment to consider your fans' possible reactions and whether there will be any adverse consequences for your career. I'm not suggesting you shouldn't do anything edgy or dangerous—just that you should consider the implications before you throw away your career.

What Do You Do if You Don't Have a Natural Fan Base?

So far this book has assumed that you are a musician who will have (or will be able to have) a direct relationship with your fan base (provided you can just get motivated). However, there are many musicians for whom this relationship is not practical, so they reach their audience through an intermediary.

There are many musicians in this situation, for instance:

- Composers and songwriters
- DJs, MCs, and beat creators

For these people, there are two options: Carry on working through an intermediary (between you and the paying public) or find another way to get your music directly to the public.

Before we look at the direct options, think for a moment about what happens if you don't have a direct relationship with a fan base—let's take the example of a songwriter. If a songwriter writes a song, then before the song can reach an audience, the songwriter (or the songwriter's publisher) has to find an artist to record the song.

This effectively puts the songwriter's income at the mercy of the artist (and the artist's fan base). If the artist makes a poor recording of the song and/or has a small fan base, then the songwriter will not see very high royalties. Now, of course, the counterarguments are that the songwriter can still place the song with another artist, and the artist can always make a great recording. Both of these options can be lucrative for the songwriter.

However, the music is being consumed because of the other artist—not because of the songwriter. With a few exceptions, people don't buy songs because of the songwriter's brand—they buy because of the artist's brand. By using an intermediary (in this case, a publisher and then a recording artist, who in turn may be dependent on managers, record companies, and so on), the songwriter is ceding control over his income and his career to a whole range of other people who won't suffer the same (financial) consequences that the songwriter will suffer if the song doesn't generate income.

If you want to take control—take responsibility—for your earnings, then the better option will always be to find a way to form a direct relationship with a source of income. In other words, create a product that can be marketed and build a community to which you can sell that product. In short, put yourself in the same situation as performing musicians and start community building.

This section looks at some of the options to do that.

Non-Performing Musicians: Products

To generate your own independent flows of income, the non-performing musician will need to start to create products.

It's not enough to simply create products, but it's the place from which to start. Without something tangible, there are no possibilities for generating independent income.

Once you can create products, then you need to build and sustain a community. Simply releasing products is not the answer. Your approach and attitude to your community will determine the success of your products. You need to work as hard—in other words, you need to spend as much time—on building and maintaining a community as performing musicians do. Getting out and gigging generates income, but it also generates publicity and helps to create, foster, and grow a community. Unless you are spending equivalent amounts of time building your community, you are unlikely to see similar results.

So what products should the non-performing musician create? There are several obvious choices:

- The first creation should be a song (or other piece of music). Hopefully, this is logical… However, it's important to do more than simply write a song—a complete release-ready track needs to be created. (In other words, the song needs to be written, recorded, produced, mastered, and so on, so that it is at a professional level—a demo recording does not constitute a product around which you can start to build a community.)

- The next logical step is for some sort of video. Clearly, if you're a non-performing artist, creating a video may pose a challenge (not least of all, a financial challenge). However, in our current world, where YouTube is so powerful—and is a potential source of income—you're going to have to be creative and find a way to create videos.

■ Once you have some traction with a growing fan base, then you can think about merchandising. However, you need to start building your interest around musical productions first.

Once you have products, then you can start converting them into income:

■ Audio tracks can be sold as downloads (individually or as part of an album). The tracks can also be sold as CDs.

■ Videos can be used for publicity and to generate advertising income. Equally, a collection of videos could be sold as a DVD.

Non-Performing Musicians: Create an Act

Non-performing musicians will always be at a disadvantage to performing musicians when it comes to building a fan base (and remember, no fan base = no career), so one possible avenue for the non-performing musician would be to form a band, create a show, and go in search of an audience.

Let's take the example of how this could apply to a songwriter who wants to remain as a non-performing musician. From a practical perspective, the songwriter would need to be both songwriter and (at least initially) the manager. With this dual role, the first tasks the songwriter would need to complete are:

■ Writing songs for the band.

■ Finding musicians.

■ Teaching the musicians the songs and getting the act into shape.

■ Developing the products that can be sold or monetized (primarily audio recordings, videos, and limited merchandising in the first instance).

■ Finding ways to reach out to the audience—finding the fan base and arranging gigs.

Clearly, this is not going to be a solution for a quick buck—this option represents a huge amount of work and a large time investment, where the songwriter will be spending the time doing things other than writing songs. However, the flip side is that it develops a community around the songwriter's music, and to a certain extent, the personalities of the band are less significant.

If the notion of years of gigging does not appeal to you, remember that just because you formed the band, that doesn't mean you have to join it. However, if you're not going to be a member of the band, then you need to consider some very practical issues.

For instance, if you are not present (either in your role as manager or as a member of the band) at a gig, then you need to have someone you can trust to collect the money and look after the arrangements (such as liaising with the promoter, keeping the band in line so they don't get drunk before the show, and so on). You could easily reach a situation where you have the same logistical concerns that a major band has for a tour (albeit on a smaller scale) and all you're doing is playing a few bars and clubs. You could then find that the band doesn't want to play your material and walks.

As I say, this could be quite a difficult situation. It could also take a considerable financial investment. However, do you like the alternatives: no career or a career that is at the mercy of other people?

In many ways this option is not new—there have been production companies around for years. For some production companies, the line between production and management is sometimes a fine one. Often, the production company will start as the de facto manager and will get a more experienced manager involved later.

The twist here is that instead of creating an act and licensing them through a record label, you would take responsibility for building and managing the fan base. In essence, the fan base would be your property to exploit. So, for instance, once you have a first act up and running, you could then establish a second act and use the same fan base to market that second act. For the songwriter, this has the advantage that she can create more than one act to perform her material. This can significantly improve the income and her exposure.

Publicity

The purpose of publicity is to generate interest, not sales.

Earlier in this chapter, I discussed the process for converting interest into fans, fans into sales, and sales into a stream of income. Publicity means nothing if it is wasted on interesting people who will not convert—you need to get money-spending punters, or at least people who will consume your output from advertising-backed hubs.

Publicity takes a lot of time and can cost a lot of money. If your publicity isn't going to reach people who you can (ultimately) convert into a stream of income, then don't bother with the publicity—you will be much better served by growing your fan base organically.

Publicity can be categorized under two very loose headings:

- **Active publicity.** Reaching out to people to try to get them interested.

- **Passive publicity.** Publicity that "just happens" without your intervention.

Figure 2.13 gives some examples of active and passive publicity.

For the remainder of this chapter, I am going to focus on active publicity. In the next chapter, I will look at passive publicity, which in certain instances can be far more valuable than active publicity.

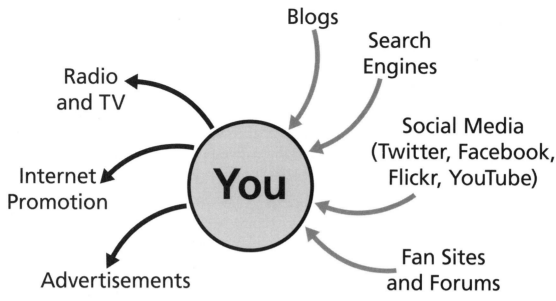

Figure 2.13 Active and passive publicity in practice.

Active Publicity

Active publicity can take many forms, but in essence it requires you to take action in order to persuade someone to expose you (and your music) to his public. This could be action that you take to get yourself into a newspaper, get your track played on the radio, or see your video played on TV.

In short, we're looking at three things here:

■ Advertising—paying someone to mention your product.

■ Getting your music played or reviewed in any media channels.

■ Publicity—creating stories that can be featured in the media. These stories can range from publicity stunts to human-interest stories.

Many people have a mistaken notion that if they sign with a record company, then that label will make them a star. This is untrue. The label will expect and will push the artist to do his or her own publicity—for instance, if you are a band, the label will expect you to tour.

The label may help focus the publicity activities by bringing in public-relations people, but ultimately all the label can do is to push an artist to do what the artist needs to do.

However, it is very easy to encourage artists to connect with their fan base in a disconnected way. Marketing can be seen as a one-way flow—from the artist to the fan—and not as a two-way communication. Equally, the wider aim—converting a relationship into a marriage—can often be forgotten when publicity professionals are involved, because these people will often be remunerated according to short-term goals (for instance, a track that needs to be publicized).

You should be aiming to foster natural, organic growth, so in many ways this form of active publicity is an anathema and a waste of resources. Although I would never suggest that you ignore any broad-based form of publicity, I think you will find that trying to connect directly with people will be more effective in the long term.

There are three main areas of active publicity that you are likely to pursue: radio, TV, the press (generally meaning the print press), and the internet. However, publicity through traditional radio, TV, and press is becoming less effective for several reasons:

- The markets are stagnant.
  - Consumer spending on TV is increasing only slowly, and the 16-to-24 age group watches less television, both in terms of the amount of television that this age group has historically watched and in relation to other age groups.
  - Consumer spending on radio services is fairly static.

- The markets are fragmenting—with many more services available, the audience is being spread more thinly.

- People are increasingly getting their information from other sources (which primarily means the internet).

Advertising

There are many places where you can advertise, including radio, TV, newspapers, magazines, billboards, and the internet.

In many cases if you want to start placing advertisements, then you are going to have to deal with advertising people. These people are the enemy: They will imply that they can bring you the world. They will not, but they will charge you a lot of money.

The statistics that advertising people can produce will suggest how effective each of the media outlets is at reaching your target audience. So for instance, they will be able to say that Show A on Radio Station B has an audience of C million people, and D% of those people are in the 18-to-45 age group.

Now, consider a conversation with your bank manager if you want to borrow money. What is going to impress her more—several million people hearing your advertisement on the radio or a known number of fans who have purchased your product and who have therefore generated a known amount of income?

In short, advertising people will not be able to deliver any measurable results. You will not be able to *prove* that their actions have increased your sales. However, they are likely to have a positive effect.

One area where a lot of money is spent is TV advertising. Many record companies will heavily advertise products where they know there is an audience and where past experience has suggested that they will recoup their advertising expenditure. However, as television becomes less significant for the younger age groups, it remains to be seen whether TV advertising will be the way that ensures music is sold in the future. And of course, for a regular musician, the budgets for TV advertising will be ludicrously high.

One place where advertising budgets can be kept to sensible levels (even to the level of a few cents per day) is the online advertising market. This is also one place where you may not need to deal with advertising people, which is an added bonus.

There are many forms of online advertising, but some of the most frequently used advertising is offered by the search engines (in particular, Google and Microsoft's Bing). This form of advertising and the options that are available are constantly changing, but in broad terms, two types of advertising are available:

- Search advertising
- Display advertising

Search Advertising

If you search on Google or Bing, above and to the right of your search results, you will see advertisements. If you've ever clicked on one of these ads, then you'll understand how effective this form of advertising can be.

The way these advertisements work is by targeting keywords. The advertiser pays to have their ad displayed whenever a certain keyword is searched for.

The ranking of each ad and the cost is determined by a bidding process. All advertisers who want to have their ad displayed against a certain search term bid. The highest bidder gets their ad displayed in the number-one slot, the second highest in the second slot, and so on.

The cost of displaying the ad is (generally) the amount bid by the next-highest bidder, plus a small amount. However, the advertiser is not charged unless someone clicks on the ad. In other words, there's no cost to display an ad, but there is a cost if someone clicks through to your site, so you only pay if the ad "works."

You can control the cost of advertising in two ways:

- First, by limiting the maximum bid. This will have implications for where an ad is ranked if it is served.

- Second, by setting a daily budget—once the daily budget has been spent, no further advertisements will be served. Therefore, the daily budget has implications for how many times an ad will be served.

For the musician, online advertising offers options to reach many people. However, the cost of advertisements when compared to the revenue generated may be disproportionate. You may need 10 people to click on an ad before you sell a download. If you make, say, 70 cents by selling a download, then if (as will be almost certain) you pay more than 7 cents for each click, you may not immediately profit from advertising. That being said, if you initiate a relationship following an advertisement, then the benefit could be immeasurable in financial terms.

There are several key advantages to advertising in this manner:

- You can reach people you may not be able to reach in any other way.

- You can target your audience (in terms of age, geography, as well as interest).

- You can find people in unusual ways. For instance, you could use the name of a similar act as a search term so your new fan finds you by accident when looking for that other act.

Display Advertising

Display advertisements are shown around websites and blogs. These ads can be text-based or have graphics, and they can be for regular-sized (full-screen) websites or sites that display on a small-sized screen (such as a smartphone screen).

Like search-based ads, these ads are placed on websites that have an affinity with the terms you specify. And again, you can bid for placement and only pay if the ad is clicked.

However, there is usually a further payment option. Instead of cost-per-click payment, you can pay on what is called a *CPM* (*cost-per-thousand*) basis, where you pay for your ad to be served and are charged irrespective of whether the ad is clicked. The advantage to this basis is that the cost of having the ad served may be lower. Clearly, the disadvantage is that you may spend a lot of money and not receive any clicks.

There are many options around this form of advertising—for instance, you can specify sites where you want your ad displayed (and equally, you can specify sites where you do not want your ad displayed). The market is very dynamic and changes rapidly, so do take a while to investigate the very latest options if this is of interest to you.

A similar form of display advertising that might be interesting to musicians may be available by buying advertising space directly on a website. If a blog or website is particularly popular with a certain demographic/interest group that chimes with your potential audience, then you may want to investigate the cost of advertising on that site.

Promotion

The line between advertising and promotion is a fine one. To make the distinction, what I mean by "promotion" is publicity work, generally for a specific project. For instance, if you have a track to promote, then you might perform that song on as many television programs as possible, or if you have an album to promote, you might perform some live gigs (or undertake a tour).

Promotion is expensive; however, it is not necessarily as expensive as advertising. It may also be more effective than advertising.

One thing that promotion may do is give you an opportunity to connect with your fan base (as well as the chance to find new fans). Clearly, you should always remember what you are promoting. However, why not use the opportunity to do something a bit special?

For instance, if you are promoting your new single and you are doing a radio interview, then why not take an acoustic guitar and perform the song live (with just a voice and a guitar)? You may not always be able to do this, but it will give you the opportunity to connect with people and to prove that you are a real performer who loves what you do.

And if you are going to perform an acoustic version of a song, then why not take your video camera and upload the video to YouTube to generate some further publicity and possible income?

The Role of PR

As you may have gathered, I'm fairly skeptical of the benefits of advertising. My skepticism is not because I think you won't get results, but because in a lot of cases I don't believe you get the results you pay for, unless those results are to raise your profile with people who will never buy your product.

I don't want to damn the whole of the marketing industry. There is one piece of marketing that I think can be very useful and that I want to single out. If you have an experienced PR person at your disposal (who may work for a record company or for an agency), that person can be very helpful. The kind of PR person you should be looking for must have lots of contacts whom he can call.

With this route, you will be getting lots of well-placed publicity, and you will be controlling the message to a much greater extent. Just taking any publicity you can get leaves you prey to whims of journalists trying to make a name for themselves.

Other Forms of Publicity

In the next chapter, "Your Presence on the Web," I will explore in detail other forms of publicity—in particular, passive publicity and the ways you can encourage the viral spread of your message.

3 Your Presence on the Web

Today, perhaps the most significant asset for any musician is intangible and cannot be controlled: the act's digital reputation.

Your digital reputation stems from many aspects, but it primarily flows from how you are represented on the internet. In other words, your digital reputation is a combination of:

- What you tell people
- What they find out about you

And what people find out about you will be greatly influenced by your search engine ranking. In other words, Google and the social networks may have a greater influence on what people think about you than you do.

However, there is still a lot you can do to influence and support a positive digital reputation and to generate income from your online activities.

Five years ago, having a presence on the internet meant having a website. That position has shifted completely, and today having a presence means being present in far more locations on the internet and proactively taking steps to manage that presence. In another five years, the position may have changed completely again, so regardless of what is written in this book, please be aware of any future developments and integrate them as appropriate.

Passive Publicity

In the previous chapter, I looked at some strategies you can employ to actively publicize your music. I now want to talk about some of the passive strategies you can consider. But before we look at the strategies, I should explain what I mean by *passive* publicity, because I definitely don't mean doing nothing.

When you actively publicize, you seek out people to receive your message: You send emails, you take out advertisements, you tweet, you approach your social-network contacts, and so on. The key being that you actively do something.

Passive publicity is all about:

- What people say about you

- How people pass on your message

- What people find when they search you out

It might be hard to influence what someone says about you on an anonymous internet forum or a social network; however, you can:

- Make it easy for people to talk about things you want them to talk about

- Provide the tools to facilitate sharing

The key issue here is that if you are creating interesting/compelling content that is easy to share, then people will share it.

If people like your content and start to share it, there's a good chance that the people who they then share your content with will share it again. This has the potential to create viral spread. Viral spread is the gold standard of passive publicity—your content suddenly catches fire and is *everywhere* over the web without you doing anything much beyond posting the content in the first place and telling a few people about it.

There are many ways you can make your content easy to share—one of the easiest is by sharing through YouTube (youtube.com; see Figure 3.1).

Perhaps the most straightforward way to encourage people to share is by creating value *for them* in sharing.

Creating Value for Other People

When it comes to getting your message out, this section is one of the most significant, so pay attention!

The Motivation to Share

To be motivated to share, there needs to be value for the person doing the sharing. This value needs to be considered in the broadest sense, so for instance, the sharer may be motivated to share by one or more of the following reasons:

- The sharer can derive a direct benefit whether financial or in terms of kudos.

- Kindness, perhaps to you but primarily to the recipient of the sharing. If someone sees something and thinks, "This will be useful/interesting for..." then they may share it.

- The item they are sharing is fun/quirky/interesting. In essence, these are variations on the theme of kindness.

Figure 3.1 YouTube makes it ridiculously easy to share videos: All you have to do is click on the Share button under the video. You can then share through many of the social networks or copy and paste a piece of text.

- It casts the sharer in a good light—for instance, it makes him look cool/educated/on the cutting edge, and so on.

- It benefits humanity. This is a subset of the themes of kindness and casting the sharer in a good light.

The Sharing Ecosystem

Let's stay with the first reason to share: direct benefit for the sharer. This may be the easiest motivation to understand. If you can create something from which the sharer can earn money, then she will share that item.

Take a practical example; say you create a video and put it on YouTube:

- When you put a video on YouTube, then other people can embed that video in their blog or website.

- If people embed your video on their site/blog, then they can sell advertising around the video, and so make money from your work.

So in short, you have created something that has value, but rather than charging you have given it away. However, someone has taken your work and is now generating income. It sort of doesn't sound fair, does it?

Well, read on:

- By putting your video on his blog/website, that other person is introducing you to all his contacts, and he is also endorsing you as an act that his contacts should pay attention to.

- You should, of course, have added some text to your video with the name of the act, your website address, and perhaps your Twitter address or your Facebook page, so anyone who sees the video will know who you are and where she can find out more (and because that information will be an integral part of the video, no one will be able to remove it).

This is a big step forward, isn't it? You are getting something in return for your hard work—you are getting access to an audience and endorsement as a credible act.

But there's more. It gets even better:

- Because you create stuff from which others can derive value, those people will follow you on YouTube (by subscribing to your channel), so they immediately pick up on any new videos. This gives you an immediate distribution network for anything new that you create.

- Moving forward, the more income that the blog/website owner can generate from your music, the more valuable (literally) you will become to that person. As you become more valuable to him, you will have more leverage, and he will promote your work harder (because he knows it generates more income). In other words, he will work harder for you, because there is a greater benefit for him.

- As well as getting access to an audience, your music is aggregated with other people (in other words, you are joining a community of other music makers). A single video (or a small number of videos) may not have critical mass (and without critical mass, sharing is harder and discoverability is lower), but through this process you are part of creating a critical mass.

Figure 3.2 illustrates this sharing ecosystem.

Any sharing is good. However, when you start connecting with people who are connected (or hyper-connected), then you start to create waves around the internet. While I will always advise people to find their own fan base, sometimes the swiftest way to find fans is by finding connected or hyper-connected people and letting them introduce you to their own following.

In this example, I've suggested a video, but that's not the only shareable product you could create. A great image will get shared (and if embedded, it can create income for

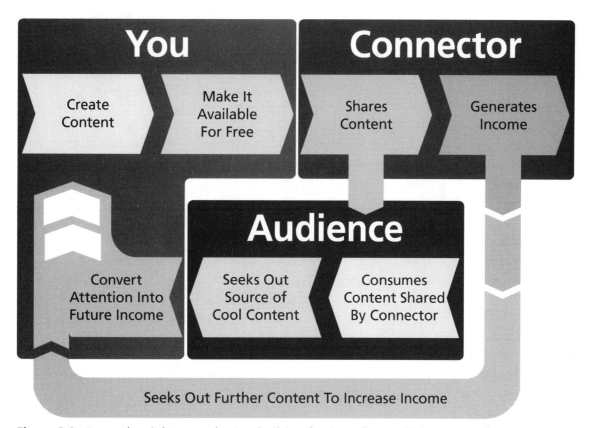

Figure 3.2 Done the right way, sharing builds a fan base from which you can then start to generate income.

others). Equally, a well-thought tweet or a relevant comment on a social network can be shared. Digitally, everything can be shared—you just have to create something that is worthy of being shared.

Now we've got that straight, let's look at how you should be present on the web.

How to Be Present on the Web

At one time, all you needed to do was have a page on the internet, and that was good enough. Then that changed, and you needed to have a whole website.

Although a website is still fundamental to your whole online presence (and I'll talk more about what your website needs to achieve later in this chapter), today the web is all pervasive, so it is necessary to have an active presence in many places. There are several reasons why you *need* multiple presences:

■ Some people live in their own social-media bubble—if you are not present within that particular bubble (such as Facebook), then they will never find you.

■ You're going to be mentioned in many different places even if you try to focus all of the comments in one place (such as your website), so you might as well try to control/shape/influence how you are represented (or at the very least make sure your view is heard firsthand). Also, if there is income to be generated, then you should be generating income. Another key reason for being present is to ensure quality control.

- Resilience. Websites, social-media sites, and the like will all suffer outages from time to time. You can minimize the outages but rarely prevent them altogether. However, if you are present in multiple locations, and one presence temporarily goes down, you are still present in many other places. The lights will always be on somewhere, so if anyone comes looking for you, they will always be able to find something.

The practical process of being present in multiple places means setting up (and maintaining) your own website, participating in discussions, and joining a number of social and sharing networks. A quick scan of the social networks will tell you there are hundreds of them, so where do you begin?

Who's Talking about You?

You could simply join every social network, website, forum, or whatever else you can find. However, this will probably take a long time. You would then spend the rest of your life (and a bit longer) trying to keep up with all the discussions going on, and that's before you spend any time making music.

A better course is to be more targeted. Go to where your fan base goes—go to where there is some buzz about you.

There are a number of easy (and free) ways for you to find out who is talking about you.

Alerts

Perhaps the most useful tool for finding out when people are talking about you is Google Alerts (google.com/alerts). Think of this as your own personal clippings service.

The way Google Alerts works is by employing the Google spider to work for you. The Google spider constantly scans the web for new material to keep the Google search up to date.

With Google Alerts, you input a search term—for instance, your name, the band's name, the name of your album, or any other significant term (you can have many terms)—and if the spider finds a new mention of any term, it will notify you immediately.

You can then follow up the mention and see where people are talking about you.

@ mentions and #hashtags

There are various conventions used to talk about people in social media.

Take Twitter as an example. If you mention @simonpcann (my Twitter name) in a tweet, then that tweet will be highlighted for me. If you get my name wrong (for instance, you miss the "P" in the middle), then I won't know that you've mentioned me (and some other Simon Cann will wonder why you're talking about him).

#hashtags are slightly different. A #hashtag is a word (or a phrase, usually combined to form one word, so instead of #giving an example you would use #givinganexample) to describe or identify the subject of the tweet, and it is preceded by the hash sign.

A #hashtag is an easy way to identify subject matter when you are tweeting, and by extension, it can also have a use if you are the subject of a discussion.

As a side issue, whenever you tweet, you should add a #hashtag to give your tweet a chance to be picked up by anyone who is interested in the subject you are discussing.

Web Analytics

There are many web analytics programs available. One of the most widely used, because it is good and free, is Google Analytics (google.com/analytics; see Figure 3.3).

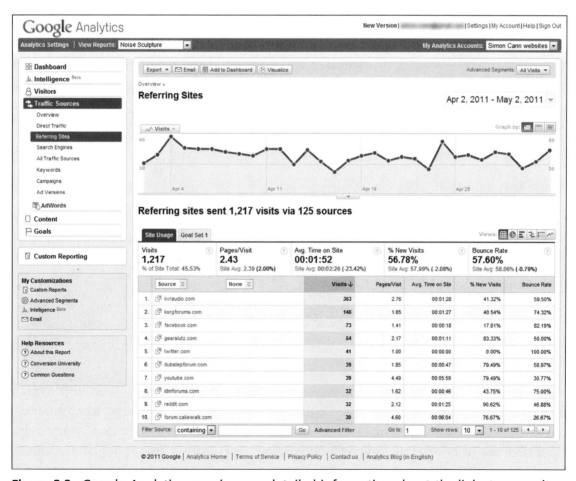

Figure 3.3 Google Analytics can give you detailed information about the links to your site.

Google Analytics (and the other analytics programs) can give you a wide range of useful and interesting data about your website. One very useful piece of information is about which sites are linking to you, and more importantly, you can usually find the specific page so that you can then (if appropriate) join in the conversation.

Inbound Links

Another simple way to find where you have been linked from is to use a search engine. Search on your domain (for instance, search for "noisesculpture.com", with the quote marks), and you will find links back to your site.

The Social Networks

Hopefully by looking at the links to your website, you will be able to figure out the most obvious places you *need* to be. However, those are not the only places—you should also appear in the popular places if you want to be available to the largest audience.

As a start, there are probably between four and six social networks where you might want to consider a presence.

Twitter

Twitter (twitter.com) is a microblogging service where you can publish short messages (up to 140 characters). People can then see your messages on a web page (see Figure 3.4) or follow you directly when your messages are aggregated in their tweet stream along with the messages from the other people they follow.

There are several benefits to being on Twitter:

■ Two-way communication is possible.

■ Interesting messages get spread. (It requires only a button press to simply re-tweet a message—it's pretty close to frictionless sharing.)

■ Trending topics—topics of widespread interest—can bring issues to the forefront of the public consciousness.

Research suggests that most (75 percent of) Twitter users use the service primarily to follow people and not to actively participate in conversations, so this makes it a place where you will find a lot of listeners.

At the time of writing this book, there was a certain concern being expressed (through the blogosphere) that with its commercialization, Twitter was effectively becoming polluted with advertisements. The issue is not that there are advertisements, but that a preponderance of tweets are effectively advertisements, rather than part of a communication between Twitter users. This may or may not be relevant, but it is always worth considering how a service is viewed before you join it.

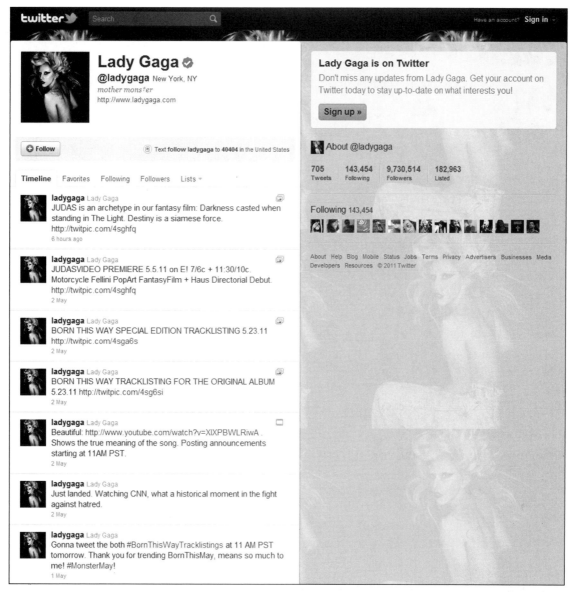

Figure 3.4 A page full of tweets—in this case, Lady Gaga's.

Facebook

Facebook (facebook.com) is a social-networking service. At the time of writing this book, it has more than 600 million users (by comparison, the United States has 305 million citizens) and is the most widely used social network.

Each user can set his own profile and share messages and images. Users can also express interests and participate in groups of like-minded individuals.

As a musician, you can set up a page dedicated to your act (see Figure 3.5). Individuals can then "like" your page and follow the postings (as well as post on your page). This starts the two-way communication process. And of course, because you are on Facebook,

Figure 3.5 The Facebook page for the boy band The Wanted.

you can participate in groups or be talked about by groups, thereby giving you immediate access to a range of people who are selecting themselves as potentially being interested in your type of act. You can also draw people to you by advertising within Facebook.

In many ways, Facebook is a closed system—once people are on the inside, they don't need to leave, because all their friends and family are there. That is perhaps the most compelling reason for joining the network.

Orkut

Orkut (orkut.com) is Google's social network. Think of it as a variant of Facebook, and you'll be getting close.

Orkut is often regarded as a failure. However, if having 51 million members and being the second largest social network (in other words, being bigger than Twitter and being the biggest network in India and Brazil, which together account for 1.4 billion people) constitutes failure, then I'm not sure what success looks like.

Buzz

Buzz (google.com/buzz) is sort of Google's version of Twitter. In many ways it is more sophisticated, but it is also less popular.

Like Twitter, you can post short messages on Buzz; these can be public or private. Unlike Twitter, there is no limit to the length of your message, and you can include photos, videos, and other content that will show in a user's stream (without the user needing to open another service).

The service is integrated into Gmail, so it is very much like sending an email but without a recipient (in the case of a public message), and it also works very well on the mobile platforms. You can geo-tag each Buzz, and then your location can be shown on Google Maps, allowing you to find and interact with people who are nearby.

In addition, you can connect readily with other services (Flickr, Twitter, and others).

However, as I said, it is less popular than Twitter, and a lot of Buzzes are simply Twitter (or other service) re-posts, where someone is posting the same message to all social networks to ensure that everything goes to everyone. This criticism can be leveled at the other services; however, there is anecdotal evidence to suggest that Buzz content is particularly heavily populated with duplicate posts.

YouTube

YouTube (youtube.com) is the most popular video-sharing site on the internet. By popular, I mean exceptionally popular—the most recent figures published by Google are that every minute, 48 hours of material is uploaded to YouTube. (Before you check for typos, yes, I do mean every single minute, 48 hours of content is uploaded—or, looked at another way, every one second, 2,880 seconds of content is uploaded.)

YouTube isn't a social network in the conventional sense, but it does offer a lot of social features:

- First and most obviously, you can share videos.

- People can subscribe to your channel and so be notified when you post new videos.

- People can vote on and rate your videos.

- People can comment on and reply to your videos.

- People can share your videos.

YouTube offers some great advantages to musicians in terms of getting discovered. Whenever a video comes up, other videos are listed on the right-hand side of the page. These videos are all related—this gives you a chance to be found. You can, of course, increase your chances of being found—for instance, if you do a cover version of a well-known (and frequently played) song, then your cover version stands more chance of being found than one of your regular songs.

If you're going to release anything on video, then you need to be on YouTube. And don't forget, as I mention elsewhere in this book, you can generate income from advertising sold against your videos.

Flickr

Flickr (flickr.com) is a photo-sharing site, and like YouTube, it isn't a social network in the conventional sense. But like YouTube, it allows you to share (photos mostly) and to build a community around you.

The sharing bit is important for community building: People will want to share with you. For instance, if you play a gig, people may want to share their photos of your performance through Flickr. It's not people sharing with *you* that is important, but rather, it's important that they share with everyone connected to you—in other words, sharing is an integral part of building a community around you.

Which to Join?

Trends change. Five years ago, MySpace was the dominant social network, and people said, "Face-what?!?" Today, for most people, MySpace is irrelevant (but that's not to say it won't have a use for you). Whatever I suggest today will be out of date by the time you read this book, so please take these recommendations with a warning.

I would suggest that you don't join all of the networks.

As a start, go with Flickr and YouTube for photo and video sharing. Both are low-impact/low-maintenance networks where you can have a presence with little work.

Facebook is hard to resist given its size, and Twitter is hard to resist given its prevalence. I'd suggest starting with one, and once you are comfortable with that, then consider the other.

Think about Orkut and Buzz, but be cautious about simply jumping in. There are very valid reasons to get involved with both networks—don't just join because you think you should.

I caution you about joining more networks than you can keep up to date, and in this context, fewer is probably better. I also caution you against considering only the networks I have suggested. There are many others out there that may better serve your needs, and you should join those before you join any mentioned here if those others are right for you. And if we're in a mood for looking into the future, let me mention one more network that seems to be growing in popularity: foursquare (foursquare.com).

foursquare is a location-based social network for use with mobile devices (and hence users need GPS-enabled smartphones or other location-tracking tools to check in at venues). Given that the service is location-based, it may not in and of itself grow your fan base; however, it will help you find people in your vicinity, which may be particularly helpful if you're touring.

What to Post?

You're a creative person; you'll figure out what to post!

All right, I'm being glib. However, there is a serious point here: I can't tell you what to post. Only you know what you're trying to promote and what your fan base wants to talk about. Bring those two issues together, and you'll have a great start. Whatever you say, you need to make it interesting *for the person hearing the message*.

When you do post, you might also want to think about two issues:

- First, if you join more than one social network, don't simply repost exactly the same content to each network. Get the message right for the medium—so for instance, you can send a number of short messages on Twitter, but maybe you could write a longer piece and post it on your Facebook page.

- Second, remember #hashtags.

Helping People Who Are Looking for You

People will find you in a range of different ways and may not necessarily find what you want them to find out or where you want them to find it. However, there are some things you can do to influence what they find.

Usually, you will want people to find your website—hopefully, this is the hub from which all your web presences flow. However, there's a good chance that your website won't be the first place someone encounters or hears about you. Indeed, if someone doesn't know about you, then how will she know to come to your website?

In reality, people are going to want to try to find you if they've heard something about you or have seen a mention, perhaps on a social media site or an internet forum, or maybe they will have seen one of your videos embedded on another site.

If you're really lucky, then in making the mention, a link to your website will be included or perhaps a link to your social-media presence (so for instance, if you get mentioned on Twitter, you might be lucky and have someone mention your @address).

In reality, you are often lucky if you get a link. Heck…just be grateful if they spell your name right or can even remember which song of yours they liked.

Unfortunately, unless people find a direct conduit to you, then you're likely to have to rely on:

■ Referrals from search engines such as Google

■ Haphazard guesses of your web address

There are a number of actions you can take to improve your chances of being that found needle in the haystack.

Getting Picked Up by Search Engines

Perhaps the most sensible thing you can do to help people find you and to guide them to relevant information about you is to think about the search engines.

Search-engine ranking is a black art. Many people will sell you services to help improve your ranking. I'm not convinced that many of these services do much good. If you want to read more about the latest thinking on search-engine optimization, one site I recommend you check out is Search Engine Watch (searchenginewatch.com).

Ignoring all of the science, there are some sensible things you can do to give search engines a chance of finding you, such as:

■ **Ensure that you use text and not graphics.** It is very tempting to use attractive graphics for key headings, such as the artists' names. If you do this, then ensure that each artist's name (in full) is included in regular text. Remember, search engines will search text—they cannot search (and read) graphics. Some sites are built entirely with graphics—while these look good, they are useless for search engines, because the text cannot be read/searched.

■ **Ensure that all of your key information is included on your site.** For instance, if you have a well-recognized song, make sure its title appears somewhere. People may search for your songs instead of just searching for you.

■ **Ensure that any unique words associated with you are included.** If there is anything that can help narrow down a search and differentiate you from other websites, then use it.

■ **Have links from other sites.** Some search engines rank the importance of a site according to the number of links to the site. As you would expect, this is one area where a strong social-network presence will pay dividends. Another way you can increase the number of links is by forum postings. Just make sure you include your site's URL in your signature, and the link will be set up for the search engine to find.

Make It Easy to Share Your Content

If you want people to link to your website, then you need to make it easy for them to link to you.

You can do two things to make this easy for people. The first is to ensure that each page has an individual URL (*universal resource locator*, or more simply, *web address*). For instance, some websites use frames and treat each piece of information as a "pane" within that frame, and the frame gets the URL, not the pane. The result of this is that people can link to the frame, but not the actual piece of information (the pane) that they want to link to.

This is a matter of website construction that I will discuss further later on in this chapter.

Second, and far more importantly, you can encourage the use of social bookmarks. The social-bookmark sites, quite literally allow people to bookmark interesting web pages (or websites) and then to share those links. The power of this arrangement, for you, is that the sharer then connects with his own community of interested people, who will often check out the link.

There are many social-bookmark sites; the most common are Delicious (delicious.com), Digg (digg.com), Slashdot (slashdot.com), Reddit (reddit.com), and StumbleUpon (stumbleupon.com). To encourage people to share, you can include buttons to link individual pages to these social sites. You will see these link buttons used on many sites—for instance, Figure 3.6 shows these buttons being used on the BBC news website.

Ideally, you should add sharing buttons to every page on your website. Several services offer tools to make this easier (and offer additional services, such as analytics, to track the sharing). The most popular services are AddThis (addthis.com), AddToAny (addtoany.com), and ShareThis (sharethis.com).

Helping People Who Want to Find Out More about You

I'm guessing that when I suggested you set up your own website, you understood my reasons completely. Indeed, I'm also guessing that you didn't need to read this book to decide that having your own website would help your career. However, you may start to wonder what I am doing when I suggest that you highlight other websites that mention you—surely by pointing people in different directions, this could get confusing and could draw income away?

And you are right to be concerned. However, remember that your success is based on a community around you, and here we're talking about publicity.

Figure 3.6 Sharing buttons on the BBC news website. (The buttons are to the right of the date—the Facebook and Twitter buttons are most prominent, and the others can be accessed by clicking on the Share button.)

Okay, enough self-justification. What am I actually suggesting you *do*, here? Well, several things:

- Find other communities that mention you. Participate in those communities and support them.

- Link to other websites/communities that have information about you. And when I say link, I don't just mean post a link on your website, I mean tweet about those places (or retweet interesting tweets) and make other mentions from your social-media presences.

Let me explain further.

Participate in Other Communities. As I've already discussed, you will be able to find whether you are mentioned in and linked from other communities (whether that be Facebook, groups, blogs, web-based forums, or something similar) by looking at your website statistics. Follow those links back, and you will find a whole array of other communities.

Take a look around these communities and then participate—drop in for a chat or just to say "hi." Be open and honest about who you are, include your URL in your signature, and perhaps use your act's logo as an avatar. (An avatar is the small image that identifies individual users on internet forums.) There's no need to spend too long, and you definitely don't want to hang around if there are any arguments. All you are trying to do is show that you are a friendly sort of person.

This sounds too simple, doesn't it? And in many ways it is. However, you have done a few things here:

- First, you have reached out to people on a human level. This gives you a certain degree of humanity.

- Second, you have added some more links back to your website. The more links there are back to your website, the more people are likely to flow toward your site. Also, the more links there are out there referring people to your website, the faster people will find you (the more links, the more your site becomes a magnet).

- Last, you have tapped into another community—in other words, a whole group of people (not just one person). Each member of that community may then bring a new group of people with him. Many communities link to other communities, and community people often bring whole communities with them, not just one or two friends. As you reach out to communities, you have the potential for the number of your fans to grow very quickly.

Other Websites/Communities That Have Information about You. As you gain popularity, people will want to write about you. One place that people may write about you is in the forums, and we have already covered this.

You may find that unofficial fan sites crop up. (Your site should be the "official" fan site.) If unofficial sites spring up, I suggest that you be very grateful and do everything you can to help these people. Just make sure their site doesn't look too much like yours, or people might think your official site is a fake.

One of the main reasons to support the unofficial sites (and to ensure that they don't look fake) is that they give you credibility. Anyone who alights upon these fan sites will be impressed by the fan's devotion and will often want to know more about the act. Hence, these other sites will help to pass more traffic to you.

When you reach a certain level (don't do it before you've played your first gig), then think about a Wikipedia (wikipedia.org) entry. Wikipedia is an online encyclopedia that is updated by anyone who wants to (which could mean you). If you do start an entry, make sure you keep it up to date. If you don't start an entry, then check Wikipedia periodically just in case anyone else has written about you (in particular, to check that they haven't accidentally got any of their facts wrong). You should, of course, check your listings in any other online encyclopedias or similar reference sources.

Building the Perfect Website

Your website is the heart, or the hub, of your online presence.

You shouldn't have a website for vanity or just because everyone else does. You should have a website to achieve specific business objectives. These objectives may include (but are not limited to):

- Giving information about the act. Acting as the central and definitive resource for the act and the members of the act.

- Highlighting the products that are available, which could include:

  - Music (whether downloads or CDs)
  - Videos (both freely available through YouTube and so on, or for sale, perhaps in DVD/Blu-ray form)
  - Merchandise
  - Gigs

- Highlighting your presence in other places, such as the social networks (or any other place where your fan base can interact with you).

A website will never have only one purpose, and as such, there will always be compromises. For instance, it may include the act's history, the members' biographies, and details about where to get gig tickets—you will have to decide which takes priority in terms of how you present the information. And to confuse matters further, there will be content that can be used in different ways (for instance, videos that can be seen for publicity purposes and that generate revenue).

There will be many discussions about what constitutes the perfect website, and to be honest, no website is ever perfect—the best you can strive for is a good work in progress.

Against that background, here are a few of my thoughts about the features of a good website. Let's start with a few general principles. Your website should be:

- Fast (in terms of load time and responsiveness when any feature is clicked)

- Easy to navigate

- Focused on you

Notice that I didn't mention the visual impact? Don't worry, I will come to that.

The Need for Speed

Your website should load quickly. Once loaded, page changes should be fast (if possible, immediate). Anyone navigating through your website should be able to get to the intended destination page quickly. If you're not fast, then people will get bored or frustrated and will go elsewhere (and you will lose the potential income that could have flowed from that person).

You can design a website to be fast. However, if you start using a professional web designer or allow "marketing" people to give their input, you will be pressured to do things that can dramatically slow down your website.

There are two things that significantly slow down a website (that is, cause it to take a long time to load and to change pages)—graphics (especially video) and audio. As you know, in your line of work, audio and visual features on a website are very important.

There is a trend to use short video clips that load automatically when you go to a website. Some of these can look quite good. Other sites have a large number of images. These, too, can be quite impressive. Some sites start to play the artist's latest tracks automatically. However, all of these approaches will dramatically slow down the loading time of the site. Some will cause the site to be so slow that you will wonder whether your computer has crashed.

There are many reasons for including impressive graphics and tracks that play automatically:

- When it finally loads, it looks good.

- People don't realize just how long the features will take to load. Often the web designer will demonstrate the features in a meeting, where she can run the video or other media feature directly from her computer, thereby avoiding showing the download time.

- Peer pressure—everybody else is doing something similar. This is coupled with a perceived need to appear fresh, new, or cutting edge.

- The belief that because it is a musician's website, music has to be stuffed down the throats of anyone who alights on the site.

Let me make a plea: Please don't do this. Please don't even think about this. Instead, please create a simple home page that loads virtually instantaneously. If you then want video, put the video on YouTube and embed it into your site.

Obviously, the home page should be visually appealing. However, you can achieve this in a quite simple and straightforward manner through some carefully chosen visual images. These images can then be optimized for web viewing so that their loading time is reduced to the absolute minimum.

It is not necessary to have animated graphics to impress people. Indeed, with animated graphics, there is a much greater chance that your site will look naff or cheesy, or will age badly, whereas with something simple there is less to get wrong in terms of design decisions.

Easy to Navigate

Too often, the navigation for a website is engineered by the website designer (who usually is a computer programmer of some sort). This is a bad, bad thing to do.

Website navigation should be designed from the perspective of the user (in other words, the fan or potential fan). It should be designed around how the fans think about you and how the fans expect to find information about you. Navigation should not be constructed on the basis of how the underlying data files are organized.

Navigation from the Home Page

The first step in helping people to find their way around your site will be the home page (the page you see when you first load your site). The home page should clearly have visual impact and should be welcoming. (In other words, it should be interesting and not crammed with lots of confusing text.)

If there is something you are particularly promoting or you have some recent breaking news, then that should be featured prominently on your home page. For instance, if you have just sent an email to your fan base about some gigs, and you have referred people to your site for the details of the dates and where the fans can get tickets, then your gigs should be prominent on the home page.

In practice, this means that words to the effect of "Gigs announced" should be immediately visible when you load the home page, and somewhere under that there should be text to the effect of "Click here for details of the dates and where you can get tickets."

Navigation Bars

Navigation bars are groups of buttons often to one side or across the top of the screen that help viewers find their way around a site. For an example of a navigation bar, see Figure 3.7, which shows a screen grab of my website. The navigation bar is on the left side. You will see there are a number of buttons, labeled home, profile, news, books, videos, widgets, FAQ, keep up-to-date, and contact.

My website has a simple aim: to promote my books (and to a lesser extent, to promote my videos, which, for me, are solely used as a marketing tool). Accordingly, my site is comparatively simple, so I need only a limited number of buttons. Each button has a text label that is fairly self-explanatory. I recommend you use the minimum number of buttons you can get away with, although you should never use fewer buttons if this will make your site counterintuitive in its operation. As a general rule of thumb, anything around six or seven buttons is fine. As I have done, you might want to have more, but I would still attempt to keep the number as low as possible.

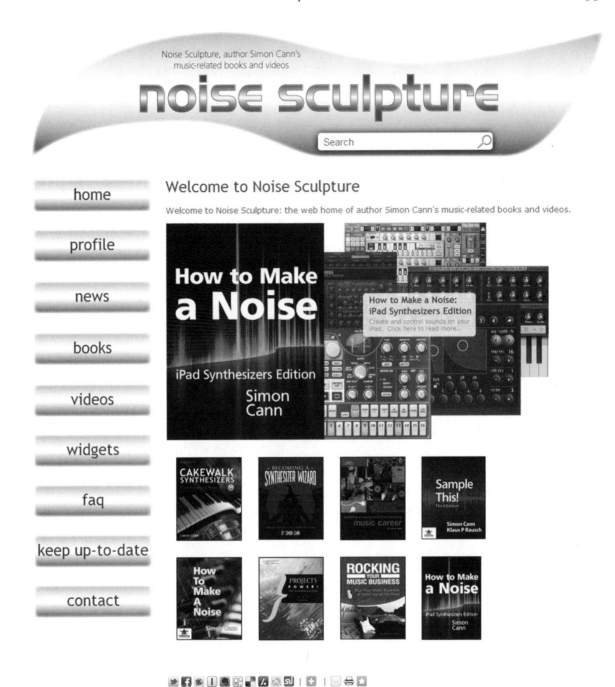

Figure 3.7 My music-related website. Note the navigation bar on the left side, which helps viewers find their way around the site.

The text on the buttons should be immediately legible and should unambiguously suggest where the viewer is being led. If the text on the button is insufficiently descriptive, you may also want to consider a rollover message (some text that displays when you roll your mouse cursor over the button).

This may all seem obvious, but I'm sure we have all seen sites that are hard to understand immediately. Remember, your fans are sensible individuals (hey—they wouldn't follow you if they weren't), and you're not making it easy because they are stupid. You are making it easy because you respect them and you want them to get to the information they want without wasting their time. If they have to waste their time or they get frustrated, they are very unlikely to spend money on you.

Structuring the Navigation

You need to give some careful consideration to how broad and deep your navigation system is. Let me elaborate. You have got some "stuff" that you want to disseminate to your fans and potential fans. The "stuff" is a mixture of different things—for instance, information about you, contact details, embedded music or video clips, pictures, and so on. You need to fit this information into a framework so that viewers can find their way around your website in a manner that immediately makes sense to them.

As a first step, that information can be split under some main headings. These main headings will become the navigation buttons. However, under these general headings, you may have a lot of different pieces of information. Those different pieces of information can be separated to make navigation clear. Under those new subheadings, you may have another grouping of information that could be separated under sub-subheadings.

As you can see, this is getting confusing! Just think how your viewers may feel. Let me give an example to try to illustrate this point. Suppose you have a button labeled About. This is where you have all of the information about the artist, including, for instance, biographies and news. You may have two different types of news: current news (news that is still relevant) and archived news (old news that you retain for completeness). Under the archived news, you may then store the news by year. With this arrangement, you could have four layers:

About > News > Archive > Year

This has a certain logic to it, and many people would be able to follow this structure. However, suppose you are looking for a press release in the 2011 archives, but you can't find it, so you want to check out the 2010 archives. You could start from the top (About) and follow the same path down the tree, and instead of selecting 2011, select 2010. However, it would be preferable if there was some way in the navigation system to step up (from 2011 to Archive) and then step down again (to 2010).

The ease with which people will be able to find their way around your site will be governed by two factors: the number of layers (in this example, there are four layers) and how you can navigate up and down between the layers. The more layers you add, the more complicated your website will be and the harder it will be for people to find what they are looking for.

The solution to ensuring that the number of layers is minimized is to have a sufficient number of main headings (in other words, a sufficient number of navigation buttons or whatever you are using to assist navigation). However, as I mentioned earlier, there is a limit to the number of navigation buttons you can have before browsing around your website becomes confusing. As you will understand, you need to strike a balance here and create a website that works for you.

Also, as you will have figured, it is pretty tedious so keep clicking links to find things. Most people will expect your site to have some sort of search functionality that will hopefully take them directly to what they are looking for.

As a general rule of thumb, if you can restrict yourself to two layers—the navigation buttons and then a layer below that—you will be able to create a website that is fast to use and simple to navigate. With some hard work, you could create a site with three layers that is reasonably fast and reasonably easy to navigate. When you get to the fourth layer, then you are likely to reach the point of confusion. You should also remember that each branch on the navigation tree does not need to be the same length.

You may be wondering about the example I gave earlier, in which the news archive was stored at the fourth level. As suggested in the preceding paragraph, if you go to the fourth level, you may reach confusion (as I illustrated). As well as going too deep, I think my example displayed another error: It put the news in a counterintuitive location. You may disagree, but I would suggest that most people looking for news about an act would not look for this under the heading About. If you regularly have news, then it is probably best to have a News navigation button and put all of the news there.

Alternatives to Navigation Bars

I've mentioned navigation bars at some length. Don't feel you must have these. With your music career, you are working in a creative industry, so you can be creative with your website, too. However, don't get too creative—if people don't understand your navigation system, you will lose customers (even if you've employed some of the most intelligent and innovative tricks that are available).

If your website is too hard to navigate (in other words, its operation is counterintuitive or people cannot find what they're looking for *immediately*) even with your best effort, then you've got too much stuff. If you've got too much stuff, then cut the content. A website should be promoting you; it is not a detailed reference of your whole performing career. (Leave those highs and lows to your biography and the documentaries that will follow after its publication.)

Amount of Information on a Page

The amount of information that any one page carries will have a dramatic effect on the comprehensibility of the page. Equally, the size of each paragraph will have a marked effect on the comprehensibility and the ease with which someone can physically read the information.

In an ideal world, you would not have a page of information take up more than one screen. (In other words, if you open any particular page on your website, all of the information should be displayed without the need to scroll down or across.)

However, there is a difficulty here. There are many different screen sizes, so the amount of information that can fit on a single screen will vary. As a minimum, a laptop screen might be 13 inches in size. (There are smaller and there are bigger, but on the whole that is the current minimum specification.) By default, most laptop screens are then between to 800×600 or $1,024 \times 768$ resolution. The larger size is fairly standard these days and is a good size to consider when thinking about how much information you can get on a screen.

There is another issue here: mobile. People increasingly view websites from their phone or from tablets (such as the iPad). Tablet screen are usually big enough to view regular websites; however, the smaller format devices can pose a challenge.

Even if we ignore mobile devices, there will obviously be times when the aspiration to keep the information on one screen is wholly impractical. At these times you should take a pragmatic approach but still do everything possible to aid navigation.

Does It Promote You?

It may sound like the most obvious thing, but your website should be about promoting you and your music. I make this point because often it gets forgotten.

People use their site to try to show off or to settle old scores. Anything that is not directly about your music is a distraction that will distance your fan base from you. As distance increases, your income will decrease.

Visual Impact

It is crucial that your website has a clear, crisp, engaging visual image. There is nothing worse than a website that looks old and tired. However, the way to ensure that you don't look old and tired is not to invest in the latest whiz-bang technology (which is likely to be advocated by old and tired web designers who are keen to try out their new toys). Instead, the answer is to design the site (visually) so that it looks as appealing as possible. The best way to do this is to find a talented designer.

You may be tempted to do the visuals for your own website. I caution against this unless you have experience in this area. So often homemade visuals just look, well, homemade. From the start you will be giving the image of an act that is cheap—in other words, not very successful and perhaps not worth following.

One last word of caution: Although your website should look great, try to ensure that it doesn't look to "corporate." By this I mean if someone could look at your site for the first time and think, "That's a website for a pharmaceutical company," or, "That's a website for an aerospace contractor," then you may not be appealing to music fans.

Things That Frustrate Your Viewers

There are lots of things you can do with your website that will really, *really* frustrate your viewers. Here is a list of just a few of those things:

- **Websites that require specific software to view.** Some web features (particularly the horrible animated graphics I have already railed against) need specific plug-ins to be installed on the viewing computer. Some people may take the time to install the plug-ins just to view your site, but many will not bother and will look elsewhere for their music.

- **Really slow websites.** Even when the necessary plug-ins are installed, you shouldn't use them automatically. Using animated graphics and automatically playing music will cause a website to slow down while the necessary files are downloading. While the files are downloading, it can appear as if the website is not working. Again, this may encourage a potential new fan to go elsewhere.

- **Websites that are incompatible with certain web browsers.** There is a wide range of web browsers, each of which will view HTML (and other web-based code) in a different way. You should ensure that your website has been checked on as many different browsers as possible before you go live. In particular, you should ensure that your website works as intended when it is viewed with Internet Explorer, Chrome, Firefox, Safari, and Opera.

- **Websites designed for a particular screen size.** As I have already mentioned, there are many different screen sizes available, and different users select different resolutions. The combination of these factors may mean your website has to fit into a very small space or a very big space. Although you can't account for all sizes, please do check that your website looks good at a range of sizes and resolutions.

Choosing a URL

A URL is a universal resource locator. In English, that means your website address.

You are likely to be constrained in your choice of URL if your act's name is not readily available. Although your choices may be limited, do try to choose a URL that is unique, memorable, and easy to communicate verbally.

I suggest you register several URLs—for instance, a .com and a .net version of your URL. You may want to register a local version (for instance, .co.uk), and although that may be a sensible idea to ensure that no one else tries to take the address, I wouldn't suggest you use it in public, because localized URLs have a habit of looking very parochial.

If you do register several URLs, then only use one (the obvious choice being .com). Only use the others to automatically transfer the viewer to your main URL.

But Where's the Interaction?

You might have noticed that I haven't suggested much in the way of fan-base interaction on the website.

Once I would have suggested setting up a forum where fans could congregate to talk about you and where, from time-to-time, members of the act might make appearances. But not anymore.

Now—in my opinion—a better solution is to interact through social media. If you run your own forum, then:

- First, you need to implement it. That will take time and may cost you money.

- Then you need to moderate any forum; in other words, you need to ensure that people are not using the forum to post hate-filled messages or advertisements for dubious pharmaceuticals.

And after that, the forum is likely to be far less popular than it could be, because first, everybody is elsewhere (on Facebook…), and second, there's too much hassle to sign up (again) to post on a forum where no one is participating.

How to Build Your Website

There are many ways to build a website, and there is definitely no single "right" way. However, let me offer one powerful and flexible option: Use a content management system.

A content management system is a tool where you feed in text, photos, dates, and so on, and it produces a website. The key being, as long as you can work a word processor—like interface, it will do everything else necessary to create a website.

There are a number of different systems available, the leading ones being Drupal (drupal.org), WordPress (wordpress.org), and Joomla! (joomla.org). There are similarities between the three systems:

- They are all open source (so they are free, and you don't need to ask permission/pay a license fee to use them).

- They are modular—you can add the bits you need and take away stuff you don't need.

- A search engine is just another module that can be engaged.

- You can create a number of RSS feeds. The significance is that you can readily syndicate content by publishing data in this format (as well as displaying content on your website). Most importantly, an RSS feed with an audio track attached gives you a podcast.

- The back end and the presentation are totally separate—these systems use what are called *themes*. A theme is the visual look of the site. This means that if you want to change the look of your site, all you need to do is change the theme—you don't need to touch the content. Equally, you can have different themes, so for instance, your content is presented in a different way for large screens and smartphone screens.

For my websites, I use Drupal. I find it hugely powerful but very flexible. Drupal powers approximately 2 percent of the internet and has some very high-profile sites, including the White House (whitehouse.gov). Although many large sites use it, it is also ideal for smaller sites, so if you're not sure where to start, check out Drupal.

Now That You've Got the Fan Base, What Are You Going to Do with Them?

Once you have found a fan base, and you are nurturing and growing that fan base, you can start to introduce them to your products. In the next part we will look at products and the issues around developing your product range.

The Product

4 Creating Products: Generating Income

The music industry convulsed during the first decade of this century.

If you listened to some of the stories, you might have thought that we were close to the end of the world. But the music industry survived, and despite what some people suggest, the major players are still making healthy profits—they have learned how to make money in different ways (often doing deals where they earn revenue from many different sources), and they promote in different ways (hence the proliferation of TV talent shows).

One of the changes to the mainstream music industry is a focus on mass-market, high-income-generating hits (hence the focus on talent shows). For the regular musician and the musician looking to build a career, this is good—the economics of small come into play. There are now many areas where small acts can earn a viable living but the big acts can't go because their overhead would make the option unprofitable.

Doing the Arithmetic

One big change, for acts both big and small, has been the diversification of income streams.

Diversi-who?

There was once a time when the main source of income for a musician was album sales. (This was in the good old days, when we had albums, and they were released on vinyl.) Touring was something bands enjoyed and needed to do to promote their album, but it didn't make money.

Today the world has changed. Income from music sales is far less significant in terms of an act's total income, and touring can make a profit (especially with sponsorship). But more significantly, income can now come from a range of sources, including music sales, video, touring, sponsorship, merchandise, licensing fees, and so on.

No one source will make you a multi-billionaire. Indeed, each individual source may seem to generate a small amount of income. However, in aggregate and taken over the long term, lots of modest sources of income will create a viable stream of income that can sustain a career. As a musician, you need to have the mindset to ensure that you are always working so that those various sources keep generating income.

This multi-income-stream approach also adds resilience. If you have only one source of income and that dries up, then you have a problem. By contrast, if no single source counts for more than, say, 10 percent of your income, and one source of income ends, then you'll still be receiving at least 90 percent of your income from all of your other sources.

There is a secondary issue here. With so many sources of income, you need to be able to identify:

■ Which activities you undertake actually generate income.

■ Which activities generate profits. (Remember, income and profit are different.) Once you understand which of your activities generate profits, then you can figure out which ones generate the best profits (the area on which you should focus).

■ Which activities don't generate income and, leading on from that, which activities result in a loss.

■ Which activities result in a loss/don't generate income but are necessary because they support or lead to activities that make money.

In other words, you shouldn't try to do everything, but if you're going to be successful, you should focus on the things that make money, and in order to do that, you need to understand the economics of each individual activity.

Let's have a look at the available sources of income. I will look at some of the commercial aspects here, but I'll get into the economics in much greater detail in the next part.

Opportunities for Income

To make money, you need to create stuff. Now, of course, *stuff* is a fairly nebulous notion, and I am intentionally using such a vague term. To generate income, that stuff needs to be turned into products—a product is something that can be consumed (in other words, purchase or viewed).

So, if you write a song, that song is stuff. However, if you record that song *and* make it available to purchase as a download in iTunes, then it is a product. But that song can be taken to market—in other words, it can generate income as a product—in many different ways. For instance, a recorded song:

■ Can be released for sale as a download.

■ Can be included within a collection of songs (an album), which might (for instance) be made available on a CD.

- Can be licensed for use on TV or in a film.

- Can generate royalties if it is played on the radio or in public.

That's before we look at any songwriter royalties...

The point being that there is not a one-to-one correlation between things and products. Each piece of stuff can ultimately lead to a range of products. If you want to dictate how your fan base *must* consume your product (for instance, if you only want them to buy your music on CD), that's fine, but you're likely to hurt sales. The more options you can give, the more likely you are to make your product available in a form that people want to consume (in other words, pay money for) and at a price that people want to pay.

I'll look at the issues around creating products (including the economics of various product options) in next chapter, but for the moment, let's look at the main possible sources of income.

Music

The most obvious source of income for a musician is by creating music. This could be music the musician has written or music that the musician has performed; it doesn't matter which. What matters is that it is put into a form that the fan can consume. The first step is to record the music and get it into a digital file, and once that is done, there are many ways in which that digital file can be sold.

Digital Downloads: MP3s and iTunes

One of the most significant changes for the music industry has been the rise of digital downloads: first illegal downloads, but in the last five years or so, legal downloads.

The behemoths in the download area are Apple's iTunes (see Figure 4.1) and Amazon (see Figure 4.2).

There are many advantages to releasing your music for digital downloads:

- There is less work involved than in creating a CD. CDs need to be manufactured—that has a cost associated, and then there is quality control (of the physical product), distribution, and so on. By contrast, for a download you only need to get a file to the retailer, and they will do the rest (and if you go through someone such as CD Baby [cdbaby.com] or TuneCore [tunecore.com], then you only need to upload one file, and they will do the distribution to all the retailers).

- You can go global. Once your songs are available for download, anyone anywhere in the world can get hold of them.

- Because there is no physical product and highly limited distribution costs, a greater proportion of the sale price comes through as profits. (Typically, you can earn up to 70 percent of the selling price.)

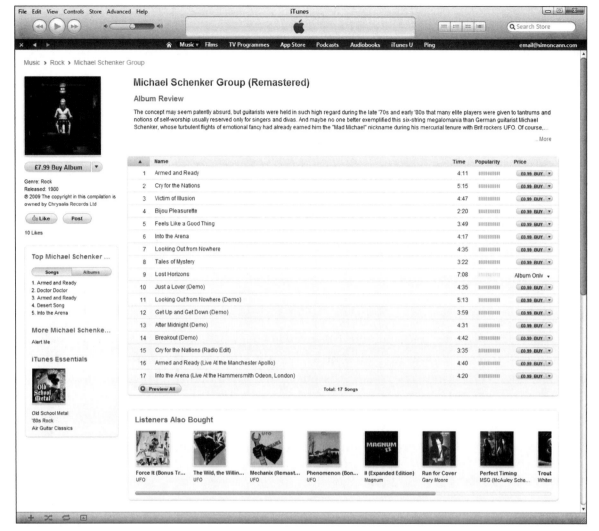

Figure 4.1   The iTunes store, which is integrated into the iTunes software. The iTunes store is the leading internet download retailer.

■ Once you are in the stores, you will have as much "shelf" space as any artist. More than that, the store will start displaying your product next to other artists (using the "people who bought this also bought…" type of arrangements).

■ If your music is easily available at a reasonable price, it is less likely to be pirated (although you are unlikely to prevent piracy).

Although the notion of selling electronic downloads may seem like a panacea, there are still many downsides. If nothing else, although your music may be carried by the major music download stores, it will not stand out. There will never be a display to highlight your latest album.

CDs
It is easy to ignore or forget CDs.

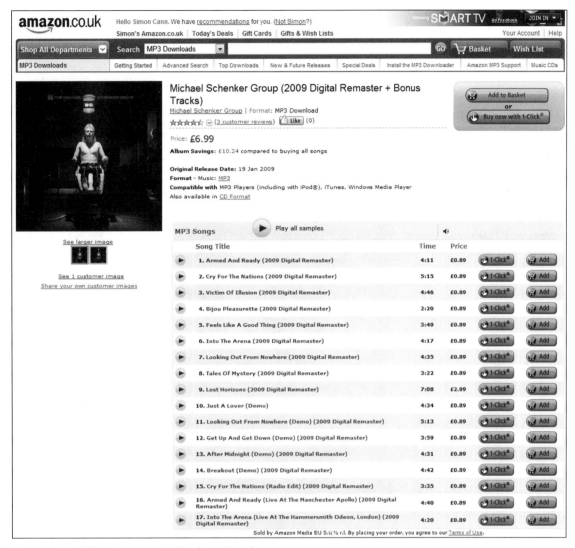

Figure 4.2 The Amazon MP3 download store.

They're expensive to make, logistically hard to distribute, and virtually every week another retailer goes out of business. Added to which, the size of the download market is growing rapidly.

However, CDs account for approximately 75 percent of the market, so it may not be wise to ignore this format.

That being said, the CD market poses some challenges:

- The first challenge is the cost of the actual product. You will have to pay for the production run before you have sold any CDs (which can be a significant commercial risk).

- You're dealing with physical products, which have to be physically shipped (to distributors, retailers, and customers).

- While prices have fallen, from a consumer's perspective they still cost more than downloads (usually), and they don't give the consumer the ability to choose the tracks he wants to buy—it's an all-or-nothing deal.

- For a smaller act, getting CDs into the retail outlets in shopping malls and so on is tough. It also requires a significant investment to get enough product that it can be widely distributed. As a result, it is often preferable to sell CDs through the online retailers.

There are a number of services to help get CDs to people who want to consume your music in this format.

On-Demand Delivery. Conventionally, if you want to sell a CD, you (or your record company) will make a recording and then go to a CD pressing plant and ask them to press several thousand CDs, which you can then sell. The downside to this arrangement is that you need to make an investment to get your CDs pressed, and if you don't sell them, you could face a loss (and you will have an awful lot of CDs sitting around your home, reminding you that you didn't sell enough CDs).

With an on-demand service, instead of pressing several thousand CDs, you wait for someone to buy your CD. The service provider then takes the money from the purchaser, presses a CD (and, of course, prints the artwork and so on), and then delivers the CD to the customer. The on-demand service provider takes its fee (which is usually fixed) and pays you the balance.

There are many other on-demand services, such as print-on-demand services. Like CD on-demand services, these will provide printed materials when the customer places an order. These services allow you to sell your own T-shirts, mugs, buttons (badges), posters, programs, and so on without incurring the upfront costs of printing/production and holding stock.

You may also find these services particularly useful for several reasons:

- You can get up and running very quickly and easily.

- When you are up and running, it is (comparatively) easy to change things. For instance, you won't have several thousand CDs sitting around if you decide you don't like your album anymore. Equally, you will usually find that if the service provider isn't up to scratch, it is comparatively painless to change the provider.

- With an on-demand service, you can compete with the major players (in other words, the established acts that are already trying to sell CDs, DVDs, and merchandise). Although you may not be able to compete in terms of revenue raised from CDs, DVDs, and merchandise (because these services are inherently inefficient, as is explained below), you will be able to have a comparable product range that should give you a certain amount of credibility.

■ Through their delivery services, they provide a way to get your CD/merchandise to a fan base over a wide geographical location.

Three examples of providers of these services are Amazon (through their CreateSpace service—createspace.com; see Figure 4.3), which provides on-demand print and CD/DVD services; Lulu (lulu.com), which provides on-demand print and CD/DVD services; and CafePress (cafepress.com), which provides on-demand merchandise (T-shirts and the like).

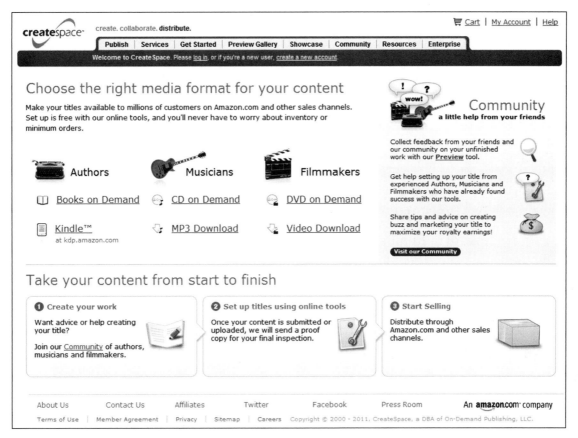

Figure 4.3 CreateSpace: Amazon's on-demand service.

The downside to the on-demand services is that they are not cheap. To give an example, a CD from an on-demand service may cost in the neighborhood of $5 to $9 (plus postage). If you're a new act looking to sell your CD at a highly competitive (in other words, low) price, with these costs you may sell a lot of CDs but not generate much profit. However, it is virtually a no-brainer to want to get your CD into Amazon, so CreateSpace is a very attractive notion.

If you do choose to use an on-demand service, you still have the option to sell your products directly. However, you then need to source your products. So, for instance, if you want to sell your own CDs at gigs, you would have to either get a batch of CDs pressed at a pressing plant or order a number from your on-demand service. In either case, you will need to make an investment, and you will then have to carry stock. If you are ordering from your on-demand service, then you will have very thin margins.

Fulfillment Services. As an alternative to using on-demand services, you may want to use a fulfillment service. These are organizations that will deliver your product to your customers. This may not be an obvious service to use—to many, it feels like paying money to have someone put your CD in the mail—however, there can be a great value to these services.

In deciding whether these services have value to you, let me ask you a question: What do you want to do—make music or spend all day processing orders, sending out CDs, and so on? If you want to make music, these services are worth considering for the benefit of the extra time that they will bring you. Seriously, think about the process a mail-order firm goes through—credit card transactions, printing invoices, packing CDs, labeling envelopes, and mailing the packages—and then decide how much it is worth for someone to do that for you.

There are also more specialized services, such as those offered by CD Baby (see Figure 4.4), who will also get your music distributed through the electronic download services (such as iTunes and Amazon).

Another example of a fulfillment service is Fulfillment by Amazon (amazonservices. com/fulfillment). The potential advantages are clear: You can sell your product(s) through Amazon and have Amazon deal with the whole process, from taking the order to shipping the product and then paying you.

The disadvantage of these services is that you still need to get your own CDs/merchandise produced, which will require an investment. You will then need to hold the stock and ship it to your delivery service. The advantage of these services is that you can make more income compared to what you can make using the on-demand services.

If you do choose to use a fulfillment service, you still have the option to sell your products directly. So, for instance, you could still sell CDs at gigs.

Music for TV/Films/Games

When I was a kid, we had three TV channels: BBC1, BBC2, and ITV (which is the independent, commercial network in the UK). That was it—there were no other options in the UK. In 1982, that choice was expanded to four channels with the addition of Channel 4. Now, with the introduction of satellite and cable services, as well as digital Freeview, there are several hundred channels available in the UK.

Anyone reading this book in the U.S. may sneer at the time when there were only three TV channels in the UK. (Just be grateful that I'm not old enough to remember when there was only one channel.) However, like the UK and the rest of the world, the U.S. has also seen a huge increase in the number of available TV channels, and I'm sure if you go back far enough, there was a time when there were only three channels in the U.S.

Figure 4.4 CD Baby offers musicians a way to get their music promoted and distributed to a wider audience.

One effect of the increase in the number of channels is the reduction in audience numbers for any particular TV program. Top-rated shows in the UK used to be able to reach viewing figures of around 25 million. Now if a show passes 10 million viewers, it is doing exceptionally well. (Even the Queen's Christmas message to the Commonwealth only gets around 6 million UK viewers.) So that's the bad news: Fewer viewers mean reduced budgets, and as you might expect, one budget that is easy to cut is the music budget.

However, the good news is that there are a lot more TV shows out there that need music. That means there are a lot more opportunities:

- To get your music heard

- To generate income from your music

These opportunities are not just available for TV. They also extend to film (especially independent films), corporate videos, and a number of other possible outlets. Like the music industry, the film industry has been undergoing many changes. Also like the music industry, it is now easier to get into the film industry. And again like the music industry, it is getting harder to reach the heights in the film industry.

However, that is not such a concern for us—what really matters here is that there are more opportunities to make money from your music on TV and in films. The commercial opportunities tend to come in a range of forms. The main options are:

- Specifically commissioned music, for which you are paid to provide an original piece of music to accompany a film, TV show, game, corporate video, and so on.

- Tracks licensed for a specific project, where (for instance) a song is licensed for synchronization with a specific piece of video (such as a TV advertisement).

- Production music or library music, as it is sometimes called. This is music that is pre-cleared for use and where the income is generated from a standardized license. This form of music is increasingly popular because it tends to be cheap, and the license terms are pre-agreed. Film/TV/video producers like using production music because they have certainty of cost and know that a synchronization license has already been granted.

Another great place for music is video games, which can provide both a source of income and a channel through which to promote your music. And if you want to be at the cutting edge of games, then the place to be at the moment is the rock band–type games, where your songs are "played" by game players.

There is much common ground between the popular music industry and the video-game market. Both are primarily marketed at a similar age group (children, teens, and young adults). The nature of video games is such that a track that is included with a game can be played hundreds of times and so can introduce a band and a track to a whole new audience. The possibilities for creating a buzz about a track (with this key audience) through a video game make video games a compelling outlet.

Another interesting facet of the video-game market is how the industry has embraced the internet—for instance, with massively multiplayer online games (MMOGs), where each player can be in a separate country playing on a computer linked to the internet.

Contrast this adoption of new technology with the music industry, which has spent years trying to stop its product from being distributed on the internet.

One last point I want to make about the video-game industry is about product life. Very often video games (which can sell for up to $50 or $60) will have a lifespan of one year. After a year, the next edition of the game is released, which again sells for $50 or $60. Then every couple of years, a whole new gaming console is introduced, necessitating another round of purchasing of new games.

Songwriting and Performing Royalties

Whenever your song is played in public (for instance, on the radio, at a gig, or on YouTube), there are royalties.

There is little you can do to increase your income from this source, other than being more popular so that more people listen to your music. As you get a large following, this income can be significant.

I talk about these royalties in Chapter 6, "Economics 101," so I won't elaborate further here.

Ringtones

I'm an old-fashioned kind of person: I like phones that ring.

Many people disagree with me and want a song to be played when someone calls them, and they are happy to pay for this privilege. From your perspective, if you've recorded the track, you might as well let people buy it as a ringtone as well as an audio track.

Video

At the time of writing, there are few opportunities to sell video downloads; however, that is likely to change over the next few years.

There are opportunities to sell DVDs and Blu-ray discs, but much like for CDs, there are logistical and cost issues.

But beyond income, there are two reasons why you're more likely to be making videos:

- To promote your act
- To connect and communicate with your fan base

Video is an excellent medium for both of those aims, but as I've mentioned several times, there are also opportunities to generate income from videos. One of the most straightforward ways is through YouTube (youtube.com).

Over the years YouTube has had several different arrangements, and the terms have continued to change, so the detail of anything written here (particularly suggested earnings levels) is likely to be out of date by the time you read it.

With YouTube, you join the partner program (youtube.com/partners) to start generating income.

YouTube earnings, like everything Google, work on a bid system, so rates will vary. There is no formal guidance about expected earnings; however, anecdotal evidence suggests that earnings will be low: typically around 70 cents per 1,000 views, although some suggest the earnings drop into the single-figure cents and can reach maybe $3 per thousand views.

Let's put this in context. At 70 cents/1,000 views, you would earn $175 if your video is played 250,000 times and $700 if it is played one million times. If you can have a video played one million times each week, then you would earn more than $36,000 in a year.

Now clearly, that $36,000 figure is not huge, and it presupposes an awful lot of plays, but remember that there will be other income and benefits: There's the publicity, you'll probably be selling tracks, and you will also be generating songwriter royalties.

If you want to make money through YouTube videos, the answer is to make short videos and to publish frequently: short videos to reduce production time, and frequent publication because shorter videos will get more views, and the advertising revenue doesn't seem to increase with longer videos.

If you're going to adopt this strategy, then you will need to learn how to create high-quality videos quickly. You'll also have to figure out how to provide enough interesting content. The content doesn't need to be perfect. For instance, as well as creating professional-level videos for your main releases, you could:

- Make an informal video about a new song you're working on

- Record your rehearsals

- Record an acoustic version of one of your songs

- Have some informal chats about what you're up to—for instance, gig plans, songs you're working on, and so on

Lots of short videos, produced for a low cost and without taking much time to make, will translate into easy income and will help to build a bond with your fan base.

Before we move on, a few words of caution.

As you will have guessed, I can see many opportunities for using YouTube. Indeed, in some ways YouTube is nearly perfect:

- It's free.

- It's fast: You can record a video, upload it immediately, and have it watched within minutes.

- YouTube can notify people about new postings automatically.

- You can link/embed videos within Twitter and Facebook.

- You can communicate directly with your fans, and they can respond directly, allowing a high degree of interaction/community building.

- Because the videos are embeddable, they can be highly viral.

- You can generate money from it (while marketing and retaining fans).

- Your output is highly discoverable.

However, relying too heavily on YouTube is risky:

- The service might change/go away.

- The business terms could change, becoming materially worse, and the rights you are expected to give up might alter.

- There might be somewhere newer/better where everyone congregates.

- You don't want all your eggs in one basket.

- You can earn more money in other ways.

My point here is simple: YouTube is great *at the moment*, and I encourage you to exploit the service to build up your business. However, it is not the only option, and it may one day be a bad option. So use the service, but don't make it the cornerstone of your business strategy, and keep the service under constant review in case it is not in your best interest to use it.

Live Performance

I don't need to explain what a live performance is, do I? You understand the basics of earning money from gigs, right?

I'll talk a bit more about some of the economic considerations with touring and live performances in Chapter 6.

Advertising

I've already mentioned advertising income, particularly in the context of video.

As your reputation grows, there will be opportunities for advertising and sponsorship. To the extent that you are seen as connecting with a certain demographic or group of people, you will have value for advertisers.

Merchandising and Other Non-Music Income Sources

As musicians have increasingly become brands, the sales of merchandise have increased.

As with any tangible object, there is an issue around the cost of buying stock. Luckily, like CDs and DVDs, there are many on-demand services to ease the production challenges.

Associates' Arrangements

In a bid to create publicity and increase sales, many online retailers offer an associates' program. An example of one retailer offering this sort of arrangement is Amazon.

The way these arrangements often work is that you create a link on your website to a certain product on the retailer's website. If someone then follows that link and purchases the product, you receive a commission, typically of a few percent of the sale price.

So how does this help you?

First, if you have a product that is widely available (such as a download, CD, or DVD) but that you are not selling directly, you can create links on your website to purchase the product(s) from the online retailer. This means that you will get paid twice: First, you get the royalty, and second, you get the commission from the retailer.

Second, this gives you another source of income. Say, for instance, you are a band performing Celtic music. This sort of music typically has a much narrower audience than a mainstream pop group could expect. However, many members of the Celtic music audience also have an interest in all things Celtic. This is where you have an opportunity to increase your income and to help your fan base connect with and learn more about the background to your music.

To give you some examples, a Celtic band could consider including links to these sorts of products:

- CDs/downloads from other bands who perform music in a similar style. Perhaps you could include links to some of your heroes or your major influences.

- Books about:

  - The origins and history of Celtic music

  - Celtic instruments

  - Celtic myths that may have influenced the subject matter of some of your songs

Choosing the Right Product

So now you've got an idea of the range of products that could be produced. Before we jump in and start creating like crazy, I think it is important for you to have an idea about who you are and what you do. If these seem like difficult questions for you, then it will be even harder to create a cohesive product that you can sell to your fan base.

Let's look at this issue from a different perspective: What does your act offer to your potential fan base, and why would the fan base pay attention to/spend money for those offerings? Take some time to think about it. It's very important.

If you're offering junk that is of no worth to a fan base, then you're going to lose your fan base and your income. No income equates to no career.

Who Are You? What Do You Do?

Have you seen or read interviews with artists who say something to the effect of, "Our album defies categorization," or "We're creative people—we don't like to be pigeonholed?"

Now, I don't want to constrain your creativity, but one thing you need to do is establish your genre. You can define the genre as broadly (or as narrowly) as you like, using whatever terms you feel appropriate (however contradictory). Equally, you can change your genre how and when you want.

But you do need a genre.

You need a genre for two reasons. First, you need a genre so you have an idea of your identity—an idea about what you actually do. Once you have defined a genre for yourself, then you will have a clearer understanding about when you are changing and developing your genre.

You also need a genre so that new people know what you do. In broad terms, people know what they like: They know that they like death metal but not freeform jazz (or vice versa). Without an identifiable genre, you may be passed by.

I love the notion of an artist who feels comfortable working in many different musical styles. However, let's look at the commercial realities for a moment. If you're a death metal band, and you suddenly start playing freeform jazz, then you're probably going to lose a large chunk of your fan base.

Very few acts can change and keep their fan base. However, many acts can develop as their fan base develops. Evolution, not revolution, is the key here. Also, very few acts can claim to be truly diverse in the way that, say, a band like Led Zeppelin was.

Zeppelin played rock (at times, heavy, thunderous rock), blues, and folk, as well as throwing in some country-tinged material while showing some reggae influences. Zeppelin disbanded in 1980, and I'm not sure that any band since then has achieved their level of success with so many diverse styles. My hunch (and it is a hunch) is that

Zeppelin's fan base accepted the wide range of styles because the band always had a cohesive, identifiable sound of their own that was very much due to the individuals in the band.

Who Is Your Market?

Once you know who you are and what you do, your next quest is to figure out who your market is.

Don't fool yourself into thinking that you will appeal to everybody. Try to really narrow down who your market is. For instance:

■ If you're producing really lightweight but highly melodic pop music, then you may well appeal to the pre-teen market.

■ If you're producing pop/R&B and you're a male singer, then you may appeal to the female teenage market.

■ If you're producing very aggressive metal/rock, then you may appeal to males aged 15 to 24.

■ If you're a middle-aged crooner singing sentimental love songs, then you may appeal to the 45+ female market.

As you have no doubt realized, these are really crude generalizations and will never be totally accurate (but just for fun, guess the audience for the people shown in Figure 4.5). Also, there will always be people who are interested in a style of music you don't expect (the grandmother at the death metal gig, and so on).

However, these broad generalizations can be useful as a starting point for thinking about your strategy for finding an audience. If you don't know who your potential fan base is, then how will you go looking for these people?

Is There an Audience?

I'm going to ask you to be really dispassionate for a moment. Try, if you can, to emotionally disconnect yourself from your music. Imagine you are hearing your music for the first time. Now answer one question: Is there an audience for this kind of music?

If there is an audience, who are these people and how big is the market?

Let me give you two examples, one musical and one not: classical guitarists and poets. No one would suggest that either of these art forms is anything other than completely worthy. However, the number of people who can actually make a living by playing classical guitar (as opposed to teaching) and writing poetry (as opposed to teaching creative writing) is tiny.

That being said, there are people who will buy classical guitar music and poetry. If you are a classical guitarist and you are reading this book and you can bring me a sublime recording (of yours) of the music of Antonio Lauro, I will buy it. As a side note, if you

Figure 4.5 Who would be this band's audience? By the way, if you're wondering, the picture is of the German band Rage.

haven't heard any of Lauro's music, you should. Check out "Natalia" and "Andreina" from his *Valses Venezolanos*.

Before you stride purposefully into the world, ask yourself how big your potential market is. Is it a Justin Bieber–sized market, or is it a classical guitarist–sized market?

If the market is on the smaller side, that shouldn't necessarily be a problem. One of the benefits to the strategies outlined in this book is that you can be very efficient from a financial perspective. This means you may be able to generate income (to sustain a career) at a much lower level than would be necessary if you signed with a record label.

Also, if you are doing something that is more obscure, then you may be able to charge higher prices. To take me as an example again—and I am not alone; this is a well-known economic phenomenon—I am happy to spend more money on acquiring the music of Antonio Lauro than I am on acquiring a regular CD, due to my liking of his music and the scarcity of good recordings. (It's basic supply and demand economics, along with my love of perfectly crafted tunes.)

Another benefit of operating in a niche is that you are likely to be working in a less crowded market, so you should be able to capture a larger share of the market.

When assessing whether there is an audience out there, be careful to ensure that there will be a suitably large audience for you. For instance, you may be in a band made up of a bunch of fat, balding guys in their 50s (no offense intended to you fat guys in your 50s—it's just a nice stereotype for illustration) who play Rolling Stones–type music (not covers, just music in a similar style). You may surmise that given the size of the audience for the Stones, there is an audience for you—and you're decades younger than Mick and Keith, so you'll be even more popular. And you would be wrong.

The Stones have their audience and will always have their audience. They have created and maintained that audience by virtue of their hard work over at least the last 50 years. People want to see the Stones; they don't want to see a bunch of fat losers (their opinion, not mine) performing second-rate "dad" music.

So I will ask you again, because this is really important: Is there an audience out there for you?

Before you answer that question, let me just add another thought. Do the people you are aiming for have the time, the money, and the inclination to buy your product and to come out and support you? For instance, if you are aiming your music at what could be lazily categorized as the "housewife" market, will that demographic support you?

Almost without exception, all of the housewives that I know are run ragged by their kids. They spend the whole day chasing and cleaning up after their kids. The priority in their lives is their kids, not music.

Although I am sure you could create music that an average housewife would like and would be happy to listen to (on the radio) while she completes her daily chores, the notion that a housewife would have time to find out about your act and support it is, I believe, misguided. Kids, teenagers, and younger adults will have more time (and, ironically, will often have more disposable income) to invest in music, and so the music market is aimed at this younger age group.

What Does Your Audience Want?

So you've decided what you do, you've identified your audience (and you're sure they'll support you), so what are you going to sell them?

This may sound like a daft question, so let me elaborate. You need to identify what the audience wants and ensure that what your act does (and produces) dovetails with what the audience wants in an act. In other words, your products need to be designed in light of your audience's needs. When you look to understand your audience's needs, this is the time when you need to understand the composition of the audience. (Don't just rely on your expectations of the makeup of the audience.)

Ask yourself a few questions: Does the fan base really want a poster? Probably not if the fans are not kids/teens. Does the fan base want a CD, or would they prefer to buy downloads? Alternatively, are they the sort of people who would value (that is, pay for) a special-edition CD that costs more than a regular CD?

You will never get the answers to these questions perfectly correct (not least since every member of your audience will have a different opinion); however, the more you know about your audience, the more informed your decision-making (and therefore your product design) will be. This is another reason why you should spend time getting to know and communicating directly with your fan base.

Tuning Your Act to Fit Your Audience

Over time, you will get to know your audience. If you don't, your career will be short. As you get to know these people (individually and collectively), you are likely to be able to fine-tune your output to match their needs (see Figure 4.6).

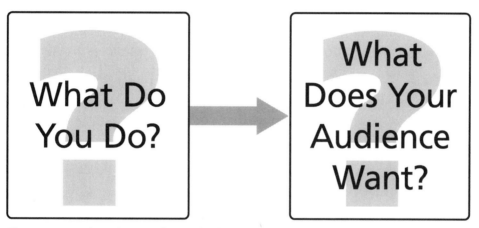

Figure 4.6 What do you do, and what does your audience want? Is there a direct link from one to the other? If not, then you may have difficulties building your career.

This is a good thing. It means that you can be more efficient in your product offerings and you will generate more income. It may also mean that you increase your fan base because you have hit a winning formula.

However, do be wary of change. With each change you could alienate your existing fans, leaving them feeling as if you have sold out. If you are making a change that you are happy with (and that may also be part of the maturing process), then I don't think you need to apologize for your changes. If this means you lose fans, then unfortunately there is little you can do to stop that. In this situation, it is important that you ensure the parting is as amicable as possible.

On the other hand, if the changes are ruthlessly commercial ones, you may find it hard to defend your position, and you may find that former fans tend to say unpleasant things in the anonymity of cyberspace.

And just to be clear, I'm not suggesting that you change everything about your act in an attempt to chase dollars. Instead, I'm suggesting that you focus on the aspects of what you do that are more popular with your audience.

Evolution

You may know your market very well. Indeed, you may know many of your fans personally. However, your audience may change over time. To oversimplify, you are likely to be in one of two situations.

Renewing Audience. If your act is focused on a particular demographic—for instance, the pre-teen market—then the individuals who make up your audience may grow out of your act. This is nothing to be too concerned about, provided you can keep renewing your audience.

In many ways, if you are renewing your audience, you can keep the same act—you don't need to do anything new, because your material will be new to the audience (but you must obviously ensure that you remain current). Although this is a bit cynical, it does illustrate an important point: With an audience that does not age (because the audience keeps renewing), you cannot change or mature as an act. It is often a big mistake to think that you can mature and carry an audience with you. Unfortunately, as the audience matures, they will just see you as either cheesy or kids' stuff (or both).

For an illustration of this, look at the boy bands that have tried to take time out and return as new, mature versions of themselves. It rarely works. Equally, look at the former boy-band members who have tried to have a lasting solo career with a more adult sound. One or two have done it, but most fail.

Maturing Audience. By contrast, you may have an audience that will let you grow with them. This is likely to be the situation if you are creating more adult-oriented music.

This audience will remain interested while you continue to provide a soundtrack that reflects their life. However, they may get diverted away from music. For instance, upon having children, many parents focus on their kids and not on music.

However, assuming you can keep the fan base over the long term, you need to ensure that you don't develop ahead of your audience or in ways that your audience doesn't appreciate. For instance, if you started life as a hell-for-leather death metal band, then your audience may be happy for you to mature into a more classic rock band over time.

Getting Stale. As your audience changes, you will have to make sure you don't change too fast if you want to ensure that you don't lose your audience.

However, you must make sure that you don't change so slowly that you become overly familiar. If you get to the point where your fan base can't be bothered to go see you because they think they will see the same show they saw last year, then you're in trouble and will probably lose your fan base.

Logistics of Creating Products

That's enough about the products you could create. The next chapter will move on and look at the logistics of actually creating products.

5 The Logistics of Creating and Developing Products

After Chapter 4, I hope you have gotten over your discomfort with the notion of "product," because you're going to have to get used to the idea.

Product is what you sell. If you don't sell any products, then you won't have any income and hence there will be no career. So make a choice: Get over your squeamishness or go and get a proper job.

We are now going to look at the business aspects of products and hence your career.

What Is a Product?

Before we go any further, let me explain what I am calling a product (see Figure 5.1).

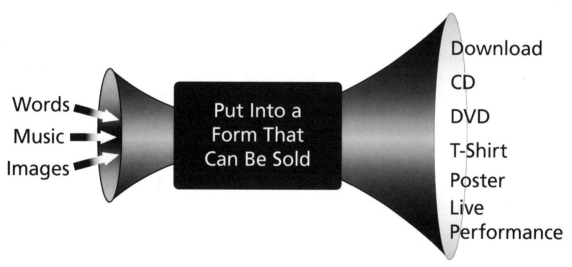

Figure 5.1 The process of product creation takes something intangible (words, music, and so on) and converts it into a form that can be sold (such as a download, CD, or DVD).

In simplistic terms, a product is something you can sell (or sell advertising against), so a few chords and a line or two from a chorus don't make a product (although they may be part of the product development process). However, more than simply being something that has the potential to be sold, a product is a freestanding item, tangible or intangible, that ideally can be sold again and again and again.

So for instance, the following are examples of products:

- A download
- A CD
- A DVD
- A T-shirt
- A poster
- A live performance

There is a strong argument that you could call a live performance a service rather than a product because you are selling entertainment (which could be deemed to be a service) to people. However, I don't want there to be any confusion in terms between products and services, so I am calling *everything* a product. If it is something that you give to your fan base in exchange for money, then it is a product.

Product Process: From Creation, through Development, to Market

When you start thinking about products, you need to think about the process, from creating a product, to selling it, to providing after-sales service. Most products will follow a process that has the following steps (see Figure 5.2). For now, I want to briefly introduce these main steps—I will then go on and discuss them in greater detail.

Product Development

The first stage of creating a product is the development stage. At this point, the product is conceived and researched. Only when you are sure that the idea is viable should the product be taken forward.

Part of the product development is obvious and natural—an example of this would be writing songs. However, other parts may be unnatural (or at least not something that you may have experienced before). For instance, you may not have familiarity with the process involved in creating a T-shirt.

Manufacturing

The manufacturing stage is when the product is created. At this point you actually make something tangible, whether that is a recording of a song or a test of a T-shirt. This is the first chance to see, hear, and touch something real.

You will often also find that there are problems at the manufacturing stage. The band may not be performing as well as you had hoped in the studio, or the T-shirt may be of a substandard quality. This may be the only opportunity you get to ensure that the quality is everything you hoped for, so take the time to ensure that the quality is perfect.

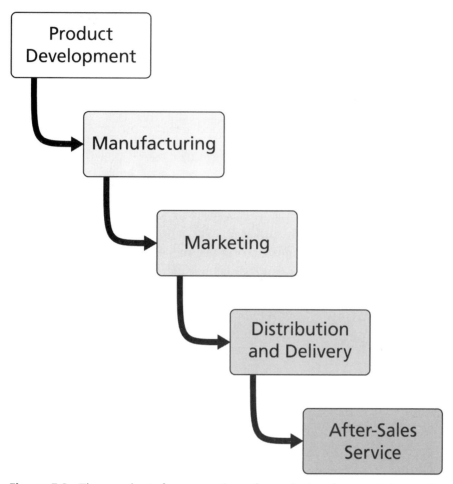

Figure 5.2 The product, from creation, through development, to market, and beyond.

Marketing

In the marketing phase, you explicitly attempt to raise awareness of your product with your fan base and the wider public. Traditionally, this is when the act goes on the road, plays live shows, and makes as many TV/radio appearances as they can. For many musicians, the two hours on stage each night are the reason they got into the business—the remaining 22 hours of each day are mindless tedium (interspersed with a hunt for willing sexual partners).

Distribution and Delivery

There is no point in creating products unless you can get the product to purchasers—in other words, if you can't find a way to get the product to a person willing to lay down cash (for instance, you can't get a CD to someone), then there is no point in creating the product in the first place.

There is no art or craft in efficient delivery; it is pure administration. That being said, when it goes wrong, it is a nightmare for you and your fans, so it is well worth finding someone who can organize this aspect of your business.

After-Sales Service

Selling your product and getting it to the fan is not the end of the story. You're going to need to respond to complaints. For instance, merchandise may not arrive, CDs may not play, or the booklet may be badly printed. Whatever the complaint and regardless of whether it's your fault, you'll be expected to ensure that these things are fixed, because ultimately a shoddy product directly translates into a bad reputation for you.

Developing the Product

Now that we have agreed on what we are calling a product, what product are you going to sell to your fan base? This is where product development comes in.

You probably looked at the products I listed in the previous section and thought that you wanted to do all of them. (This is not unreasonable; most musicians do want to produce downloads, CDs, DVDs, T-shirts, posters, and live performances.) You probably also got lots of other ideas for products you would like to create.

Let's look at some of the factors that should influence your choice of which products to develop.

Size of the Product Range

Although it may seem like an odd consideration, the number of products you offer is an important issue.

You should aim to have a reasonably wide range of products so that you can offer something for most of your fan base. If you limit your product range, then you are limiting your potential income. If there is nothing more for people to buy—perhaps because they've already bought everything you have to offer—then they won't give you any more of their money.

And while we're talking about money, let me mention price—as in the price you charge for your product. I'll talk about this subject in more detail later in this chapter, but for the moment, please remember that different people want to pay different amounts for what is apparently the same product—this is why people buy expensive cars that perform the same function as cheap cars. Taken to its extreme at the other end of the spectrum, some people will believe that the correct price for your content is zero. To address the differing attitudes to price, as well as a range of products, you need a range of prices (which I'll come to later).

By contrast, if your product range is too broad, that will create other problems—for instance, if you are dealing with real products (such as CDs), you will have large amounts of stock to store, insure, and keep track of. Also, with a wide product range, you may end up spending more time on your products and less time on your music.

When you first start out, it will be quite easy to limit your product range because you will be starting from zero. Perhaps a bigger problem will be charging for products.

Only you can decide what is right for you in light of your fan base. To the extent that you are uncertain about the scope of your product range and the number of each product that you will stock (and you should be uncertain about developing any product for which you don't have an order that has been paid for), then don't be too ambitious: Start small and grow.

Which Products Do You Need? Setting Your Priorities

Now that you have an idea about some of the products you can develop, it's probably a good idea to prioritize the development of these products. This will ensure that you have a steady flow of new products rather than everything arriving in one lump, and that you don't spend all of your time thinking about products and none of your time making music.

Planning will also help you to think about future products. You may have just released your latest album, so it would seem a sensible approach to plan when the next album will be released, given that it may take a year from conception to release (and that's presupposing that an album is right for you—for many acts, single songs are more appropriate). With a bit of planning, you can ensure that you get everything you want sorted out. For instance, with some planning you could find a time when the producer you've always wanted to work with is available.

As a first step in the planning process, split your ideas into two piles: those things you should do and those things you should think twice about.

The things that you might think about developing include:

- Products you need because they define who and what you are. Two examples of products that define you are recorded tracks (available as downloads or CDs) and gigs. I can't see many people existing as musicians without developing one or both of these.

- Products that generate a healthy income and a profit. I will talk more about this issue under the section "The Cost of Developing Products," later in this chapter.

- Products that advertise you or raise your profile. A great example of this is T-shirts. Think about it: People will pay you money to advertise your brand on their body!

Then there are some things that you should think twice about (and then think again). As a start, this category will include products for which you need to carry a large stock, which have low margins, or which you just don't understand.

So what products should you create? That depends on your fan base and what you actually do. If you are creating a product that your fan base wants to buy, then you won't have to work hard to make sales, but you may have to work hard to ensure that your fan base knows about the availability of the product—especially if you don't have a direct line of communication with your fan base.

By contrast, if you create a product that your audience doesn't want, then you're likely to have a lot of stock on your hands. Think about the notion of "want" in human terms, not just in relation to a general demographic. Ultimately, you should develop products you are passionate about—develop things that really matter to you and things that you care about. These are the items your fan base is far more likely to be interested in and will want to buy.

In this book I don't offer you money, but I *am* trying to help you find a way to do what you love and to generate sufficient income to live. It is your career, and you need to feel good about yourself. If you develop products that you are truly passionate about and that you truly believe are good, then it doesn't matter whether you sell 1,000 or 10 million (or just a few to your family and friends)—you will still believe you have a good product and will feel proud. And you will know that you haven't ripped off your fan base with second-rate tat.

Market Testing

One of the biggest difficulties in developing a new product is knowing what your fan base wants and what they will buy. It's pointless to develop a new product if no one is ever going to buy it.

One way to find out what products would interest your fan base is to carry out some research—in other words, ask people directly. This can be useful to a certain extent; however, one of the downsides of market research is that people aren't always straightforward. If you ask people whether they would buy a certain product, they may say they would. However, this doesn't mean that they will buy the product.

For instance, the person you surveyed might have been willing to buy when surveyed, but may have run out of money by the time the product is available. Alternatively, people may change their minds, or the product might not be what they expected from the description given when they were surveyed.

Whatever the reason, they won't buy.

And just to be clear here, I'm not suggesting that if you're a death metal band, you should ask whether your audience wants you to create bubblegum pop. What I'm looking at here is focusing your options.

A better way to know what the fan base might want is to know the fan base. If you get to know your fan base over a sustained period of time, and you have conversations with individuals (two-way conversations, asking questions and listening), you may get a better feel for what they want than you would get if you followed the survey approach. However, you still will not get a perfect idea.

You will only truly know what sells once it has sold.

Research can be helpful, and I always suggest that you get as close as possible to your fan base; however, if you want to know whether something sells, then the best course is to try selling it. If you start small, so that you don't take too much of a loss (perhaps only releasing a product through an on-demand service), you will be able to gauge interest. Then, on the basis of actual sales figures, you can grow your product.

So for instance, you may know that your fans will buy T-shirts, but you don't know whether they will buy baseball caps. You could set up a baseball cap with an on-demand service and order, say, 50 caps to try to sell at gigs. If they don't sell, then you won't have lost too much. However, if they do sell, then you could look into having them produced at a lower cost (in other words, at a cost that may allow you to generate some profits).

And of course, your main product—your music—doesn't really lend itself to market testing!

Making Your Product the Best You Can

There are several elements in the strategy I am setting out in this book. For the moment, I want to look at two pieces: the direct relationship with your fan base and making excellent music. By bringing these two focal points together, you are getting close to developing a product that will sell itself. This is a good thing, because as you will have noticed, the strategy in this book does not rely on extensive advertising and hard selling. Instead, it relies on people wanting to buy.

Before I look at other products, let me look at your music products and take the example of producing a CD.

There are many elements that affect the overall quality of a CD, including:

- **The songs.** You need well-written, properly structured songs with instantly memorable tunes and lyrics to draw in the listener immediately. Songwriting is an art and a craft, and you should continually seek to improve your writing ability, whether through courses, a songwriting consultant, reading about other songwriters, continuing to practice your skill, or working with other writers.

- **The songs should be well performed.** There is no excuse for an average or lackluster performance. Remember, your recording could be available in 10, 20, 30, 40, or more years' time, and you could still be receiving income over this period. Surely, for a work that will have that longevity, the extra take just to nail the track is worthwhile.

  When it comes to performance, are all the musicians as good as they could be? Are you recording with a singer who has never had a singing lesson in her life? Does the bassist have trouble with the notion of 4/4 time? Does the guitarist keep old, dull strings on his guitar? You need to do anything and everything you can to improve the quality of your product before you sign off on a recording.

- **The songs need to be well recorded.** This doesn't mean that you need an expensive recording studio; it just means that you need to ensure the absolute highest audio fidelity—and don't kid yourself that your ropey old computer will do. Equally, don't kid yourself that a shiny new computer will make you sound great when there are more fundamental problems (such as lack of talent, a poor recording room, or similar factors).

I also have to question your commitment to creating a product of the very highest quality if you're not going into a studio with the best producer you can find (and, of course, afford). You may be good, but ask yourself how many hit record there have been over the last few years that haven't had a top-flight producer? Some, but maybe not that many who have gone on to have a lasting career. You really need to find a producer who will ensure that you sound like a bunch of slick professionals and not like a group of highly talented amateurs who don't quite make the grade.

- **Once the tracks have been recorded, they need to be mixed and mastered.** You may be able to record yourself. You may have even bluffed the production bit. However, before you go any further, ask yourself whether you have the talent to mix and master your material. I'm sure there must be some artists somewhere who record, produce, mix, and master their own work, but I think these people are few and far between and may not sell huge numbers of records.

  If you want the best product that you can have, then find the best mixer you can afford and find the best mastering engineer.

- **The final step (in this example) when the recording, mixing, and mastering has been completed is to get the CD pressed.** All your hard work will be in vain if the reproduction, printing, and packing are not completed to the highest standard.

Although you may get each element right on its own, it is also fundamentally important that the elements work together. For instance, if you have the best producer, the best mixing engineer, and the best mastering engineer working on your project, then they all need to know what you want and expect. If each individual has his or her own separate vision of where your product is heading, then these individuals may work against each other. The producer may add lots of bass parts, the mixing engineer may feel that the bass end is too muddy, and the mastering engineer may feel the track lacks body, and so he boosts the middle of the audio frequency.

Someone needs to take hold of a project and ensure that all of the parties understand what you want. (When I say "you," I mean you the client—the person who is paying everyone's salaries.) If they then don't do what they're told, don't pay them.

To succeed, your product must be of the very highest quality. You won't sell just because you've sent an email to your fan base. You have to create something that your fan base wants to buy—this is very much the strategy of "build a better mouse-trap, and the world will beat a path to your door." Remember, you are not stuffing your product down people's throats with advertisements, so you need something that is really good in order to convert interest into sales (and quickly). If you create a stinker of a product, the word will spread very quickly.

I have discussed one particular musical product here (the production of a CD). The principle of producing the best product you can applies to any product, whether it is a gig or a mug. If you're not selling top-of-the-line products, then life is going to be tough for you.

Releasing the Product

One of the biggest problems will be deciding when a product is ready to be released to the public.

For an artist signed to a major record label, the decision to release an album is usually fairly simple. If the producer says it's ready, and the label thinks it's ready, then it is ready, and the album (or whatever) will be released.

If you're trying to release a product (any product, not just a CD) without having someone with that level of financial involvement, then you need to be really certain that you aren't releasing your product too soon. When you think that you may be close to release, make sure you distance yourself from the product (as far as you can) in order to stay as objective as possible.

Also, again to the extent possible, consider other people's opinions. In particular, if you have paid someone to be involved with a product (for instance, a producer), and her reputation is on the line too, then make sure she believes you are ready to release.

Product Renewal

Products get renewed: In other words, production of old products ceases, and a new product comes in its place.

Outside of the music industry, product renewal comes in two forms:

- Giving additional features to an existing product to make it more attractive

- Launching a whole new product to replace an existing product that is withdrawn from the market

This sort of product renewal can be difficult in the music industry, so let's look at the example of how the video-game industry renews some of its products:

- To encourage new purchases of an existing game console, further titles can be released. This creates more reason to buy the console. In addition, giving away free games when a console is purchased lengthens the lifespan of the console by increasing demand.

- To encourage renewal, a whole new console can be released that is incompatible with existing games. Of course, the stated reason for the incompatibility is to give new features.

The key difference between these two approaches is that with the first option you are getting more sales from the original product, so you are widening your user base. With the second approach, the existing user base is being asked to replace a product that has become obsolete (and all of the games for the obsolete product can be regarded as obsolete, too)—in other words, people are being asked to buy the product for a second (or third or fourth) time.

These sorts of practices do happen in the music industry. Here are a few examples:

- Greatest-hits albums bring in new fans (and can sometimes sell to existing fans who want to own all of an artist's catalogue).

- Greatest-hits albums with new tracks bring in new fans and sell to existing fans who are keen to get the new tracks.

- Remixed and remastered versions of old (usually classic) albums are intended to be sold to existing fans as an "upgrade" to their existing album.

- Live albums sell the same songs to existing fans. The same principle applies for acoustic versions of existing songs.

- Limited-edition merchandise, such as a tour T-shirt, becomes available. Because availability of the T-shirt is limited to a certain timeframe, a new T-shirt can be sold when this one has become obsolete. Any piece of merchandise can easily be made into a limited-edition product that can then be replaced by new limited-edition products. Perhaps the most obvious limited-edition product (that will generate income every year) is a calendar.

The complete renewal of a product (such as the new video-game console) is a harder task to achieve. The music industry last did this very effectively when it made vinyl obsolete with the introduction of CDs. However, since then it has not managed to renew its products so well. That is not to say it hasn't renewed—for instance, MP3s, remastered albums, and attempts at higher-quality audio (such as 5.1 mixes) have had some effect.

For your early products, just focus on getting a successful product launched and ensuring that you make a profit. Remember the possibilities of renewal, and don't make any decisions that would make it harder for you to renew your products.

When you have a portfolio of products, then you can consider whether it is feasible to produce a version two or a version three of any products. Before you renew your products, consider two issues:

- Will renewing the product make it easier to sell the renewed product? In other words, will the existing product already be recognized/established in the market? Alternatively, will it being renewable make it easier to reach a wider fan base?

- Will renewing the product make it harder to sell in the market? Will the renewed product just be seen as a re-tread of a tired old product that should simply be dropped? Equally, will renewal tarnish your reputation?

Only you know how your fan base will react, and only you can decide upon the right course for your business.

Development Time

I now want to focus on some of the logistics of product development. As I discussed earlier in this chapter, as a crude rule of thumb, the more products you can produce, the higher your income will be (within reason). However, to develop a high-quality product that will enhance your reputation and will sell, you need to invest a lot of time.

You need to balance these two competing interests to ensure that you have time to do what you love (make music) and generate sufficient income.

Planning

You need to take development time into account to organize your life. Historically, most artists follow a structure in which they record an album, release the album, and then tour to promote the album. The tour is usually booked before the album is finished, so a few months' gap is left for overruns. If you don't plan well enough, you could be touring before you have finished and released the album you are meant to be promoting.

Without wanting to belabor the point too much, remember that planning also takes time, so you should include an allowance for planning. (I know it sounds like planning how to plan, but it's better to remember it than to get it all badly wrong.)

Critical Path

When you are planning a project, there are some activities that can happen only after something else has happened. For instance, you cannot mix a track until it has been recorded, and you can't press a CD until the songs have been written.

Equally, there are plenty of activities that are not dependent on other activities. For instance, you don't need to have completed the mix of an album to commission the artwork.

The key to successful planning is ensuring that you have a timescale for each part of the project and then recognizing which parts are dependent on a previous task having been completed and which tasks can be completed independently. Clearly, the tasks that are dependent on a previous task are the hardest to plan, particularly when you are trying to schedule several people together (such as a producer, a mixing engineer, and a mastering engineer).

Logistics of Product Development

Turning to focus on the logistics of product development, as a musician you know that there are no shortcuts when you create music. You cannot half-write a song and hope that you are inspired to write the remaining part when you get up on stage and start playing the song. If you've only half-written a song, you will find it is impossible to teach the rest of the band the song.

If you are a songwriter, you know that songs get written in many different ways. Sometimes inspiration comes to you, and the song writes itself in as long as it takes you to play it. Other times, you need to keep returning to a song over a long period of time, perhaps agonizing over one word or one note for several weeks. Maybe you write with a partner, or you and the whole band all get in the room and play. Everyone throws in lines and melodies, and together you create perfection that could not be created by any of you individually.

You also know there is no right or wrong way to write a song, although it often feels as if you are using only the wrong ways. This is the nature of the creative process, and how you create is up to you.

However, although I do not wish to put any constraints on your creativity, I would like to make a few suggestions:

- First, understand your creative process. If you are a songwriter and you can write 10 hit songs in an afternoon, that's great. However, if, like normal people, it takes you a lot longer to write songs—perhaps a couple of days, or maybe each song is written over several weeks—that's fine. Just make sure you have factored the writing into the product-development process.

  Equally, if you ask someone else to get creative on your behalf—for instance, you might ask someone to create some artwork for a poster—then try to understand the person's creative process and the timescales to which he works.

- In the 1950s and 1960s, whole albums could be recorded in a matter of hours. I think the Beatles' first album was recorded in three hours. Those days are gone—I don't think you could get a kick drum set up in less than three hours these days.

  You should always ensure that there is sufficient time to record, but you may want to constrain this time if you are working to a tight budget. It is very easy to sit around and say, "We should be able to record this whole album in a few days, as long as we have rehearsed enough." However, it will always take longer than you expect, especially if you are aiming to create the highest quality product. Unfortunately, the only way you will learn exactly how much time you need is to spend the time.

- As well as understanding the creative process, develop a thorough understanding of all of the other aspects involved in making the product happen. Make sure you (or whoever is running the project) understand which function each person involved in the project fulfills and how much time her process will add to the project.

Product Pricing

Product pricing is crucial. Charge too much, and no one will buy the product. Charge too little, and you won't make a profit.

In the next section ("The Cost of Developing Products"), I will discuss the cost of developing products and the economics that determine when a product starts to make a profit (or, more importantly, the point at which a product ceases to make a loss).

Development costs will have a significant influence on pricing. However, there are many other influences—some are scientific, but most are less so. Perhaps the two most significant questions when it comes to pricing are:

- **What price will people pay?** In other words, how much can you charge before people will refuse to buy your product? The secondary issue here is at what level your fans will think you are abusing their good nature and taking money straight out of their pockets. If you reach this price point, you will lose fans quickly.

- **What price will make the product sell?** In other words, how low do you have to go to encourage sales? You should also remember that there is a point at which your product will look "bargain bin"—if you reach this, then you will lose credibility. You should also remember that rubbish never sells.

You might be thinking that you'll set the price of each product according to the manufacturing costs, then add a bit for profit, and perhaps give the retailer some margin. This is admirable but probably rather naïve. As the next section about the cost of product development will demonstrate, it is difficult to know when a product will break even, and once you've broken even, what do you do then? Drop the price. Also, even if you price a product on the most reasonable basis, people will still feel ripped off.

People feel ripped off because they will ascribe a value to your product based on their own beliefs and values. In other words, they will value your product based on what they feel it is worth for them, not based on what *you* feel/know it is worth. It is for this reason that manufacturers apply differential pricing.

Let me give you an example of differential pricing from Apple. Take the iPad 2, and look at the price/features set out in Table 5.1. (Please note these are the UK prices quoted today on the Apple website, including VAT [value-added tax] but excluding any carrier costs associated with the wireless connection.)

Table 5.1 Apple iPad 2 Prices and Features

Model	Memory	Wireless	UK List Price
iPad 2	16 GB	Wi-Fi only	£399
iPad 2	32 GB	Wi-Fi only	£479
iPad 2	64 GB	Wi-Fi only	£559
iPad 2	16 GB	Wi-Fi and 3G	£499
iPad 2	32 GB	Wi-Fi and 3G	£579
iPad 2	64 GB	Wi-Fi and 3G	£659

So, what does this show us? Well, first off, you will see there is a price range, from £399 to £659.

Is the most expensive model really worth £260 more than the cheapest model? That's a 65 percent price increase.

Look at the factors affecting the price: memory and wireless connectivity. With either model, it costs £60 to increase the memory from 16 GB to 32 GB, and a further £80 to increase the memory from 32 GB to 64 GB (so you're paying £3.75 per gigabyte and £2.50 per gigabyte, respectively, for the memory boost). You're also paying £100 to have the option of 3G connectivity (before you pay any carrier charges).

So does it cost more to manufacture a model with more memory? Is the 3G wireless really that expensive? Are the higher-priced models a better value?

First, let me give you some price comparisons. If I wanted to buy a 16-GB SD memory card on Amazon, I could get one for £13.99, and a 32-GB SD memory card for £28.88. For the wireless difference, look at the Kindle, where the Kindle Wi-Fi costs £111 and the Wi-Fi/3G model costs £152. Now, of course, this is a slightly bogus comparison, but you see that others seem to think that memory and 3G wireless may cost less to add to a product.

Although these comparisons are interesting, let's get back to the main point: Why the price differences?

The simple answer is because people will pay what they think the product is worth. If someone thinks that an iPad is worth £400, then they'll buy the base model. If they think it's worth £500, then they might by the Wi-Fi and 3G base model, or perhaps the Wi-Fi-only, 32-GB version. Sure, they might justify that they need the extra memory or the 3G connectivity, but at the end of the day, it all comes down to what they want to pay.

Whatever your perception, price is a matter of what people *want* to pay; it has virtually nothing to do with the cost of the component materials or the manufacturing costs. Sure, the manufacturer will "explain" the price difference in different ways (for instance with more memory or 3G wireless). Do you want some more examples? Here are a few:

- **Bottled water.** How much does that cost? Seriously, how much? People drink bottled water because they want to.

- **Soda.** All you are buying is carbonated water, sugar, and some coloring. Where's the value that you're paying for? If you're thirsty, why not just drink from the tap?

- **Cars.** Take the BMW 3 Series range as an example, where the base model (the 318i ES) lists for £22.690 and the top (petrol) model (335i M Sport) lists for £36,900. Does a bigger engine really justify the extra £14,000?

- **Microsoft Windows.** What justifies the price differential between the various versions (Home Premium, Professional, and so on)?

And let me get to perhaps the most interesting issue. Apple is a premium brand—it sells its reputation on producing expensive gear. You will notice that for all the discussion about the pricing of the models relative to each other, one issue that I have not raised is the actual value. Having a range with a base model and a top-end model means no one questions the price of the base model (because it will always look like a bargain when compared to the top model).

Now think how this principle could be applied to your products. Let's take the example of a group of songs to create an album. Think of the range of price-differentiated products you could create:

- As a first step, you could give away a track or two for the people who think all music should be free. This giveaway could also act as a marketing tool.

- You could then make individual tracks available for download (and the whole album also available for download, but at less than the price of the sum of the individual tracks).

- You could create a cheap CD with a cardboard sleeve and a plain label.

- You could create a regular CD with a jewel case.

- You could create a collector's edition CD with a special booklet, and perhaps include a DVD with videos of you performing some of the tracks. The videos could, of course, also be made available on YouTube at a later date.

The downloads would cost nothing to manufacture, because they are digital files. Pressing a CD might cost you $1 per unit for a short run. This price would include a jewel case and a printed booklet. You could produce this at a lower cost by dropping the leaflet and using a cardboard sleeve. Perhaps this would come out at $0.80 per unit. The collector's edition of the CD might come in a DVD-sized case and could cost $1.50 per unit to produce.

When it comes to selling these products, you might be able to sell individual tracks for 99 cents, a download album for $8, the regular CD for $10, the cheap version for $7, and the collector's edition for $20. If you could achieve these prices, then the income from the collector's edition CD would be three times the income from the cardboard-sleeved CD (see Table 5.2). However, the bigger point to note is the range of purchasing options—you have products with a price range going from free to $20. In short, everyone can choose the price they want to pay.

Table 5.2 An Example of Differential CD Pricing

	Manufacturing Cost	Retail Price	Profit ($)	Profit (as a Percentage of Manufacturing Cost)
Free Songs Given Away	$0	$0	$0	0%
Individual Tracks for Download	$0	$0.99	$0.70	infinite %
Album for Download	$0	$8	$5.60	infinite %
CD with a Cardboard Sleeve	$0.80	$7.00	$6.20	775%
Regular CD	$1.00	$10.00	$9.00	900%
Collector's Edition CD	$1.50	$20.00	$18.50	1,235%

Before you get too carried away looking at the big numbers, remember that I will talk more about profit margins in the next section. However, you will see that you have options to create different products so that you are selling essentially the same product (the album) for four different prices, depending on what people want to pay (and you're also splitting off individual tracks too, for those who won't buy a whole album).

One issue that concerns people when they start looking at differential pricing is cannibalization—in other words, does making something available at a lower price mean that someone won't buy the more expensive item? To an extent, this is a reasonable concern; however, in practice, cannibalization is less frequent than you might expect, because people pay what they want to pay.

If you are concerned about cannibalization, then ensure that there is always a reason for the more expensive items to be bought. So, in the example above, include some additional songs on the regular CD and the collector's edition CD.

Albums aren't the only products for which you can apply differential pricing. For instance, you could charge more for a long-sleeved T-shirt than you would for a short-sleeved T-shirt. Perhaps you could charge $5 more, or perhaps $10, since you are likely to find that your T-shirt supplier will charge you more for the raw materials. There is no real logic for this—if suppliers felt the need to charge more for materials, then they would charge more depending on whether you buy small, medium, large, or extra-large T-shirts—however, you will pay more, so they will charge you more.

Are you starting to see how it all works now? Okay, now go away and think about how you can create a range of products that will be valued differently by different fans with different spending power.

The Cost of Developing Products

In the next chapter ("Economics 101"), I will discuss the economics of a career in the music industry. For the moment, I want to talk about the economics of products.

Time Is Money

How many times have you heard that phrase and wanted to scream? Unfortunately, it is true.

There are things you can do as an artist that will generate money (for instance, writing a hit song), and there are things that do not generate money (sleeping, for example).

Every minute that you are alive has a certain cost. You have to buy food, you have to put a roof over your head, you have to put gas in your car if you want to drive anywhere, and so on. Although you may not be spending money at any one particular moment, over the course of time you do have to spend money.

Therefore, your time as an artist is valuable. If you spend an hour on one project and a year on another project, you will have incurred different costs. Hopefully, the longer project will generate more income. If it doesn't, then I suggest you complete more of the single-hour projects—they are far more lucrative for you.

When I talk about the cost of time, this is the principle that I am discussing.

The Profit Margin on Products

When you sell a product, you will receive income—in other words, money. This is great; money is really useful for buying stuff like food. However, you can't spend all the money you receive, because you will have incurred costs in getting your product to your fans; even if your product is digital (such as a download), there will be costs. In really crude terms, the difference between the wholesale selling price for the product (in other words, the price you are paid for it) and the cost of producing the product is the profit.

The profit is money that you can spend (or money that you can invest to develop more products). If the cost of producing the product exceeds the price you get for selling a product, then you have incurred a loss (which is a bad thing—if you do it too often, you become bankrupt). I make no excuses for spelling out in detail many of the costs you may encounter. If you don't recognize and factor in these costs, you run the risk of incurring a loss.

There are many costs in developing a product; these fall into the broad categories of development, manufacturing, distribution, marketing, and after-sales service (which I discussed at the start of this chapter). Let's look at how these may apply to you in a real-life situation. Please bear in mind that many of these areas overlap and may be difficult to separate if you are working on a project, so some of the distinctions I have made may seem slightly artificial.

The Cost of Developing Your New Product

The development stage of any product is the really creative stage. The most obvious example of product development for a musician is writing songs. New material is the quintessential core of a musician's new product. For the non-writing musician, finding the right material can be as time-consuming as writing music for other musicians.

Writing new songs can take considerable time. Many artists who sit down to write an album's worth of material will spend many months honing their material before they are ready to go anywhere near a studio, and even then the songs may need a lot of polishing.

In music, the costs of development are usually the cost of the artist's time (which usually equates to his living expenses for the development period). However, there may be other costs—for instance, if a band is writing an album, they may hire a studio in which to write. They may need roadies to look after their gear, and the studio may provide an engineer. All of these costs need to be factored into the development of the product.

Not all products have a development cost. For instance, if you write an album's worth of songs and then use those same songs for live shows, there is no new development cost for the second use of the same piece of development. In other words, you don't have to write the songs again to perform them in a live setting.

As you use your raw material (in this example, your songs) in more ways (album, live shows, DVD, film soundtrack, and so on), your development costs as an absolute figure will not reduce; however, the costs, set against the total income from the development work, will look far more efficient.

I have given only one example of a development cost. There are clearly others. You can also think about research costs under this banner—for instance, if you are researching the market for producing merchandise.

One of the key factors to note about development costs is that they are usually fixed. In other words, the amount does not change based on the quantity of product you sell, and once you have spent the money, it is gone and cannot be recouped. Also, it is rare to be able to change the selling price of the final product if the development costs are greater than expected. Therefore, you need to think about a development budget before you spend the money, not after.

Manufacturing Costs

Manufacturing is the process of taking the raw material (often the song) and turning it into a form that can be sold (such as a digital download or a CD). There can be several stages to the process (and there are different cost implications associated with each stage). Take the example of producing a new CD for which the songwriting stage has been completed. There are then two manufacturing stages:

- Recording
- Pressing

Recording may be part of the writing process, and there may be little cost if the artist self-records. If this is the case, the main costs are likely to be the artist's time, electricity, and the investment in recording technology. However, for larger projects, it is common for an artist to record in a studio, in which case the costs will include the studio hire, roadies, engineers, a producer, and so on.

Within the recording costs, there is also the expense of mixing, mastering, and getting the music into a format that can be sent to the CD pressing plant (or uploaded to a download store, such as iTunes).

As with product development, once these manufacturing costs have been incurred, the money has gone, so stringent budgeting will help ensure that you at least stand a chance of making a profit.

There are many costs involved in arranging for a CD to be pressed, beyond those associated with the purely mechanical process of stamping out a number of CDs. These additional costs include everything from preparing glass masters from which the stamp (that is used to stamp the CD) is prepared, to preparing the casing and the artwork.

The costs will vary depending on a range of factors; however, the costs of pressing are generally very controllable. Assuming you are going the glass-master route, there are some fixed setup costs, but after that most of the costs are dependent on the numbers of

CDs pressed. The more CDs that are pressed, the higher your costs will be (because you will be buying a greater number). However, with greater numbers you will probably be quoted a cheaper per-unit cost.

The key mechanism for controlling costs (for CD reproduction) is to control the number of CDs that are pressed. By controlling the number of CDs you order, you can also control your cash flow. If you split one large CD run into two smaller batches, then you will probably increase your overall cost. However, by following this course, you can use income generated from selling the first batch to fund the costs for the second batch.

There are, of course, many different products you can offer, and for each product there will be a different and unique manufacturing process. For instance, if the product you will be offering is a live show, then the manufacturing process will revolve around pulling the show together, rehearsing the musicians, and so on.

Marketing Expenses

Marketing is the process by which you make potential purchasers aware of your product. Marketing costs can vary hugely. However, if you were paying attention in the earlier chapters of this book, then you will have built up a database of your fans, and you will know how to contact these people directly (whether through the social networks or by SMS message, email, or some other system).

However, if you feel your database doesn't include all of your fans (and there is a good chance that it won't), or you want to expand the size of your fan base, then you may decide on a more elaborate marketing campaign. This may involve advertising and promotion work. In crude terms, advertising will cost you money, while promotion work will take your time (and require you to spend money getting to the location of the promotion).

The amount of marketing you do is likely to have a very direct effect on the success of your product. It should also have an indirect effect of growing your fan base over time.

Provided you have a way to connect with your (growing) fan base to guarantee a certain level of product consumption/sales, you can have a successful product without spending significant amounts on marketing. Beyond that point, your marketing budget can be controlled quite tightly, but once you do start spending on marketing, there is always the temptation to spend "just a little bit more" to get a slightly better result.

Distribution and Delivery Costs

Distribution and delivery are about getting the product to the purchaser. This is a simple matter of logistics. However, when you include the human factor and multiply the possibilities for unintended errors by a whole fan base, you will understand why this can be one of the most frustrating parts of the process from a fan's perspective.

You are likely to get your products to people in different ways. Here are some of the examples of the means of distribution and the costs that will affect your pricing:

- If you sell your tracks as digital downloads through iTunes or Amazon, then you will be paid a percentage of the selling price (usually around 70 percent), and if you also use an agent to interface with the vendor, then they may cost/take commission.

- If you send CDs and DVDs by mail, then the costs will include the postage, the packaging, and the human costs involved in processing the order and preparing the package to be mailed. You will also incur costs in processing payments. Typically, if you receive money by credit card, then you will receive an amount equal to the price of the product less a credit card processing fee.

  With mail order, the customer usually will be charged for postage and packaging, so you may not see this as something that should be included when you are thinking about pricing your product. However, if you don't get your mail-order pricing right, you will incur a loss, and that loss will need to be funded from somewhere, so I recommend you get the pricing right before you start sending out products. And if you do find that you have gotten the mail-order pricing wrong, then change it at the earliest opportunity.

- If your CDs and DVDs are distributed by a fulfillment company, then they will also charge a fee for postage, packaging, processing, and the humans involved in their process. There will also be the cost of getting your CDs/DVDs to the fulfillment service. A whole stack of CDs can be quite heavy, and this can make courier charges quite steep (especially if your fulfillment service is overseas).

- If you sell CDs/DVDs at gigs, then you will need to keep a certain level of stock, and the storage space may cost (even if that cost only appears to be the stress of having your stock sitting around at home).

- If you sell CDs/DVDs through record stores, then there will be a cost of physically getting the product to the record stores. There will be another hidden cost in that the record store may not pay you for a while (perhaps not for several months). In this situation, while not an explicit cost, there is a price that you will pay for effectively giving the record store a loan.

- If your product is a live show, then you will have a large number of expenses associated with putting on the show. These could include the cost of the venue, security staff, getting equipment to the show and getting it set up, as well as transportation and accommodations for everyone involved.

After-Sales Service: The Hidden Costs

After-sales service may not be something you think about—it's not as if you're selling a toaster. However, this is an area you will have to consider even if it is virtually impossible to budget accurately for it. For instance, what happens if a CD you have sold doesn't play? Or what happens if the mug your on-demand supplier sells is chipped or has a blurred photo?

In many cases, after-sales service will not cost very much money; however, it will take an awful lot of time and may divert you from other activities from which you could be generating income. That being said, replacing one or two CDs may not cost much, but replacing a whole batch of 25,000 could have a significant impact on your profitability if you have to pack and mail out each CD.

Shoddy goods and failure to attend to after-sales service also can do a lot of damage to your reputation.

Making Money from Products

The purpose of a product is to turn your ideas into something that can make money. The amount of money you can make from your products is determined by a range of factors:

- The number of products you sell

- The profit you make on each product

The Number of Products You Sell

There are two factors determining the number of products you can sell:

- The number of people who will buy your product

- The number of products you have available for sale

It may sound simple, but the more people you can sell to, the higher your income will be (provided you are selling your product at a profit). Although you may have an excellent product, if your market is limited (for example, taking the illustration I used earlier, if you are a classical guitarist), then there will be a ceiling on the number of people who are likely to buy your product. Therefore, to generate more interest, you need more products (so your income per fan rises).

Only you will know your particular situation and your fan base. In light of this knowledge, you will need to decide whether you should spend more time marketing or more time developing a wider product range if you want to positively influence your income stream.

As a side note, do remember that the rule that selling more products leads to more income is true only if you are making a profit. If you have priced your product at a level that creates a loss, then higher sales equates to greater losses.

The Profit per Product

At the individual product level, one control you have over the income that flows from each product is your profit margin. Irrespective of the cost of production, many products will have a maximum price above which no one (or only a few people) will buy them. For instance, if you are selling a CD, most people might expect to pay in the range of $8 to $15, and you will find only a few who would be prepared to pay more than $20.

Usually you can't break the ceiling price for a product. However, at other times you can. For instance, if you are playing a gig, then there is probably a ceiling on the maximum price you can charge for tickets. The solution to generating more income in this situation is to sell more tickets, which you can do by using a bigger venue. Obviously, a bigger venue will lead to higher costs, but you should be able to factor these in to ensure that you make greater profits. Also, somewhat ironically, as you move up to bigger venues, your gigs will become more of an event, which will allow you to price the tickets at a higher level.

Profit Levels

In broad terms, the profit you will make from any product is the income from sales (which, if you're selling through a vendor, will be the wholesale cost, not the sticker price), less the costs.

Some of your costs will be fixed; for instance, once you have recorded an album, any studio costs that need to be recouped through the project will be fixed. As we have also seen, other costs can be managed on an ongoing basis—for instance, you can control the cost of CD duplication by limiting the CD run.

The difficulty with costs is that they tend to be big numbers—they're usually followed by three zeros, denoting amounts in the thousands. By contrast, income tends to come in small amounts—typically, you're selling single-digit products (if not less, in the case of downloads). This disparity means that it can take a long time to recoup your investment in a project. If you don't have any money to fund yourself until you are making a profit, you run the risk of bankruptcy.

I will look at some of the ways you can finance your career and your products while you are waiting for your income to start flowing in the next part, as well as consider the wider issue of income and profitability.

At this point I want to illustrate the costs and potential income from a product with the example of a CD project. For this example, I have invented numbers to illustrate my point. You should not assume these numbers are anything close to realistic. More realistic numbers will be discussed in the next chapter. Also, to make this example easier, I have assumed that you are earning all of the income from the CD (in other words, you are selling it directly and are not giving a cut to a retailer). My final main assumption is that you have a source of income to fund your project. To make the illustration more straightforward, I'm ignoring other sources of income that might flow from the recording (for instance, download sales).

For this project, I am assuming we have an established band of four members, who each draw living expenses from band funds of $2,500 per month (in other words, $10,000 per month for the whole band or $30,000 per year per band member—no one is going to buy a Rolls-Royce on that salary).

I will assume that the time spent during the development phase and the recording phase (up to the point that the CD can be released) is 12 months. In other words, the band's living expenses will have reached $120,000 over that period.

I am assuming that the band has a reasonable following and that there is a manager who will take 20 percent of the net income (which I am defining as the income less the recording costs, but not including the band's living expenses). I will talk more about managers in Chapter 8, "Building the Team around You." There may also be office staff (running the fan club, updating the website, and so on) and other miscellaneous unaccounted-for expenses, but let's not get too detailed yet.

Anyway, for this album project, let us assume that:

- The recording studio plus engineer costs $50,000.

- The producer costs $35,000.

- Mastering costs are $5,000.

- The artwork costs $2,000.

- There were miscellaneous costs of $8,000 (such as pizzas and beer for everyone when the recording sessions ran over).

In total, the recording costs come to $100,000. This figure has to be recouped before the band can see any income.

For the manufacturing costs, let's assume that the band gets the CD pressed in batches with the following costs (including shipping from the plant to the band's distribution center):

- The cost for the first 10,000 CDs comes in at $10,000.

- The next 15,000 CDs cost $10,000.

- Subsequent batches of 25,000 CDs come in at $16,000.

We'll assume each CD is sold for $10, and I'm also assuming the fan will pay for postage and packing. Let's assume that there is a credit card charge of 60 cents for each sale, meaning that each CD will bring in $9.40. To make things simple, I am not making any allowance for sales tax (such a VAT or any state or national equivalent).

Before a solitary CD can be sold, the recording costs have come in at $100,000, and the first batch of 10,000 CDs has cost $10,000. Added to this, there is the expense of running the band, which came in at $120,000, so the total spent before any money has been earned is $230,000 (see Table 5.3).

Table 5.3 The Costs of Recording a CD and Getting the First Pressing

	Income	Expenditure	Total
Earnings during recording	$0		
Band expenses during recording		$120,000	
Recording studio plus engineer		$50,000	
Producer's fee		$35,000	
Mastering costs		$5,000	
Artwork		$2,000	
Miscellaneous expenses		$8,000	
Pressing the first 10,000 CDs		$10,000	
Total expenses to date			−$230,000

Assuming the first 10,000 CDs can be sold at $10 (bringing in $9.40 after credit card charges), this will generate $94,000. From this, the manager will take nothing because the recording costs have yet to be recouped. After the sale of 10,000 CDs, the project is running at a loss of $136,000.

With the pressing of the next 15,000 CDs, a further $10,000 will be spent, giving a total loss for the project of $146,000 (see Table 5.4).

Table 5.4 The Costs Incurred after Selling 10,000 CDs and Arranging for a Second Pressing

	Income	Expenditure	Total
Loss on recording (see Table 5.3)			−$230,000
Cash generated from selling 10,000 CDs (income after credit card charges)	$94,000		
Pressing next 15,000 CDs		$10,000	
Profit generated by project to date			−$146,000

When this batch of 15,000 CDs is sold, they will generate an income of $141,000. At this stage, the recording and CD pressing costs will come to $120,000 ($100,000 recording costs, plus $20,000 for pressing 25,000 CDs to date), so the manager will start taking her fee. In this instance, the manager's fee is 20 percent of the income above recording costs (in other words, $94,000 + $141,000 − $120,000).

After deducting the manager's fee of $23,000, the project is still running at a loss of $28,000. This means that after 25,000 CDs have been sold, each CD now equates to just over $1.00 lost. To generate more income, more CDs need to be pressed. This time 25,000 will be pressed at a cost of $16,000, leading to a total loss to date of $44,000 (see Table 5.5).

Table 5.5 The Costs after Selling 25,000 CDs and Arranging for a Further 25,000 CDs to Be Pressed

	Income	Expenditure	Total
Losses to date (see Table 5.4)			−$146,000
Cash generated from selling next 15,000 CDs (income after credit card charges)	$141,000		
Manager's fee (20% on income over $120,000)		$23,000*	
Pressing next 25,000 CDs		$16,000	
Profit generated by project to date			−$44,000

*Note that the manager is taking her fee while the project is still running at a loss.

If this next batch of 25,000 CD is all sold (making total sales of 50,000), it will generate $235,000, from which the manager will take $43,800 (in other words, 20 percent of the income from the sales less the production cost).

The break-even point is when the expenses have been recouped and therefore any further income is profit (refer to Figure 5.3). At the point that the project sells 29,095 CDs, it will break even, and the band will start to make a profit (in other words, the act will start to generate some income for themselves). However, due to the nature of the product that is being sold here, there is a cost associated with each CD (for instance, the cost of manufacturing and the credit card charge). Accordingly, the break-even point is not as simple as Figure 5.3 may suggest. A more detailed explanation of the break-even point is contained later in this section.

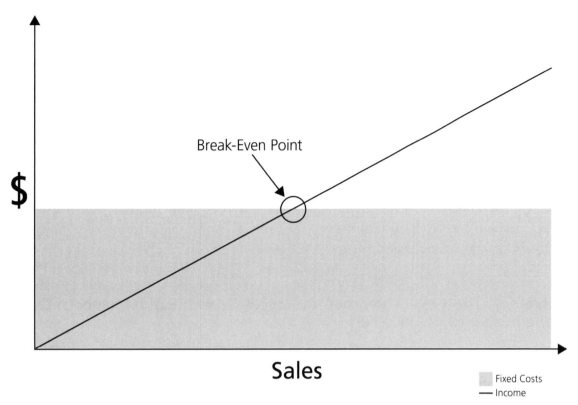

Figure 5.3 An example break-even point. Unfortunately, break-even points are never as simple as this graph may suggest. See Figure 5.4 for a more detailed example.

Having sold 50,000, the CD has now made a profit of $147,200 for the band members —in other words, $36,800 per member (see Table 5.6).

Table 5.6 The Project Finally Moves into Profit

	Income	Expenditure	Total
Losses to date (see Table 5.5)			−$44,000
Cash generated from selling next 25,000 CDs (income after credit card charges)	$235,000		
Manager's fee (taking account of the cost of pressing 25,000 CDs)		$43,800	
Profit generated by project to date			$147,200

This implies an income for each member of the band of around $66,000 (including the $30,000 living expenses) for just over a year's work. However, let me add some caveats here.

First, there will be more expenses—for instance, accounting costs, warehousing costs for storing the CDs, and insurance, to give three examples. There could be quite large expenses, such as hotel costs and transportation for the band and their equipment (with roadies) while working at the studio. Second, the band is likely to have to tour extensively to support this album and generate this level of sales. At this level, the income from touring may be quite volatile.

Added to this, it may be two years before the next album is released, which implies the profit would need to be split over two years, giving an income (including the money used to fund living expenses) in the region of $33,000.

Perhaps the most significant caveat is that it is really hard work to sell 50,000 CDs. However, I wouldn't wish to discourage you from your aim. In fact, why not work even harder and try to sell 100,000? Look at Table 5.7 for an illustration of the income that this sales figure could generate.

Table 5.7 The Project Reaches the Level Where Band Members Can Generate a Healthy Income

	Income	Expenditure	Total
Profits to date (see Table 5.6)			$147,200
Pressing next 50,000 CDs		$32,000	
Cash generated from selling next 50,000 CDs (income after credit card charges)	$480,000		
Manager's fee (taking account of cost of pressing 50,000 CDs)		$89,600	
Profit generated by project to date			$505,600

As Table 5.7 shows for this example, selling 100,000 CDs could generate a profit for each band member of $126,400, which equates to $63,200 per year if it is split over two years. However, do remember that you may not sell all of your CDs immediately once they have been pressed.

At the start of this example, I put in an allowance of $2,500 per month for band living expenses during recording. If this amount is removed to show the total profit for the project, then the total profit on the project would amount to $625,600. If this figure is split over two years for each band member, it equates to a monthly income of $6,500 (before taxes, savings, or any other deductions).

I will discuss the level of earnings you need to achieve to live on in greater detail in Chapter 7, "Your Pay Packet." I will also discuss the comparative income you could generate under a typical contract with a record company.

Expenditure

Before we move on, I want to draw to your attention some of the large amounts that have been spent in this project. Some of these charges are explicit (the band has to pay them directly—an example of this would be the studio costs), and others are implicit (and cause a reduction in the band's income—an example of these would be the credit card charges).

Selling 100,000 CDs at $10 should have generated an income of $1 million. However, the band received only $505,600—in other words, half of the income (and remember that this example assumes the act sells its music directly—the income would have been greatly reduced if sales went through retailers). Let's have a look at where the rest went.

- $120,000 (12 percent of the income) was drawn by the band as living expenses.

- $100,000 (10 percent of the income) was spent on recording costs.

- $156,400 (15 percent of the income) was charged as the manager's fee.

- $52,000 (5 percent of the income) was spent on CD manufacturing.

- $60,000 (6 percent of the income) was spent on credit card fees.

The figure that leaps out here is the charge by the manager, which accounts for 15 percent of the income (although, do remember that the manager's charge is 20 percent—the discrepancy arises because some expenses have been set against the income before the fee is calculated). However, before you judge the manager too harshly, remember that this is not straight profit for the manager. From this figure, the manager will need to fund her office and many of the costs of running the band. Also remember that in this example, the manager doesn't take a cent until the recording costs have been recouped, so there is a risk that the manager may not generate any income.

You should also note that in some ways this is a slightly unrealistic number. Conventionally, a manager will take around 20 percent of gross earnings (that is, earnings before any deduction). However, that percentage is normal when a band may be on a royalty of 18 to 23 percent of the price that the CD is sold to a retailer. In other words, if a CD is sold into a shop at $6.00, then the band might receive $1.20 (before the manager's cut), and the manager would take $0.24 per CD sold.

By contrast, under the business model set out here, the manager could be taking $1.79 per CD sold. This may sound like a large number until you remember that calculated on the same basis, the band could be taking $7.17 per CD *after* the manager has taken her cut.

If you are going to adopt this business model, you may want to have a discussion with your manager about what expenses should be included or excluded when calculating her fee.

Just to close off this discussion, if the manager was looking after a band with a major recording company, then she could expect perhaps 1 million albums to be sold, generating a fee of $240,000. However, using this business model, we have assumed that 100,000 CDs are sold, which will generate a fee of $179,000. Although $61,000 isn't an amount to be sneezed at, the fees for the manager in both scenarios are in the same ballpark, suggesting that the fee level may be reasonable.

I will talk more about managers in Chapter 8.

For me, the next charge that leaps out is the cost of the credit card company. You will see that the credit card charges exceed the cost of manufacturing the CDs. This is not an abnormally high fee (although I did round it up). For illustration, a credit card company may charge 2.9 percent of the purchase price plus $0.30 per transaction. If the CD had been priced at $14, then the credit card fee would have been $0.70. Unfortunately, this is one of the charges you have to accept because there really isn't a viable alternative.

As you read earlier in this book, one of the benefits of running your own career is that you can retain control. To a large extent, you can decide who you work with and how much money you want to spend. This example has illustrated the costs for producing and selling a CD. However, many of the expenses could have been managed in a different way.

For instance, if you had recorded the album in your own studio, you could have cut approximately $100,000 from the budget (although there will be a cost associated with setting up and running your own studio). By contrast, you could have chosen to work with a producer with a world-class reputation and paid $1 million plus for his services.

Break-Even Point on a Project

One of the most important factors in the project I have just illustrated is the break-even point. This is the point at which the project ceases to make a loss and starts to generate a profit.

In simplistic terms, once you have covered the expenses, then the project will move into profit. (Figure 5.3 illustrated this principle.) However, in reality, the break-even point is actually a moving target, because the expenses get larger over time. With the example I have just illustrated, this is particularly so in two areas:

- Each time a new consignment of CDs is pressed, there is an expense.

- The manager takes a cut of the profit once the cost of producing the recording and pressing the CDs has been met.

You will also have noticed from this example that there was no way that costs would be covered with the first consignment of CDs. Indeed, costs were not covered with the second consignment. It was only after the delivery of the third batch of CDs that the project moved into profit.

There was a logic for ordering insufficient product to cover the costs (in other words, there was a logic why a conscious decision was made to order an amount of product that could *never* bring the project into profit): controlling cash flow (in other words, not spending more money than was on hand so that as much money could be retained in the business as possible). Keeping a tight rein on spending also has the effect of controlling potential losses. If all of the CDs had been purchased in one lump, it would have cost an additional $42,000 (or perhaps slightly less with a discount for bulk). This would have made a total expenditure of $52,000 on the CDs. Splitting the purchases meant that the band was not left with $52,000 worth of unsold stock (and didn't have to store and insure the stock).

As a side note, you should also remember that there are other sources of income that could be derived from the music (for instance, online sales, licensing for inclusion on compilation albums, and licensing for use in film and television). All of these additional sources of income could be used to offset any losses.

To return to the subject of the break-even point, this is probably best illustrated by the graph set out in Figure 5.4.

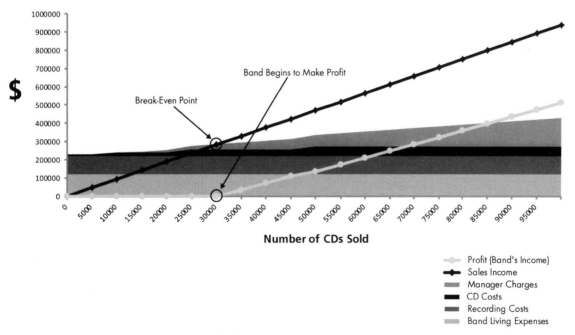

Figure 5.4 This graph shows how the break-even point is a moving target due to the increasing level of expenses. When sales income exceeds expenses, then the band starts to generate some income.

As you can see:

- The recording costs and the band expenses are fixed, as is the cost of the first CD pressing.

- The costs rise after 10,000 sales, when the second batch of CDs is ordered. In reality, this second batch of CDs would be ordered before 10,000 sales had been achieved to ensure that the product was always available.

- The manager's fee kicks in at 12,766 CD sales, when the costs of recording (excluding the band expenses) and the costs of the CD pressings have been recouped.

- The costs rise again after 25,000 CD sales, when the third batch of CDs is ordered.

- There are no profits until the income exceeds the expenses (which, as we have seen, continue to rise). This occurs when the project has sold 29,095 CDs. This is the break-even point. If we had ordered, for instance, 100,000 CDs at the start of the project, then the break-even point would have been much later.

- Although the break-even point has been passed, expenses continue to be incurred, which is why the profits increase at a lesser rate than the income.

Lastly, do remember that some expenses are included by way of a reduction to income (specifically credit card charges, which are not explicitly shown in Figure 5.4).

Profitability

In Figure 5.4, it may look like the band doesn't fare particularly well. In this business model, the band takes the greatest risk and finances the project. Unlike under a conventional recording contract, the band will also get the greatest reward. Figure 5.5 illustrates this point.

This graph shows how significant each financial element is as sales increase. You will see that initially, all of the income is dedicated to meeting the costs. As the income grows, the manager's charges are also paid. When the project has broken even, then profits are generated and the band can share in the gains.

However, you will see that as sales continue to increase, the profits increase considerably, too. If you were to extrapolate this graph, you would see that the fixed recording costs (including the band expenses) would become comparatively tiny, and the band's profitability would increase further. Indeed, as the sales increase, the band's profits tend toward 80 percent of the net income (but will not reach that figure because there is always the expense of pressing further CDs to meet increased demand). The band will never reach 100 percent income because the manager will always take 20 percent.

One point you should note about Figure 5.5 is that the graph is intended to show the main proportions and does not show (for instance) the expense of credit card

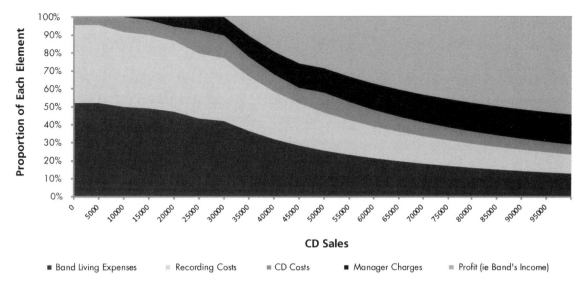

Figure 5.5 This chart shows how the respective proportions of the income are split as sales increase. With greater sales, the fixed costs become less significant, and the band's profits increase.

transactions. Also, until the break-even point, remember that the expenses will exceed income. Until this point, the graph illustrates the relative proportions of the losses.

As a last point, could I remind you that this is a book about building a career in music, not a manual about releasing your own CD? If you are going to release your own CD, then you will need to undertake considerable research (and hopefully, this chapter gave you some pointers about some of the financial aspects that you should be considering).

Hard-Core Finances

This chapter looked at the issues around creating products, including some of the financial issues. In the next chapter ("Economics 101"), I'll delve more deeply into all of the financial aspects around your career.

The Nasty Commercial Bits

6 Economics 101

As I have discussed throughout this book, the musician looking to build a successful career today has many more options than were available in the past.

One of the key differences between the old approach and the new approach is that before, the musician could have expected his income to come from one or two sources, and now there are many more possible sources of income, with each source producing a less significant flow of income.

On their own, many (perhaps most) of these sources will not be sufficient to sustain a reasonable standard of living. However, the musician has the opportunity to aggregate these sources and to increase the period over which the income is received and so can obtain maximum value from each product. In this way, a musician can develop a sustainable career.

I have spent a lot of time focusing on the proactive actions that musicians can take. I have advocated this approach for a number of reasons:

- Major corporations have major overheads (and smaller organizations have overheads, too). Although there may be efficiencies that the majors can negotiate, you can often earn more money (as a percentage of each product sold) if you take a proactive approach. For instance, a self-released CD can generate more income than the royalties paid by a major label if it releases your CD.

- A self-managed approach gives more people an opportunity to have a viable music career. This should have the effect of making music more diverse and less driven by the commercial imperative (not that I have any problems with commercial and popular music).

- You learn and understand the business.

- Your career begins immediately and is a long-term undertaking, not something that will end when you cease to be flavor of the month.

- You keep control of every aspect (from financial to artistic).

- This is simply a better way to promote yourself if you want to deal with the majors (or any other business partner for that matter). They come to you because you have something highly valuable to offer.

- Fans are treated with respect.

However, this approach is not the only way, and I would not wish you to think that you shouldn't deal with the major entertainment companies. Just deal with them from a point of strength!

Having control and having negotiating power means you can start your career in a self-managed fashion. Once you reach a certain level of success, it may be in your interest to work with a major record label—only you can make that decision.

However, if you do decide to deal with a major, don't abandon the principles set out in this book. There will almost certainly come a time when both you and the record company want to end the deal. If you don't have a direct relationship with your fan base, then you may not be able to sustain a career after the deal ends.

Sources of Income: How Much Can I Earn?

In the previous chapter, within the context of product design, we looked at the economics of releasing your own CD. In this chapter I'm going to go further and look in more detail at the economics of more products. In doing this, I will try to compare the income you can generate by taking different approaches. For instance, I will compare the income you could expect if you release a CD through an on-demand service or with a record label.

In illustrating each option, I will use figures that are within the bounds of reasonableness at the date of this writing. Although reasonable, they are definitely not the lowest-cost/highest-income figures you would be able to find after commercial negotiation. You should not regard these figures as accurate, because they will be out of date by the time you read them, and local conditions (including local taxation) will almost certainly affect your position if and when you are in a position to undertake any of these activities.

In Chapter 7, "Your Pay Packet," I will look at how much you need to earn to sustain your lifestyle. This may influence the amount you feel you need to earn.

Before we go any further, I want to warn you about many of these figures. This warning is especially relevant if you are selling in the European Union.

Many jurisdictions, particularly within the European Union, have purchase taxes (a tax levied on the sale of goods). In the EU, this tax is value added tax (VAT). The rates of VAT vary, but they are generally around 20 percent of the purchase price. To give an example of how VAT works in the UK (where VAT stands at

20 percent), if you sell a CD for £10, then after you have accounted for VAT, you will receive £8.33 (£8.33 + 20 percent = £10).

Your credit card processor will charge its fee based on the full selling price (in other words, what you receive and VAT), so this can be something of a double-whammy: As well as paying tax, you will be charged to collect tax on the government's behalf.

The figures in this section do not (except where specifically noted) take any account of VAT, so you are getting an inflated idea of potential earnings in jurisdictions where this tax is payable. However, where you are looking at royalties, VAT will have been dealt with at the retail level, and you do not need to worry about having to further account for VAT. This means that some of the figures shown here may not be comparing similar situations.

Earnings from Music

If you have just read the introductory paragraphs, you might be forgiven for thinking there is only one way to generate income from music: to release a CD. However, there are, of course, many ways. Let's have a look at the main options.

Downloads

In the last few years, the music download market has matured. Today, it is a significant part of the music market—within a few years it will almost certainly be the way most people buy music. And naturally, downloads are a great option for smaller acts, because you don't have the logistical challenges of creating and distributing CDs.

As part of the maturation process, many of the smaller download players have fallen by the wayside, leaving a lesser number of more significant players. The two biggest are, of course, Apple's iTunes and Amazon. Although the market has narrowed, there is still a range of options beyond these two.

There are two factors that will affect what you get from any download service:

- The first factor is how much the retailer pays (which can be affected by the price charged for a download). Most retailers pay around 65 percent of the sale price (in other words, for a 99-cent download, you will receive 65 cents before deductions).

- The second factor affecting the income is how you access the retailer—if you access the retailer through an aggregator or middleman, then there will be additional costs that affect your income. By equal measure, if you access the retailer as part of your contract with a record company, then your royalty will be considerably less.

Getting into the Download Stores

Let's look at the second factor (how you access the download stores) in a bit more detail.

The figures in this section are for the recording artist. If you also wrote the track, then there will be a separate payment from your songwriting royalty collector (which is discussed later in this chapter—as a side issue, the amount of the songwriting royalty is around 8 percent of the sale price in addition to the figures set out here).

If you've been paying attention, you will have noticed that I have railed against middlemen (and middle-women), as they tend to add too much overhead. One place where an intermediary can be very useful is in submitting tracks to the download stores. There are several companies who provide this sort of service, including CD Baby (cdbaby. com), TuneCore (tunecore.com), and Ditto Music (dittomusic.com).

The companies all provide a similar service, including:

■ Encoding your audio into the appropriate format for each store.

■ Uploading the audio to each store (and remember, this may be no small task—for instance, the iTunes store has a number of different stores).

■ Entering into a contract with each of the retailers.

■ Collecting your earnings from each of the retailers.

■ Paying out your earnings.

The key issues to note are that instead of dealing with each store on a case-by-case basis, you have to deal only with the aggregator, who will handle everything for you. So you will have only one contract, and you will need to upload only one file. If you would rather spend your time making music instead of messing around with files and administration, then use an aggregator.

But consider the cost levied by the aggregators before you do.

Some charge a flat fee and then pass all of the earnings directly to you (for instance, TuneCore charges $9.99 to upload a track). Others take a percentage (for instance, CD Baby takes 9 percent). Some have tiered levels of services, offering more if you pay more (for instance, Ditto Music charges £88 for a chart-registered release). Only you can decide what is right for you. And in addition to the direct cost, you should also look at the time they take to pay. If the aggregator holds your money for longer, then that is money you can't spend.

As you can see, there is a break-even cost associated with TuneCore and Ditto Music, but for CD Baby the situation is far simpler: You will get an income of 59 cents for each 99-cent download (99 cents – 34 cents – 6 cents; in other words, 9 percent of 65 cents), which still is a pretty reasonable income (and may be better or worse than one of the fixed-cost arrangements).

However, if you have a deal with a record company, you are likely to receive considerably less. Sales through iTunes and the other download stores are (generally) regarded by many labels in the same manner as sales from record stores. In other words, iTunes buys the track wholesale (for 65 cents) and then sells it at whatever price it wants. The record company will then treat that 65-cent income (which may be less if there are expenses) in the same manner as if it had sold a physical product and will make the same deductions as if a product had been sold (for instance, for container charges, even though there was no packaging—this is explained later in the chapter) and will then pay a royalty on the income. This could give an income of around 10 cents.

As you would expect, there are other deals out there. For instance, some download services treat tracks as if they had been licensed, so a license fee can be paid. However, because some labels have figured this may generate more money for the artist, these deals are becoming less common.

Your Own Download Solution

Just because there are many commercial download services, that doesn't mean you can't adopt your own system. You could adopt an off-the-shelf solution for selling digital goods, such as E-Junkie (e-junkie.com).

Alternatively, you could commission some custom programming on your website and come up with your own arrangement for selling your tracks and for ensuring that you get paid immediately.

However, I wouldn't follow either of these courses. To my mind, if you want to sell music, then your music needs to be where other people have their music: You need to be in a virtual record shop.

Subscription Services

For the consumer who wants to get her music in digital form, there is an alternative to paid downloads: subscriptions.

These services offer access to millions of tracks (literally millions, depending on the store). The consumer pays a flat fee (maybe $10 a month) and can then stream as many tracks as she wants. At the end of the month, either the subscription is renewed or the individual has no further access to the music.

There are variations on a theme within these services. Some allow a very limited number of tracks to be downloaded and kept, some offer different tiers of service, and others generate income from a range of sources (including by inserting advertisements).

Although there are differences, there is a broad similarity in how the income is split with the copyright holder. Each month, the download service has a pool of money. This is essentially its income over a period less its expenses (for instance, the expenses of running the business, including credit card fees, the cost of paying the songwriter levies, plus an element of profit). This pool of money is then shared between everyone whose track is streamed during the period that the pool of money has been earned, and the more a track is streamed, the greater the share of the pool that the track takes.

Ringtones

A few years ago, the ringtone market was huge. Now it's still a healthy market, but it is nowhere near as significant as it was.

The royalties generated from ringtones are a bit of a mishmash of arrangements. Some royalties are negotiated on a license-by-license basis. In other territories, there is a prescribed rate. For instance, in the UK, the MCPS (*Mechanical-Copyright Protection Society*) has set a rate for the use of music on mobile phones. This rate is the greater of:

- 12 percent of the gross revenue received by the licensee

- 10 pence (approximately 17 cents)

CD Sales

A CD release perhaps gives another good illustration of how your income (and your cost control) can change depending on how you produce the product. For instance, your income will differ hugely depending on whether you release the CD yourself or a major record company releases it. Not only can your income vary, but so can the financial risks you are taking.

You should note that in all of these examples, I am not comparing (I cannot compare) like with like. Look at a self-released CD compared to a CD released through a major. On your own, you could take 100 percent of the profit, where with a major you might get 15 percent of the list price. One hundred percent may look better than 15 percent, but if you don't recoup your costs, then you are getting 100 percent of nothing.

You should also note that the charts I am about to use illustrate proportions. (Broadly, they illustrate what proportion of the income from a CD's sales translates into profit, or income, for you.) They do not illustrate how much income you can make from each source. So if you're looking at how much income you can generate (and trying to calculate whether it will be enough to live on), remember that 100 percent of $1 is a lot less than 1 percent of $1 million.

To see the significance of the proportions, you have to multiply the proportion, by the number of sales, by the price of the CD (or whatever other product you are selling). The benefit of being able to take a greater proportion of the revenue means you need far fewer sales to generate sufficient income to sustain your lifestyle.

However, when you start scaling up your operations (in other words, when you start selling sufficient quantities of product to earn a living for yourself and everyone else involved in the project), then you may find that administration and logistics become far more significant if you are dealing with tangible products, such as CDs. (There are no such analogous problems if you scale up your sales of downloads, especially if you use an aggregator to handle the files.)

If you spend all you time fulfilling orders, you will stop making music, so the only practical option that will be left to you is to take on staff. When you take on staff, your costs will rise, so you will need to sell more products. With the additional expense of staff salaries, you will find it becomes a fine balancing act to make money.

On-Demand CDs

Let's start by looking at on-demand CD production, since this is one area where you can generate immediate profits (once you have met your recording costs). For the musician, this offers the nearest thing you will find to a zero-risk self-released CD.

Let me just be clear about the term "profit." What I am implying here is that you *can* set up an on-demand CD without costs, so you can start selling without having to buy stock. All costs of the service would be implicit and charged on each CD purchased, so there will be little benefit to be gained from scale. You may want to go with a service that charges a setup fee if this gives a better profit.

To give an example of a price being quoted by an on-demand delivery service today (with no setup costs for you), if you sell a CD for $10 using this service (direct mail order from the service—your customer pays for postage), then for each sale, you would generate a profit of $4.50.

With this example, there is a benefit from scale, which would be applicable if you were ordering stock to sell directly. Orders for five or more CDs (and I'm not sure why you would order fewer than five) generate a profit of $5.50.

There are many reasons not to go with an on-demand service. For instance, the CDs will be produced on CD-R discs (in other words, the same sort of disc that you would burn in your computer's CD drive). This may not give quite the professional image you are after, although I would guess that not many people will notice or care.

However, on-demand delivery gives you a way to get your CDs out very quickly and with little cost.

You should also remember that sales tax (such as VAT) may be payable on CDs, depending on the jurisdiction. If you are offering your CD at a price that includes VAT, then (using an example VAT rate of 20 percent and assuming you buy more than five CDs), you could see your profit from a $10 CD drop from $5.50 to $4.60.

Figure 6.1 shows the respective proportions relating to the production, sales tax, and profit for an on-demand CD sold for $10 (assuming you get the bulk discount). If the price were to be raised, then the VAT would increase (since it is price-related), but the production cost would remain at a similar dollar amount, hence the profit would increase.

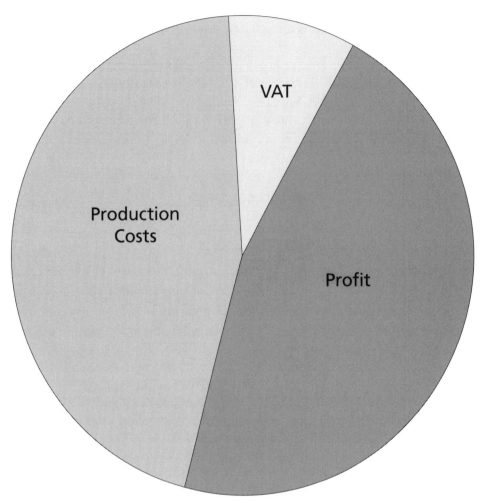

Figure 6.1 The costs and profits associated with the production of an on-demand CD (including VAT).

Pressing Your Own CDs

I looked at the economics of arranging for pressing your own CD in Chapter 4. I will repeat the comment that I mentioned then: This is not a book about pressing your own CDs. If that is a route you wish to follow, you should remember that there are many issues involved. (For instance, if you want your CD to show up in the charts, you are likely to need a barcode.) I suggest you seek advice from a local expert about the requirements in your jurisdiction if this is an option you intend to follow.

One key feature of this option is that you have to make an investment—you have to purchase your initial stock before you can sell it. As I noted in the earlier chapter, you don't need to buy all of your stock immediately; however, you will probably be able to negotiate better discounts with larger orders.

If you are getting your CDs pressed (rather than getting a number of CD-Rs reproduced, which you might do for short runs), then there is the upfront cost of a glass master. Many pressing plants will factor this cost into their quote.

Another factor to bear in mind is that once you have your product, you will need to store it and insure it. (Most household insurance policies will not cover this sort of commercial activity.) In addition, there will be a cost associated with the distribution of the product—this cost would be in terms of physical distribution (in other words, paying a courier/postage) and, assuming your sales are sufficient, human fees (in other words, paying someone to undertake the work—if you sell 100,000 CDs, you probably won't want to send them all out yourself).

I have not added these additional costs in this illustration. You should make an appropriate allowance before you make any price comparisons with other methods of CD production.

For this illustration, I am using figures that were quoted for 25,000 CDs to be produced in the UK. The price I was given was £8,700 (including VAT on the purchase of the CDs), or roughly $15,000, which equates to 60 cents per CD. (Compare that to the cost of on-demand CDs.) At this U.S. price, if each CD is sold for $10, then you would make a profit of $9.40 per CD. However, as illustrated in the earlier chapter, there are a lot of other charges that could reduce that apparently large profit by a considerable amount.

If we take the effect of VAT on the sale of the CD into account (you have to pay VAT if you sell in Europe, and for this example I've assumed VAT is 20 percent) and add in the credit card processing charges, then you could reduce your profit to $7.79. I do realize I'm mixing apples and oranges by applying a European tax to a U.S. dollar amount; however, I want to illustrate how VAT (and other sales taxes) can chew into your earnings. By the way, for those of you outside Europe, it is a legal requirement to quote prices *including* VAT—there should be no surprise at the checkout for the customer.

If you're trying to follow these figures, then you may have difficulties because I have offset VAT inputs and outputs (to give the technical term to the VAT you pay and the VAT you must charge). This is a practice so that you don't pay VAT twice. This is not a book about tax, so for once may I ask that you trust me on this number without further explanation?

Also, you have to actually sell your CDs to make that profit. If you don't, then you've wasted $15,000. If you are intending to sell your CD through record stores, then, as an example, you are likely to find your distribution costs are disproportionately high when compared to those of the majors, who will have quite a slick distribution operation in place and will be able to negotiate much better deals than you can.

The chart in Figure 6.2 illustrates the proportions of income that would be attributable to the costs of producing and selling 25,000 CDs. This chart also shows the proportion that would be profit. To add some realism, the chart shows an allowance (of 15 percent of the sale price) for distribution expenses. I will talk more about distribution costs in a moment. I have also added in an allowance for a manager to take his or her cut, because you may well have a manager involved by the time you are selling this number of CDs.

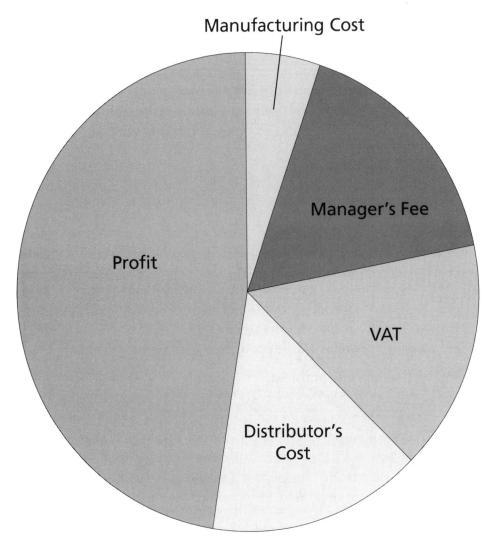

Figure 6.2 The costs and profits associated with pressing your own CD.

Before you get carried away looking at the profit, remember that to make this proportion of profit, you have to sell 25,000 CDs. That is a huge number of CDs to shift. If you don't sell that number, then until you have passed the break-even point, you will be working at a loss.

I said I would mention distribution costs. If you're going to get 1,000 CDs pressed, then you are unlikely to be at a level at which the major record stores will pay any attention to you. That probably won't concern you, because you would probably be selling CDs to friends and at gigs. Even at 25,000 CDs, the national record-store chains are unlikely to be interested in you; however, this number does vary depending on your jurisdiction and the market for which you are aiming.

When you start selling in big numbers, then you will probably need a distributor, because you're not going to be able to pack the number of CDs you want to sell into the back of your car and deliver them all by hand—take some time to think about the logistics of distributing 1 million CDs by hand. Unfortunately, when you get other people involved, huge chunks of your profit get swallowed up, as you will see when we look at the income you can generate by releasing a record with a major record label.

One form of distribution that is likely to be appealing to you is mail order; this is perhaps the only practical way (until you are a very well-established artist) to get a CD to a fan base that is spread over a very wide geographical area. If you want proof that mail order is a viable option, look at how Amazon (and the like) continue to grow while the number of record stores is decreasing.

To give you an idea about distribution costs for mail order, let me talk about CD Baby for a moment. For a one-time setup fee of $39 per CD and a fee of $4 per CD sold, CD Baby will handle your mail-order distribution. You set the price and then CD Baby will take orders, send out the CD, and charge you $4 for each transaction. As far as fulfillment of the order goes, all you have to do is sit back and wait for payment (which comes every week).

The other expense you will incur in using a service like this is the cost associated with delivering your CDs to CD Baby. However, when you order your CDs from the pressing plant, you can always arrange for the plant to deliver the CDs directly to CD Baby. This won't cut costs, but it will ensure that you are not charged twice for delivery.

Using CD Baby (but ignoring the cost of getting your CDs to CD Baby), each $10 CD would generate $6 for you. If you then deduct the manufacturing costs (based on 25,000 CDs being pressed), that would give you a net income of $5.40 per CD.

CD Sales with a Record Label

Income from CD sales is very different if you release through a record label.

The main purpose of including this information is to give a broad overview of what you might expect from a recording deal so that you can make a comparison between your financial expectations working on your own and working with a label. There's no point in trying to get a deal just to find that really what is in your best interest is to go it alone.

If the notion of a deal with a record label doesn't appeal to you, then please feel free to jump to the next section ("Moving Images").

The income you may be able to generate from a deal with a record company depends very much on the nature of any particular deal, your status as a recording artist, and the type of label with which you are dealing. However, there are certain characteristics of different types of deals, and I have used these characteristics to give an illustration of the different royalties that you could expect in different situations.

I have given a few brief pointers about the different sorts of deals and the different commercial considerations that may apply; however, for details about the nature of the different types of recording deals and the financial expectations under each, I suggest you check out *All You Need to Know about the Music Business* by Donald Passman.

When trying to make comparisons—particularly when trying to compare the apparently generous levels of profit you can generate by pressing your own CDs—remember that record companies have very large expenses associated with the release of a CD.

In addition, record companies will usually pay some sort of advance. I will look at alternative ways of raising financing later in this chapter. These alternative forms of funding could replace an advance and fund a project—including the marketing and distribution costs—if you would still prefer to release a CD on your own terms.

One last point: If you enter into a deal with a record company, they won't just want the CD rights, they will want all rights, so you can't keep your download rights and make a deal with a major to release CDs. The major would expect to release your downloads and your CDs (and anything else it can find to release).

Size of Record Label and Your Status in the Industry

Two factors that will have a considerable bearing on the deal you can negotiate are:

- The size of the record label you are dealing with

- Your status (and therefore negotiating power) within the industry

With a smaller label, you may be able to negotiate a better deal, perhaps even a profit-sharing deal, which may be beneficial to you in certain circumstances. In this context, when I talk about a "better" deal, I mean one with higher percentages and more artistic control. However, the downsides to dealing with a smaller record label are that they are likely to have less money to pay an advance and to fund marketing activities.

You may also find that although the label you are dealing with is smaller, it will have done a deal with a larger label. This may arise when you are signing with a production company of some sort, rather than a record label.

The other side of the coin when looking at deals is your clout. Your status is likely to fall into one of three groupings:

- **A new act with little negotiating power.** If you're at this stage, then you probably haven't read the rest of this book (or if you have, you haven't acted upon it). If you don't have a fan base and you have no proven track record of generating income, then you have little clout and will probably take any deal that is offered to you because it is your only way of getting money. Unless you are a very lucky person, you could end up disappointed by this deal.

- **An act with some clout.** In this situation, you could be an act looking for your first deal with a record company or an existing act looking to re-sign. Either way, if you are bringing something to the party, then you stand a much better chance of negotiating a satisfactory deal, provided you have the right team around you to guide you. See Chapter 8, "Building the Team around You," for further details about getting the right team.

- **An established star/superstar.** If you fall into this category, you're probably too busy/famous/rich to read this book, although you may find that one of your "people" has read it. Given that this category of artists is unlikely to be reading this book, I won't focus on them too much.

As I've already discussed, negotiating power comes through having the option to walk away. If you have your own fan base, and you are already making a living in the music industry, then you are in a position to walk away from an unfavorable deal. This gives you huge negotiating clout.

Another factor giving you clout is whether anyone else is bidding to sign you. In competitive bidding situations, people are likely to pay more to ensure that they sign you. This may be good for you (because you can negotiate more money and better terms), but it may also be bad. For instance, you may negotiate yourself into a position where you will never live up to your own hype, so the relationship will go sour when expectations (on both sides) cannot be met.

You are most likely to find yourself with several bids if you are a proven commercial proposition (in other words, you can demonstrate that you have a fan base and you have a proven track record of selling CDs).

Type of Deal

There are many different forms of deals that may be on offer to you. All of these deals are likely to involve you selling your copyright to the sound recordings to the record label. Some deals where you may not need to assign your copyright are considered briefly under the heading "Other Types of Deals," which follows this section.

Don't get too hung up on the differences between these deals. The differences are not always as black and white as this section may suggest. What is important—if you are offered a deal—is that you understand the nature of what has been offered to you, and you understand (in minute detail) what this deal means for you both financially and in terms of your career. But until you have that offer, these descriptions are here to give you an idea about the alternatives to forging your own path.

Exclusive Recording Contract

For many musicians, the exclusive recording contract is the Holy Grail and is regarded as the first step to superstardom.

An exclusive recording contract is what most people understand (or think they understand) when they talk about a recording contract: The act signs with a record label, who then funds several albums. The reality is, of course, somewhat different.

In practice, the record company is likely to fund a few singles or an album. Depending on the success of the recording, the label will then decide whether to release the product —often the label will be under no legal obligation to release. However, if it does and the recording sells well, then record company will exercise its options (for further albums).

Often, the most that a record company will commit to is to release an album (if even that). If that album is seen as not being a commercial success, then the act may be dropped. When an act is dropped, the record company rarely breaks its contract. Instead, it simply decides not to exercise its option to commission another album. In effect, the future contract simply lapses.

Generally, you would only expect to take another form of deal (one that isn't a long-term exclusive recording contract) if no other deal is on the table. If no other deal is available, then you probably haven't made yourself sufficiently attractive. If this is the case, then I suggest you walk away. I suggest this not because the deal will be bad (although it is unlikely to be the best deal that you will ever see), but because you don't have the fan base that is necessary to make your career work. Go back and build the fan base, and then approach the record label when you have proved your commercial worth.

Production Deals

A production deal is similar to an exclusive recording contract. The key difference relates to the record company with which you are signing. Typically, the record company will be owned by a manager, a producer, or even a recording studio. In reality, therefore, the "record company" is a production company, rather than a record company. Sometimes these production companies will be funded by a larger record company and will act as a talent scout for that label, bringing them a finished "product" that can be launched without any significant investment in developing the artist on the part of the larger label.

For the production company, this is often a very attractive deal. The company gets to do what it wants to do and what it does best: develop talent. Even better, this is funded by someone else. The company then has a guaranteed outlet for its product. The company can choose to work with artists it likes and believes in. These are all positives for the artist.

However, the profit that the production company generates is based on the fee that it is paid by the larger label, less an amount to fund the production company's expenses and also less some profit for the production company. The net result of this may be that you will usually generate less income by signing with a production company than you would if you signed directly with the larger label, and you may also miss out on the larger label's marketing muscle.

If you have a fan base and some success behind you, then a production deal may not be the most enticing deal for you. You should have already done a lot of your own development and will already know what your fan base wants. However, there are features of this style of deal that may be appealing.

Primarily, this form of deal may be interesting if the production company is your own company. In this case, the deal would probably work more like a licensing deal (which is discussed in the "Other Types of Deals" section). You may also find this sort of deal appealing if you are using your infrastructure to promote another act (in other words, you are starting to act as a record/production company). Some more of these options are discussed later in this chapter, under the section "Income from Your Infrastructure."

Demo Deal

With a demo deal, a record company (or production company) will pay for you to record some demos in a professional studio, with a professional producer. This sounds good, but the downside is that you are actually entering into a recording contract. The record company will own your recordings and will probably want the right to release those recordings if they see fit.

In many ways, a demo deal is a cheap way to get you under contract.

Other Types of Deals

The next three types of deal have, at various times, had a bad press. However, for the self-promoting musician, these deals may be very attractive, especially since you can maintain high levels of control, and you may be able to either keep your copyrights or get them back after a set period.

Licensing Deal

With a licensing deal, you grant a record company permission to release and market your product. In return, they will pay a license fee, which may be similar to the royalty you could expect under an exclusive recording contract. However, since you will be meeting the development costs and the cost of recording, and then presenting the final product to the record company, who can decide whether to license the product, the record company's risk will be greatly reduced. This may mean that you can expect a better percentage than would otherwise be payable.

Under a licensing deal, you may be able to retain your copyrights. However, you would likely have to enter into an agreement that would tie up your copyright on an exclusive basis for a number of years (usually between five and ten). At the end of the license period, you may get full use of your copyrights; so for instance, you could re-release an album or enter into another licensing agreement with your music.

Joint Venture

With a joint venture, the artist and the record label create a separate business entity. (Its precise legal structure is irrelevant.) This entity is a joint venture owned by the artist and the label. The joint venture will generate income and will have costs. Once the costs have been met and the profits calculated, these are then shared between the artist and the record company.

Joint-venture arrangements are usually more favorable to:

- The record label when sales are modest.

- The artist when sales are higher. However, in this case, the record label is less likely to be concerned about what it is paying you, since it will be generating a healthy income itself.

Pressing and Distribution Agreement

As its name suggests, a pressing and distribution deal is an arrangement where you can tap into a record label's logistical expertise.

Under these arrangements, you give your finished masters to the label/distributor, and in return they will get your CDs pressed and into the shops. All you then have to do is promote your CD! In many ways, this arrangement is very similar to a self-pressing setup, but instead of you getting your CD pressed, you are using the record company's expertise. You are also avoiding the hassles of distribution, which, if you are intending to play on an international stage, will save you from considerable stress.

Typically with pressing and distribution deals, the record label will charge a percentage for distribution (perhaps 20 percent), and production costs will then be deducted. The profit is the wholesale cost, less the distribution charge and less the production cost. As you can see, this is likely to give you the highest proportion of income for any of the deals that may be available with a record label.

However, this option also gives you the highest risk. CDs are generally sold on a sale or return basis. If your CDs don't sell and they are returned to you, then you will be charged for the distribution and return costs (as well as the production cost), but you will have no sales to fund those expenses. You will also have a lot of unwanted CDs to store.

The nature of pressing and distribution deals is different in different territories. As an example, the practices in the UK and the U.S. differ. In the U.S., the big distributors are the record labels, so you would make a pressing and distribution deal with one of these labels. In the UK, the labels contract out their distribution to specialized firms, so you would likely make a pressing and distribution deal with one of these specialized companies.

Clawbacks under Recording Contracts

For anyone not familiar with the term "clawback," let me explain.

A clawback is a way to take money back from people. For instance, a record label may say, "We'll pay you $1 million" and then find a way to claw back most of this and only pay you (for instance) $10.

Once you have your deal with a record label, you will find that while you are getting creative with your music, the record label is getting creative with ways to keep hold of the money and avoid paying it to you. In addition to what you'll read in the following subsections, you will find there are many other ways the record label can keep hold of your money—for instance, by keeping a reserve against any returned CDs (a practice that is adopted because all record companies allow dealers to return unsold CDs).

Advances

One of the main reasons to take a deal with a record label is the advance that will often be paid. An advance is an immediate chunk of money that you can spend as you want, but from a practical point of view it is intended to pay for necessities, such as food and accommodations, until you receive your royalties. The advance will also be applied to meet business costs, which could include studio time, the cost for a producer, and touring expenses.

An advance is similar to a loan. However, unlike a loan, there is no interest payable. Also, unlike a loan, the record label usually can't ask for an advance to be repaid. Instead, it takes the advance out of the artist's royalties, and artists do not receive royalties until the advance has been fully recouped. For this reason, one of the most significant clawbacks from royalties is the repayment of this advance.

You will see that in this book I don't outline the level of advances you can expect. My reasons for this are twofold. First, the amount you can expect is highly dependent on your situation. Second, advances are not real money. Now, this is a slightly rash statement—many times, all an artist will receive under a recording contract is an advance—so let me explain. Ninety-five percent of artists don't recoup their advance, so the royalties on offer are just an illusion. The advance is an amount of money designed to get an artist into debt with the record label and then to keep the artist working for the label.

Advances tend to come in two flavors: one that includes the cost of recording (often called a *recording fund*) and another that doesn't (*personal advances*). Including the cost of recording an album gives the artist a certain degree of control. However, any overspends will cut directly into any money that the artist would have used to fund day-to-day living expenses (such as food). Recording-fund deals tend to be less generous when compared to personal advances, plus the associated cost of recording an album.

One of the main reasons why artists look for a deal with a major record label is to secure an advance to provide income and to fund the recording of an album. As you will see later in this chapter (in the "Sources of Finance" section), there are other options instead of an advance, and you don't need an advance to kick-start your career. However, these other options may include an expectation of interest and repayment.

Producer and Recording Costs

The artist will meet the cost of recording an album. The cost of the album has many factors; as you might expect, the largest costs are people and places.

The people are the engineer(s) and the producer. In particular, producers are often paid an advance and also receive a percentage. The producer's percentage is nearly always met from the artist's royalties, so if you're on a 16 percent royalty and the producer gets 3 points (in other words, 3 percent of the income, not 3 percent of your royalty), then your royalties will be cut to 13 percent.

The places that cost money are recording studios and any accommodation that is used during the recording process (such as hotels or properties that may be rented in the vicinity of the studio to house the artists during the recording). These expenses are all recouped before royalties are paid.

Usually, the costs of the studio will need to be met before the facility will release the master recording. The deals for producers usually provide that, unlike the artist's royalty, the producer's royalty will not take account of recording costs. This often will mean that a producer starts to earn his royalties before the act does.

Overseas Sales

You might think you're signing to a global entity when you sign with a multinational record company. In reality, these businesses are usually managed as a group of individual businesses, and hence, each separate business has to make its own profit. This means that each overseas company will take its own cut. For you, the artist, this means you can expect a reduced royalty rate from overseas income.

Another downside to having each territory working as a separate entity is that you usually won't be able to force an overseas arm of the company to release your product. However, this is an issue that goes beyond the scope of this chapter.

You may find that in overseas territories, your royalties are cut to around 75 percent of the royalty in your home country. Sometimes the royalty can go as low as 50 percent of your home-country royalty (so if you have a home-country royalty of 16 percent, then you may get only an 8 percent royalty for overseas earnings).

Sometimes, particularly when you are dealing with a smaller label, there will not be an overseas office. In this case your label will often license your music to a local label in each territory. Sometimes this licensing can generate an advance (which the record label will be keen to snaffle up). When tracks are licensed, it is unlikely that you will make as much money as you could if there were a local arm of your label.

Container Charges

A significant deduction from an artist's royalties is made for container charges.

This is an amount intended to cover the packaging of CDs (the argument being you get your royalties on the CD, not on the packaging) and is usually set between 15 and 25 percent. This charge is usually levied before the royalty is calculated, so if you have a 20 percent royalty that is based on a CD price of $15, and a 25 percent packaging deduction is applied, you can expect to receive $2.25 per CD sold (before the other deductions that I discuss in this section).

Breakages

Until the 1950s, records were made out of shellac. These discs were comparatively fragile and were liable to break. Due to the high number of breakages, it was assumed that a certain number of discs would break, so a discount was given. A conventional discount to allow for breakages was 10 percent.

In these days of CDs and downloads, breakages are comparatively rare. However, the practice of giving a 10 percent discount for breakages still remains with certain labels (and the breakages allowance can even be applied to downloads).

New Technologies

Historically, record contracts have had a provision for new technologies. Essentially, the provision works so that a reduced royalty rate is paid for any releases that use new technology. Typically, the royalty paid will be 75 percent of the full royalty. (For instance, if the full royalty is 16 percent, the new technology royalty will be 12 percent.)

Depending on the nature of the deal, new technologies may include CDs (the technology may be more than 25 years old, but some record companies still regard it as new) and digital downloads (where there is no cost to physically manufacture the product).

Promotional and Free Copies

Record labels legitimately need to give away a number of free copies of the CDs they are promoting. If they don't give CDs to radio stations, then the music won't be heard on the radio. Equally, it can be helpful for record stores to have a copy of the music to play for their customers.

However, labels go further than giving away a few free copies here and there. Often they will give away a large number of CDs (perhaps 5 percent or more of a total order) to retailers. The effect of this practice is to give retailers a discount, and because the CDs are given away, no royalties are paid on them. This discount won't particularly hurt the label's income (it's a marketing expense), but it will hit the artist's royalties because the artist won't get paid on these CDs if they are sold.

Cross-Collateralization

Under a cross-collateralization arrangement, a record label may take a profit you have made in one area to fund a loss you have made in another area. So for instance, if you don't recoup your advance on your first CD, but your second CD propels you into the stratosphere, the record label may use your earnings from the second CD to fund your loss on the first CD.

In practice, this means you won't see any royalties from your second CD until the debt on your first CD has been met.

Videos

For many artists, videos are an integral part of marketing their music. However, videos are a very expensive luxury—some cost more than $1 million to make—and videos don't necessarily generate any significant income in their own right when taken as individual videos.

Although videos fall under the marketing budget, and therefore the costs usually would be met by the record label, very often the label will split the cost with the artist, or sometimes, especially when a budget exceeds a predetermined limit, they may charge the whole cost of the video to the artist.

When the artist is charged for the video, the record label meets the cost, and this cost is then recouped from the artist's earnings.

Independent Promotion and Other Specialized Marketing Activities

Most record companies have their own promotion department. The cost of promotion by a record label's in-house promotions department is usually met by the label as part of its business cost.

Labels will also hire in promotions specialists who will be paid a large chunk of money to get your record played (usually on the radio). Often the fee that the promotion firm will be paid is linked to the record's chart success.

Unlike the in-house promotion department, the artist usually meets the cost of independent promotion specialists, although like the situation for videos, the cost will be met by the label and recouped from the artist's earnings.

Tour Support

Touring is another one of those highly expensive activities with which musicians get involved. Conventionally, until you reach superstar status and can sell out a tour and bolster your income with merchandising and sponsorship, touring results in a loss.

Although touring can result in a loss, it is often encouraged because it is a great way to build a fan base. However, if you build your fan base slowly and progressively and interact directly with your fans, then you can tour in a small-scale manner without incurring a loss.

For acts that don't have an established fan base, record labels will often underwrite tour losses to a pre-agreed level. Anything beyond the agreed level of loss will usually be met directly by the artist. Again, although the cost will be met by the record label, any spending will be charged straight back to the artist as a deduction from royalties.

So What Will I Actually Get Paid under a Recording Contract?

I don't know.

Seriously! Have you been paying attention?

I don't know what deal you could negotiate. However, I can give you an indication of what might be considered "average" and what your expectations could be given a certain starting point.

Royalty Percentage: Percentage of What?

Once you've generated some income, and the record label has clawed back as much as it can, then you can start looking at your percentage. Unfortunately, the figure on which your percentage will be based is not necessarily a straightforward one.

In most of Europe, royalty percentages usually are calculated as a percentage of the price that the dealer pays for a CD (in other words, the wholesale price). In the U.S. and some other territories, the percentage is driven off a suggested retail list price (usually called the *SRLP*). Ironically, the SRLP is often not the recommended list price, but the wholesale price increased by 30 percent.

Royalty rates will differ depending on your status and depending on what the royalty is based on. When royalties are based on the suggested retail price, they will be lower than if they were based on wholesale prices.

For artists whose royalties are based on suggested retail prices, royalties are usually in the region of 10 to 20 percent. For artists whose royalties are based on retail prices, royalties are usually in the region of 15 to 30 percent. The lower amounts are for new artists signed to a smaller label, and the higher amounts are payable to more successful artists with a track record of success.

Example of Possible Royalties

Here's an example of earnings from a CD release with a record label. For this example, I'm going to make some assumptions.

- Number of CDs sold: 250,000. (This would represent a low number of sales for a record label; however, it would also take a lot of work to reach this number.)

- Suggested retail price of CD: $15.

- Artist's royalty rate: 15 percent.

- Container charges: 20 percent.

- Breakages: 10 percent.

- Free CDs: 10 percent.

- New Technology: 100 percent. (In other words, there is no clawback.)

- Recording costs: $100,000.

- Video costs: $250,000.

- Producer's royalty rate: 3 percent.

Take a look at Table 6.1 to see how this income translates to income for the artist.

Table 6.1 An Example of Earnings from a CD Release

Item	Calculation	Cost
Royalty base		$12
suggested retail price, less	$15	
20% container charge	−$3	
CDs on which royalties are based		200,000
number of CDs sold	250,000	
less free CDs	− 10%	
less breakages	−10%	
Artist royalty		12%
royalty rate, less	15%	
producer's royalty rate	−3%	
Income from CD sales for royalty calculation purposes	$12.00 × 200,000	$2,400,000
Artist's royalty	12% of $2,400,000	$288,000
Less		$350,000
recording, and	$100,000	
video costs	$250,000	
Total income for the artist		−$62,000

So after selling 250,000 CDs, the artist is still in debt to the tune of $62,000. This is probably a highly unrealistic figure—you will see that many costs have not been included. For instance, there is no fee included for the manager, and the artist is likely to have had an advance that would also be recouped from royalties.

Let's take the same figures, but assume:

- The artist had an advance of $100,000 (which does not cover recording costs—in other words, recording costs plus the advance equal $200,000).

- Five-hundred thousand CDs were sold.

- An independent promoter was paid $200,000. (Without the promoter, sales of 500,000 may be unlikely.)

- The manager charges a fee of 20 percent.

Table 6.2 shows what the position could look like.

Table 6.2 A Slightly More Realistic Illustration of Possible Earnings from a CD Release with a Major Record Label

Item	Calculation	Cost
Royalty base		$12
suggested retail price, less	$15	
20% container charge	−$3	
CDs on which royalties are based		400,000
number of CDs sold	500,000	
less free CDs	−10%	
less breakages	−10%	
Artist royalty		12%
royalty rate, less	15%	
producer's royalty rate	−3%	
Income from CD sales for royalty calculation purposes	$12 × 400,000	$4,800,000
Artist's royalty	12% of $4,800,000	$576,000
Less		$765,200
recording costs	$100,000	
video costs	$250,000	
advance	$100,000	
manager's fee, and	$115,200	
promoter's fee	$200,000	
Total income for the artist		−$189,200

Again, this figure may not be realistic because it does not include any costs incurred in touring. However, you can see that although the artist has sold a lot of CDs, he is still in a worse position than when he started (owing the record label nearly $200,000).

I don't like unhappy endings, so let's take the last scenario and assume that instead of selling 500,000 CDs, the artist sold 705,500. Weird number, I know, but this would be enough to give a profit, as Table 6.3 shows.

Table 6.3 After Selling 705,500 CDs, the Artist Finally Shows a (Very) Modest Profit

Item	Calculation	Cost
Royalty base		$12
suggested retail price, less	$15	
20% container charge	−$3	
CDs on which royalties are based		564,400
number of CDs sold	705,500	
less free CDs	−10%	
less breakages	− 10%	
Artist royalty		12%
royalty rate, less	15%	
producer's royalty rate	−3%	
Income from CD sales for royalty calculation purposes	$12 × 564,400	$6,772,800
Artist's royalty	12% of $6,772,800	$812,736
Less		$812,547
recording costs	$100,000	
video costs	$250,000	
advance	$100,000	
manager's fee, and	$162,547	
Independent Promoter's fee	$200,000	
Total income for the artist		$189

And that's not a typo—after selling more than 700,000 CDs, the act will have earned less than $200 (but don't forget the $100,000 advance—they're not starving). That's 200 bucks; there are no thousands here.

Now let's have a look where the money in Table 6.3 goes: Figure 6.3 sets out the respective proportions of each expense. For this chart, I am assuming that the whole-sale price is $6 and distribution costs make up $2.50 of that $6.

As you can see in Figure 6.3, the artist's earnings could account for nearly one-quarter of the income that arises from the sale of each CD (but then they get spent).

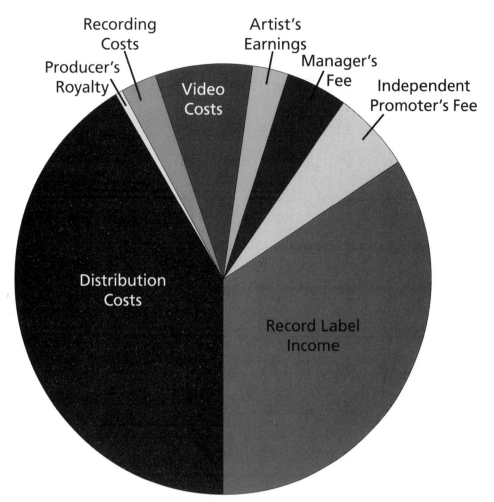

Figure 6.3 How the income is split for a successful CD (successful financially, for everyone except the artist).

If an artist could take that one-quarter of the income, she would become very rich very quickly. However, as you can see, there are costs that are taken from the artist's royalty (meaning that the artist is left with $189 profit, excluding her $100,000 advance). Figure 6.4 shows how the artist's royalty is spent (in other words, how the costs that are charged against the artist's royalties eat into those earnings).

So there you have it. If each CD is sold for $15, then the artist will have generated an income of $10,582,500 but will only see $100,189 (including the advance). In other words, a 15 percent royalty will have equated to 0.95 percent. And as I keep belaboring, that is after selling more than 700,000 CDs, which is a large number to sell.

In the real world, the artist would be much more likely to still be in debt after selling 700,000 CDs. As a general rule of thumb, an artist will start to make a profit under a recording contract after selling more than 1.5 million CDs.

I hope this illustrates why many artists rage against current business practices. I also hope this explains why you may be better off following your own path.

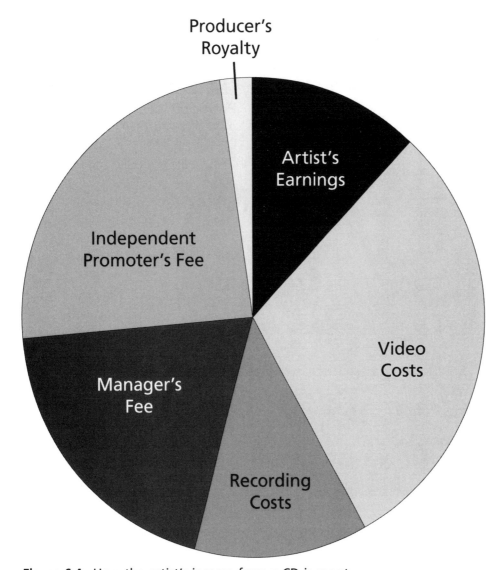

Figure 6.4 How the artist's income from a CD is spent.

Moving Images

You can make money from putting your music with moving images in a number of ways. The two main options are putting out your own video and allowing your music to be used as part of a soundtrack. There is a third option that I covered in some more detail in the previous chapter—selling advertising against your videos through You-Tube (or similar services). I'm not going to elaborate on that option any further.

Songwriters can also make money from royalties generated from video sources. Song-writing royalties are considered in greater depth later in this chapter.

DVD (and Video)

If you are signed to a record label, then your video rights will almost certainly be signed up, too. In this case, if you release a DVD (or a Blu-ray)—for instance, of your recent live tour—you can expect a royalty (perhaps up to 20 percent of the wholesale price) in a similar way to how you get a royalty on CDs.

Alternatively, you (or your label) could license someone to create a DVD and generate income in that manner. If a record company licenses the creation of a DVD, then your royalty usually would be based on the income that the record company generates.

By contrast, if you are running your own show, then you could get 30,000 DVDs pressed for around $60,000 (in other words, about $2 per DVD). This might sound good, but remember, there are considerable costs in the production of a DVD (such as the camera-crew costs and editing). This isn't YouTube, and you are unlikely to have the expertise (or sufficient number of talented friends) to be able to create a video of merchantable quality without making a significant investment. How much you then spend on production is really up to you.

Also, remember that 30,000 DVDs is a large number. It could be really hard work to sell this number of DVDs, and if you don't sell them, you're going to need a lot of storage space. This was the lowest quote (in terms of numbers to be pressed) that I could readily find for pressing from a glass master. You may find quotes for DVD-R duplication, but the unit cost is likely to be higher.

Synchronization Fees

Another source of income in connection with moving pictures comes from what is called a *synchronization license*. This is, quite literally, a license to add your original sound recording to a soundtrack of a video, film, TV show, corporate video, game, and so on.

The license fee is dependent on a number of factors, largely your negotiating clout and the ability of the licensor to pay. The amount the licensor will want to pay is likely to depend on the use of the music. For instance, an advertiser who wants to feature your song in a global advertising campaign (think "Start Me Up" by the Rolling Stones when Microsoft launched Windows 95) will pay much more than a TV company producing a daytime soap in which your music is playing on a radio in the background. The fee is also likely to be governed by local agreements and practices.

Merchandising

Merchandising is an area where the costs and possible income are ever variable. The notion of what actually constitutes merchandising is quite tough, because it can cover a wide range of products branded with your logo (or other image). In practice, it probably includes:

- Clothing, such as T-shirts, sweatshirts, hoodies, jackets, caps, and so on

- Printed materials, such as calendars, books, photos, posters, and programs

- Stationery, such as pens, pencils, paper, rulers, and erasers

- Dolls and other figures

- Chinaware, such as mugs and plates

- Bags, buttons (that is, badges if you speak British English), fridge magnets, clocks, coasters, mouse pads, pillows, and candles

- Anything else your creative mind can come up with and for which you believe there is a market

You have three main choices if you want to generate income from merchandising:

- Use an on-demand service that can create a product when the customer orders it. (This is the same principle that applies for on-demand CDs.)

- Create and sell your own product (which probably means you need to commission someone else to produce the product for you).

- License someone else to create and sell your branded merchandise.

As always, you can mix and match these options. However, if you license a third party to create and sell merchandising, that party is likely to expect an exclusive contract (even if only for a limited territory). This requirement may constrain your more entrepreneurial merchandising avenues.

As you may expect, as a general rule of thumb an on-demand service will have the advantage of allowing you to create a range of products at a one-stop shop. By contrast, creating your own product may give higher profits, but you will have to find product suppliers, spend money up front, store the goods, sell the goods, and then deliver them to your customer. For both of these routes, you will have to commission or create your own artwork.

With a licensing deal, all you have to do is sit back and wait for the money to roll in—it will be in your licensor's interest to proactively sell as much product as possible. This is obviously an oversimplification of the position; however, the work involved is much reduced. For instance, you may not have to create your own artwork. If you follow this route, you will need to spend more time approving the quality of the products to which you are licensing your images.

When you license the production of merchandising, you can expect a royalty of between 50 and 80 percent of the profit. The licensor is likely to be able to obtain the raw materials and create the product for a far lower cost than you can, so you may find this share of profit exceeds the profit you could make by creating your own products. You may also find a licensor will pay you an advance.

Whether you go down the on-demand-service route or arrange for printing yourself, T-shirts tend to come out between about $5.80 and $6.80 once you order around 100. This is a very rough pricing based on my local sources—in your market, you may find a better price with some work. If you order fewer, the price per unit goes up, and again there's little to separate the prices. If you obtain the T-shirts yourself, you can probably get the cost down, but the setup costs for screen printing are fixed. For anything greater than 100, screen printing tends to be cheaper.

You may be wondering why I showed a price for 30,000 DVDs but only considered a run of 100 T-shirts. This is largely because the markets for DVDs and T-shirts are influenced by different factors. There are many reasons why you are likely to purchase T-shirts in smaller numbers.

- First, at the time I got the quote, the minimum run of DVDs using a glass master that I could find was 30,000.

- Although T-shirts are not perishable, they are harder to store than DVDs. For instance, T-shirts can rot and go moldy if kept in an inappropriate storage facility. Also, DVDs are less likely to be eaten by mice. Hence, you can order more DVDs.

- Styles and fashions change, so the lifespan of a T-shirt design is shorter than the lifespan of a DVD (or a CD, for that matter). Added to this, T-shirts are often linked to certain events (for example, World Tour of Iceland 1993).

- You may be able to produce one or two new T-shirt designs each year, whereas you may get an album or DVD out only every other year.

- Fans may well buy your whole album collection. They are far less likely to want to buy your entire selection of T-shirts (although some may).

In practice, you will probably find that a sensible approach is to use an on-demand service to provide your mail-order T-shirts. For gigs, you may be able to get a supply of T-shirts more cheaply. Alternatively, you could bulk buy (which usually means more than 100, but it can mean as few as 25) from your on-demand provider.

Ideally, you will probably want to do a deal to license someone to provide your merchandise, because this is likely to generate the most income for you. If you do, then ensure that you get commission on any sales you generate (for instance, any sales generated or initiated from your website).

Live Performances

You have two main choices for putting on a live performance:

- Hire the venue yourself and take all of the risk.

- Get hired by a promoter who will put on the gig.

As a general principle, you are likely to hire the venue and put on your own gigs only when:

- You are first starting out.

- You reach superstar level.

Apart from that, the benefits of using a booking agent and promoter are likely to outweigh the effort, risk, and difficulty in putting on your own gigs. However, don't let me stop you putting on your own gigs (and acting as the promoter), especially in your own territory. For an explanation about the roles of booking agents and promoters, see Chapter 8.

If you are going to act as the promoter for your gigs, then you need to be reasonably certain about the numbers who may come; otherwise, your economic plans may be thrown into disarray. Also, you must have the logistical infrastructure in place to be able to put on a gig at a particular venue in a particular territory.

So for instance, you may be a band based in Paris and have a large fan base in Japan. But, do you know where all of these people are? Are they all in Tokyo, or are they spread over the country? Suppose you choose to put on a gig in Tokyo—do you have the necessary skills to put on a gig? Can you speak the language? Do you know the level at which tickets should be priced? Do you know where to hire a PA system? Are you aware of any local legislation that may impinge on the gig?

If you're going to go the booking agent/promoter route, then you will probably find that the agent will take somewhere between 15 and 20 percent of your income. The amount you can squeeze out of the promoter will vary depending on the size of the venue and your negotiating power. You may find that a promoter will pay a fixed fee—this is particularly likely when you have less pulling power. When you can guarantee an audience, you may be able to negotiate a profit split with the promoter. You may even be able to negotiate a share of the profit and a guarantee (which, like an advance from a record label, is non-returnable).

Touring also provides an excellent outlet for selling your merchandising. If you have appointed a merchandising firm, then they will expect to be able to sell at your gigs. (However, your promoter may want a cut of this income.)

You should also remember that each time a song is performed, it generates performance royalties for the songwriter, which may be another stream of income for the artist.

Although there are many opportunities for generating income from touring, there are even more opportunities to lose a lot of money. The drains on your finances while you are touring arise in the following areas. You can control all of these expenses to a certain extent; however, they are unfortunately expenses that do need to be incurred.

- Travel, which is mostly the cost of transportation between each gig. At one extreme, you can hitchhike to gigs, but this may prove impractical, especially if you are the drummer. At the other extreme, you can have a private chauffeur for each musician, some helicopters, and a private jet. From a practical perspective, you are likely to have a van or bus. The time when you switch from a van to a bus, and the size and luxury of the bus, will vary depending on your finances.

- You may be able to avoid hotel costs by sleeping in your van or sleeping on friends' and fans' floors. However, you are more likely to need some form of hotel accommodation, which could be a cheap motel or a suite in a five-star hotel. When looking at hotel costs, remember that you need a bed for every member of the tour, not just the musicians.

- Staff, in the broadest sense, cost money. Except when you are on the tightest budget, you will need a road crew (technicians to look after the equipment) and possibly other musicians, who will all need paying. As your act grows, so will your entourage grow to encompass caterers, wardrobe people, stylists, as well as personal gurus.

- An army marches on its stomach, and every member of your tour will need feeding (probably several times a day). Even if you're eating only cheap takeout (which is not a healthy diet!), those costs could still mount. Ten people on a 45-day tour, each eating a $5 meal three times a day, would cost nearly $7,000 for the tour.

- Insurance. I'm sorry to be tedious, but you're going to need insurance. In some areas you may feel you can take a gamble. If someone steals your favorite stage hat, then you may just have to swallow that cost. However, there are areas in which you cannot gamble, particularly with public liability and third-party insurances. These insure against any liability that arises against you for any injury suffered by another person—for instance, if the tour bus runs someone over or someone gets injured at a gig. You need insurance, so go find a specialized music-industry insurance broker who can help you get the right coverage.

As I have said—and hopefully the outline of the main costs illustrates—the costs of touring can be considerable. Most artists do not make any profit from touring until they get toward superstar level. Instead, they regard touring as a way to build up a fan base. It is for this reason that record labels have historically been agreeable to providing tour support (in other words, meeting some of the losses you incur while touring). Any tour-support expenses are then deducted from future royalties, so think of this as a further advance.

There are, of course, other options. If you know where your fans are and they will come to your shows, then you can be more selective about which gigs you play. If you only play gigs where you are going to make a profit or break even, then you won't incur a loss from touring. However, it is difficult to take this approach.

For instance, if you're a band from London, and you know that you are big in New York, Seattle, and Kansas, then it may not be practical to "tour" the U.S. just to play three cities. Equally, you would probably find the hassle of arranging a tour of three U.S. cities plus the cost of shipping your gear to the U.S. would far outweigh the benefit of playing three gigs. Also, by limiting the geographical spread of your tour, you are limiting your opportunities for reaching a wider fan base.

For these reasons (and because you're a musician whose role is defined by being on the road), you may decide to take the short-term loss on touring for the long-term gain. If you do that, in addition to the sources of income I have already discussed, look at opportunities for using your fan base to offset some of your losses. I'll share some more thoughts about how you can marshal your fan base to come to your aid in the "Commission" section later in this chapter.

Sponsorship/Endorsements

When I mention sponsorship, my first thought is always about gigs. Gigs are perhaps your most visible public appearances and so are one of the easiest ways for a product or brand to associate itself with you.

Sponsors want to be associated with you because they believe the demographic of your fan base is the same demographic at which they are aiming their product. So for instance, if you are a female singer whose fan base is predominantly younger teenage girls, then you may find that a makeup firm wants to be associated with you. Alternatively, if you are a hard-rock band with a reputation for raucous hard living, then you may find that a hard-liquor firm wants to be associated with you. You're unlikely to find a teen princess sponsored by a whiskey brand or some hard rockers advertising mascara (unless 1970s glam makes another return)… You get the idea.

You should remember that sponsorship deals are not simply a case of someone giving you money for free (although it may feel like that at times). Sponsors are going to want something in return. The nature of the something may be the subject of negotiation. Naturally, if your tour is sponsored, then the sponsor is going to want to see its name on the advertising and on the tickets. It is also going to want to see its banners strung liberally around the venue.

However, a sponsor may want more than that. For instance, it may want a block of tickets to give to staff as a reward or to impress clients (thereby filling your gig with corporate stiffs). A sponsor may want you to meet some competition winners, or it may want you to meet some of its key executives. The sponsor may want to go further and gain access to backstage areas before and after the gig. Some executives from potential sponsors may want to be your friend. These are usually sad, lonely, deluded people you should run away from. Seriously, you do need to think about what you are giving up in order to get money.

As for the amount of money, as you would expect, it is very much dependent on your status and the marketing budget of your sponsor. This is one reason to use a sponsorship agent (discussed in a moment). These are the people who know and understand the deals that have been done and should be able to find you the best sponsors and squeeze the most financially rewarding deals out of them.

Endorsements take the idea further. Instead of simply associating a product with you, you will be asked to imply that you use a certain product. For musicians, the most obvious form of endorsement is when you state your use of a certain musical instrument and allow photos of you using the instrument to be included in advertising for the product. However, this practice can go much further. When you reach the superstar level, you will find people endorsing clothing, fragrances, cars, alcoholic and non-alcoholic beverages, food (and restaurants), as well as personal care items, such as razors.

There are two ways to find sponsorship and endorsements. First, go out and find it. Second, wait for the advertisers to come knocking. They're only likely to come knocking when you're a megastar and your brand has reached the consciousness of the mass media.

When you do not figure on most people's radars, then you will have to find your own deals. You can do this either by knocking on doors yourself (or getting your manager to do some knocking) or by using an agent who specializes in arranging sponsorship. These people will usually work for a percentage, anything up to 20 percent.

If you are going to knock on doors yourself, then you need to have a strong reason why the potential sponsor would be interested in sponsoring you and what the benefit would be to their business—this will be the business proposition that any sponsorship agent would be putting to potential sponsors.

Just because you are a lower-profile act, don't think there are no opportunities for you. There will be—it's just that the potential sponsors are (like you) likely to be slightly lower down in the hierarchy. This means you may need to look to local sponsors and specialized niche sponsors.

Commission

There are a wide range of commissions you can capture to generate income. Some of these sources are formal arrangements, and the details are published. For others, you'll have to ask and negotiate a deal. You are likely to find that the formal arrangements are with larger organizations, and you won't be able to negotiate a specific deal for yourself or your fans. Instead, you will be able to take commission, and the commission won't affect the price that your fans pay.

With the individually negotiated arrangements, you will sometimes be able to negotiate discounts for your fans (which won't do anything directly for your income, but might encourage more people to spend money, which will help your cash flow indirectly).

Perhaps the most widespread (and easy-to-use) commission arrangement is the Amazon Associates arrangement. Under this plan, you can direct people from your website to specific products on the Amazon website through customized links. (It's all very easy—Amazon will give you the HTML code for this, and you cut and paste it into your website.) If the person you have directed to Amazon then spends money, you get a commission. Better still, the commission is based on all products the person purchases at Amazon after following one of your links.

The rates payable vary depending on the Amazon to which you are linking. For instance, Amazon.com (Amazon U.S.) has rates between 4 and 8.5 percent, depending on the volume of sales you generate, while Amazon.co.uk rates are between 5 and 9 percent. These are percentages of the Amazon selling price. The breakpoints at which you qualify for higher rates differ by location, too. These are just two Amazon examples; each separate Amazon has its own rates.

The one downside to this arrangement with Amazon is that you need to provide a link for each separate Amazon, so if you want (for instance) to get credit for sales with Amazon U.S., UK, and Canada, then you need to provide a separate link for each.

Once you have signed up as an associate, it really is very quick to set up the links. (As I said, Amazon will generate the HTML code for you.) All you have to do is drop the code into your website and then sit back and wait for the commission to roll in. Clearly, you won't become a millionaire from this arrangement; however, you may generate more income from an Amazon sale of your CD than you would generate from royalties from a record label. Eight-and-a-half percent of the Amazon retail price for a CD could be more than 20 percent of the wholesale price that a record label may pay you.

Amazon is just one of the organizations that has an associates arrangement. The other major opportunity you should think about is the Google Affiliate Network. The advantage of the Google network is that you will have the opportunity to advertise a much wider range of vendors, meaning that you can tailor your advertisements more closely to your audience's demographic/interests.

Also, as noted earlier in the book, remember that you don't just have to create links to your own products. You can link to other merchandise that may be of interest to your fan base and other people who browse your website. So, for instance, you could include links to the music of bands that have influenced you.

When thinking about some of the commissions that you could generate yourself, you need to bring your creative skills and negotiating power to the forefront. Perhaps the most obvious commission you should generate is anything that you can sell through your website. So, for instance, if you have licensed your merchandising to someone else, then any sales through your website should generate commission.

Equally, if you are not promoting your own gigs, then you could get a commission on all ticket sales that you generate. Ticket agencies would take a cut, so why shouldn't you? Perhaps you could go further and arrange accommodations near, and transportation to and from, the gig. You could then take a cut of each element that you have organized.

I am sure there are many other activities you can think of that could generate commission by leveraging the spending power of your fan base. All you have to do is figure out what these opportunities are and negotiate a cut of the action (or rather, get your manager, who will be taking 20 percent of all your income anyway, to negotiate a cut of the action).

Songwriting Royalties

If you write a song and it is used (that is, recorded or performed), then you are due royalties from a number of areas. In particular, you are due:

- Mechanical royalties, which are royalties from sales of CDs, DVDs, and the like

- Performance royalties when your music is performed live or broadcast

The amount of the royalties depends on the territory, the type of license that is issued for the use of your music, and whether you have entered into any deals to share your income with anyone else or to allow them to pay you less than the going rate.

You've probably heard many urban myths about songwriters making a fortune. Although not necessarily based on fact, there is a potential for songwriters to make a lot of money. Two of the main reasons for the earning capacity of songwriters are:

- There are many outlets (for instance, there are many radio stations that play records).

- With certain exceptions, there are no clawbacks against songwriting earnings. The main clawback is a practice adopted in the U.S. called *controlled composition clauses*, whereby record labels restrict the amount of earnings a songwriter can make from releasing her own songs.

Let's look at songwriting royalties in a bit more detail, starting with mechanical royalties.

Mechanical Royalties: How Much Do I Get from Writing Songs?

There are two main approaches to calculating mechanical songwriting royalties (royalties that arise from downloads, CDs, DVDs, and other sound recordings of your songs). In very broad terms, there is one approach taken in the U.S. and Canada and another approach taken in the rest of the world. Naturally, each separate jurisdiction will have its own quirks.

U.S. and Canada Mechanical Royalties

I'll use U.S. figures for this example and will ignore the effects of controlled composition clauses.

In the U.S., the songwriter (or writers) may get paid 9.1 cents per track on a CD. This royalty is paid for each CD sold. Therefore, if you have written songs on a CD that sells 100,000, you will get paid $72,800 (100,000 × 8 × $0.091). I say "may" get paid, not "will" get paid because this is the statutory (compulsory) rate.

The statutory rate is payable in certain circumstances. One of those circumstances is *not* the first recording of a song. Therefore, on first recording, the record label can negotiate a separate deal and screw you to the ground. However, the statutory rate does give you a yardstick to see how much you aren't being paid.

Video royalties can be individually negotiated (although again, controlled composition clauses do come into play).

Rest-of-the-World Mechanical Royalties

Much of the rest of the world operates a system in which royalties are paid on the sale price of the CD or DVD. Let me use the UK as an example.

In the UK, songwriting royalties at the rate of 8.5 percent of wholesale (or 6.5 percent of retail excluding VAT) price are paid to songwriters. Where the CD contains more than one song, each song gets a pro-rata share, so if there are 10 tracks, then each song gets 0.85 percent of wholesale (or 0.65 percent of retail).

The rates are the same for videos and DVDs, although there are some rate reductions in certain circumstances, depending on the nature of the content of the DVD. For details of the varying rates, check to the website of the Mechanical-Copyright Protection Society (prsformusic.com).

Performance Royalties: How Much Do I Get from Writing Songs?

Performance royalties arise when your music is performed or played in public. There are many sources of performance royalties; the main ones are:

- Radio

- Television

- Internet

- Live performances

- Public playing of your music (for instance, if your CD is played in a bar)

The amount you get paid from each of these sources will depend on the venue of the performance. With most sources, there is a vaguely scientific attempt to attribute the extent to which your music has been played. The income this will generate then depends on how that source pays royalties.

Some sources pay a set fee according to how many minutes of music are used—this fee can then be allocated to give you a share of the distributed income. Other sources pay a more generalized license. Again, this license fee can be allocated to give each songwriter a share of the income that relates to songs that he has written.

To put it bluntly, someone somewhere does a calculation and pays you money. Unless you are very wealthy, you are going to be hard-pressed to challenge the payment that you receive.

Collecting Songwriting Royalties

Songwriting royalties are collected by a range of collection societies. Most of these societies relate to a specific territory, and some relate only to certain income streams within their territory—for instance, the Performing Right Society in the UK collects income in the UK relating to performed music. The collection societies then remit their payments to music publishers.

It should go without saying that music publishers will then take their cut. Typically, a publisher may take 25 percent, but they could take anything between 10 and 40 percent. There are other options—for instance, you can cut out the middleman completely and join each collection society yourself, so royalties will be paid directly to you. Alternatively, you could appoint a collection agent (who, for a fee usually in the region of 10 to 15 percent, will collect your royalties).

You may also find that if you are using a publisher, your overseas earnings are reduced still further, as the publisher will subcontract the collection of publishing rights to a publisher in each jurisdiction. The overseas (in relation to you) publisher will take a share of the income it collects before sending the money to your publisher, who will take another cut and then pay you.

In Chapter 8, I will look at some of the options for collecting royalties with a lesser percentage being deducted. However, don't go leaping ahead, expecting a panacea: Music publishers tend to take much less than their record-label counterparts. Also, if you are looking to have your song placed with other artists, then you probably will need someone to go out and find those other artists to record your songs. This is a service where a music publisher really will earn their fees.

There is one other wrinkle you should be aware of: If you are self-releasing your own download/CD/DVD, then depending on the restrictions in the territory where you are releasing, you may not have to pay yourself. In certain territories (such as the UK), you can avoid paying royalties to yourself by confirming that you are the copyright holder and that you do not require royalties (which will be the case if you are receiving all of the profits from the release). Usually the paperwork to regularize this process needs to be put into place before a license can be granted for the production of the CD (assuming that a license is necessary).

Gifts

I went to a seminar a while back. All of the attendees were given goodie bags as we left. Among other things, the bag contained a CD.

There is a market out there for gifts. These may be gifts to customers, or these may be gifts to staff. Most of the people who are buying are corporate buyers. These are not people looking to buy a single CD, who will worry about whether it is priced at $14.99 or $15. Typically, these are people who have budgets of thousands of dollars and who want a lot of your product.

The hard work is finding these people. Needless to say, if you can find an agent to look for opportunities, your life may be easier. However, even with an agent you're going to need to understand the market in which the potential purchaser works. So, for instance, if you produce ambient music, then you may be able to sell your CDs to a health-food store to offer as a special gift to their customers. If you're a hard-living heavy-metal band, then the health-food store is probably less likely to be interested in your CD.

As well as finding these people, you'll also have to figure out what else you may be able to sell them. For instance, someone in a corporation may be keener to purchase a job lot of your CD if she also sees you perform. The idea of a corporate gig may not appeal, but it will provide reasonable money where you can have a fair expectation of being paid.

Income from Your Infrastructure

I briefly want to talk about an area where you can make comparatively easy money. However, this is an area where you can lose your fan base very quickly through greed and crass stupidity. It is also an area where your business practices will be indistinguishable from those of the record companies from whom you have so cleverly run away.

If you have been following some of the suggestions I have set out in this book and have pursued your own course into the music industry, then you will have two things:

- A fan base

- An infrastructure (that is, a means by which you can create product and get that product to your fan base)

These are two highly valuable business assets. However, you may find that these two business assets are being underutilized. *Underutilized* is a business term that, broadly translated, means "somewhere where we can easily earn more money."

Before we go any further, let me refer you back to Chapter 2 and remind you about the expectations of your fan base.

Okay. If you've read and have heeded the messages of the earlier chapter, then I'll continue.

One way you can make more money is by selling more things to your fan base. You will find that you can create only a finite amount of product (and there is a point at which most of your reasonable fans will feel as if they have enough of your stuff). However, your fan base will be open to purchasing music and merchandise from other people.

So, for instance, here are some of the things you could do to generate income from your fan base:

- Sell music from other artists. For instance, if you swap gigs with another act, you could also swap CDs. If you give each other a certain number of (non-returnable) CDs, any you sell would then be direct profit for you. Done with some care, this could also work as a service for your fan base.

- You could help other acts to record and release their own album. The risk and the reward you take for being involved in this activity would be up to you. However, you have a range of options, from working as a purely benevolent facilitator to becoming a record label releasing other people's product.

- Alternatively, you could find other acts who have recorded and pressed their own CDs and help them with distribution and order fulfillment.

When you start looking at the options, you will find that there are many ways you can generate income from your infrastructure. However, before you move ahead too quickly, do remember that you are taking very different sorts of risks and risks that you may not fully understand, so please proceed with caution.

Sources of Finance

If you were thinking about opening a candy store, you would probably consider getting a loan. So if you're going to run your music career as a business, why not raise some finance to fund it?

If you genuinely believe in what you're doing, then it would be a reasonable business decision to finance your business with a loan. However, many banks may perceive that music-related businesses are too much of a risk and so would be very cautious about considering your application. I now want to look at some of the options for raising money and some of the practicalities around this action.

If you are going to borrow money, then the person you borrow from will want to make a profit. This is not an unreasonable attitude. Therefore, to borrow money you are going to have to put a business proposition to the other party that explains how you will make money—and therefore, how they will make money. In putting forward this proposition, it is important that you understand how the lender's/investor's business is structured and how they make money.

I should also point out that this section is not something to contemplate on day one: If you've only just learned how to tune your guitar, then a bank will not give you a loan, and a venture capitalist will not be interested. This is for people who are serious about building a business.

What Are You Getting? What Are You Giving Up?

There are two main forms of finance:

- Loans

- Equity

The difference between the two is significant.

Loans

With a loan, you borrow money. Your only obligation is to pay back the money that you have borrowed, with interest. Typically, the lender will not have anything to do with the running of your business—all they will want from you is timely repayment.

A lender may ask for security (particularly if you are perceived as a high risk, which you most certainly are). The purpose of the security is to give the lender an asset that it can sell to raise money if you do not repay your loan. The security may be a business asset (which could include your copyrights) or a personal asset (such as your home).

A lender will make money by charging interest on the loan.

Equity

When you sell the equity in your business to an investor, you sell part (or all) of your business.

As a creative person, there are huge implications in selling part of your business. You will be selling rights to the income that arises from your copyrights. In addition, your investor will then have same rights as the other shareholders, and so, for instance, will be able to influence strategy.

To sell equity, you would probably need to structure your business as a company with shares (although this may not be necessary). This company would then need to become the legal owner of the rights to your income—I would expect the investor would want this to be *all* sources of income (including recordings, publishing, merchandising, and so on) or as many sources as possible. You would hold some shares, and the investor would hold some shares.

An equity investor will make money by selling their shares in your business. In essence, the investor will not expect to make serious money until they sell their shares. When they do sell their shares, they will look to get back their original investment and some profit. Typically, the level of profit will be much higher than the level of interest that you would pay on a loan.

You will hear equity investors talking about their "exit strategy." This strategy is the process by which they will sell their shares (hopefully for a profit). A concern for the equity investors is who will buy their shares. Unless the potential investor can see that there will be a reasonable prospect that someone will buy their shares when they want to get out and leave your business, then they are unlikely to invest.

Although you are selling rights to the income that derives from your copyrights, equity investors differ from record companies and music publishers in a significant way: The equity investor will always look for a time when the deal ends and they can sell their shares. Record companies and music publishers will often hold the copyright until the end of the copyright period (which, in the case of certain copyrights, can be 70 years after the death of the creator).

Initial Financing

When you are first starting out, you are unlikely to find any bank or other financial institution that will lend you money. This is not unreasonable—you have no track record and probably have no assets to offer as security to back any loan.

Accordingly, if you need money you will need to raise it from:

- Your own resources (so if you're not independently wealthy, you will need to get a job, even if that means flipping burgers at McDonald's)
- Family
- Friends

This may sound like a fearfully unscientific way to raise capital. However, this is the way that many businesses start.

Taking money from family and friends should make you aware of the risks you are taking. If you can't repay your debts, then it will be your family and your friends who are out of luck due to your stupidity.

Initial financing of this form can take the form of loans (where repayment may or may not be demanded) or equity.

The Fan Base as a Source of Finance

A unique source of financing could be your fan base.

There are many ways to use the fan base as a source of finance; for one example, take Marillion (marillion.com), who borrowed money from their fans to finance an album. The band was smart and didn't structure the borrowing as a loan. Instead, they asked fans to preorder the album 12 months before release. The band was quite honest about what they were doing. Fans weren't left expecting a CD to turn up any day soon because, in fact, the album had yet to be recorded. Using their loyal fan base, the band encouraged 12,000 fans to preorder the CD.

Banks

Once you have a viable business, banks will consider loaning you money.

In addition to their conventional form, where a bank will lend you money, loans can take many different forms, which may include an overdraft facility and factoring (where the bank will advance you against invoices you are waiting to be paid).

If you want a loan, don't just go to your nearest branch and ask for a loan. Instead, you need to find a bank with a specialized creative industries department and where there are people who will understand your business. While your business is small (in the bank's eyes), a specialized creative industries department may not want to deal with you. If this is the case, they should be able to recommend another part of the bank that can deal with you more sympathetically.

Business Angels and Private Investors

This is where we are getting into risky territory. First, some of the deals suggested from now on may have implications that could kill your business if you make the wrong deal and the deal then goes sour. Second, you're going to be dealing with serious business-people who will be very dismissive unless they can see a way to make serious amounts of money.

Business angels and private investors are essentially the same beast, although they may behave slightly differently. Try not to get too hung up on the terminology, because anyone can apply either of these labels to himself. People who apply an "angel" tag to themselves usually like to be thought of as being more benevolent and less money-grabbing. For this section, I will use the term "private investor" to refer to both types of investors.

Private investors are individuals who are happy to buy equity in small companies and to support the companies in other more practical ways—for instance, by helping with the finances or marketing. These investors do not necessarily expect to see a return on their investment in the short term but will usually hope to sell their shares at some point. However, they may also be interested in the business and enjoy the kudos that come from being associated with their investment. Accordingly, they may not be quite so aggressive and demanding about their exit strategy.

You may also find some private investors who are companies. It's unlikely that many companies would want to invest in your business; however, I am mentioning this for completeness.

Venture Capital

Venture capitalists are equity investors who specialize in investing in higher-risk businesses that often do not have a long track record.

Venture capitalists will expect to make a return that is a multiple of their original investment and will expect to see this return over a comparatively short period of time (perhaps three to seven years). Unlike some private investors, venture capitalists will need a very definite exit strategy.

Venture capitalists look for businesses that have very good growth potential and that can produce an ongoing stream of income. The chances of getting an investment from a venture capitalist are practically nonexistent, but don't let that stop you if you have a solid business. However, unless you can demonstrate that your business has immense growth potential, you will not get any venture capital interest.

Business Partners

You may well find that your business partners can be a useful form of finance; however, this will very much depend on the nature of your business. For instance, a record company may be interested in investing in your business to gain a share of your income from areas where it may not usually receive income (such as merchandising—but, in any event, it is becoming more common for record labels to enter into deals where they take a share of every stream of income that the artist generates).

When you first start your business, you are unlikely to have any business partners, so this will not be a useful avenue for you to pursue. However, as your business grows and you develop more business relationships, you should look for financing opportunities. It should go without saying that if you sell your rights (for instance, as part of a record deal or a publishing deal), then a large part of your business will already have gone, and you won't be able to sell an interest to another business partner.

What Sort of Investment Should I Go For?

You may have finished reading the last section and be sitting there scratching your head, not really knowing how to go forward. Raising financing is a highly complex subject, so let me give you my overly simplistic view about the options that are out there.

- First (with thanks to Polonius), neither a borrower nor a lender be. If you are able to survive without borrowing, do. Borrowing costs money and so reduces your income. (The same principle is also true for investment.)

- If you need to raise financing, then follow the simplest course. This will usually involve taking out a loan of some variety. If you take out a loan, then get the smallest loan you can, at the most beneficial rate of interest, and combine it with more flexible sources of income (such as an overdraft or money borrowed from family and friends).

- Be very wary about any equity investment. You are selling something very valuable (which, if you make it to the big time, will be worth an awful lot more). If you are dealing with private investors, they understand a lot about investment and very little about the music business.

- The Marillion idea of seeking funding from the fan base is interesting and may be appealing. However, you need a very loyal fan base to raise sufficient funds, and then you need to deliver a truly remarkable product. Marillion did this; not everyone can. If you get it wrong, you'll probably never see any of your fan base ever again.

Also, take some time to consider the situation from the investor's/lender's perspective and look at the returns they will be expecting. Take a look at Figure 6.5. This graph shows how over time the value of a typical growing business and the risk associated with a business may change.

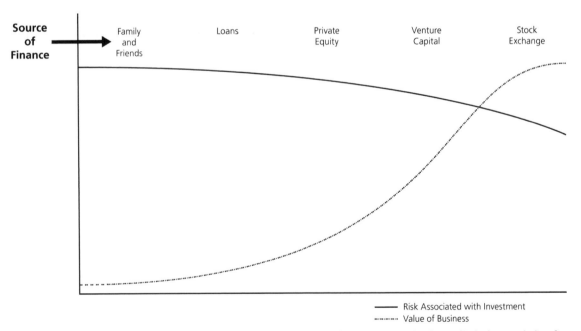

Figure 6.5 As the value of a business grows, its risk profile tends to decline slightly, and the form of investment that would be suitable changes.

At different stages of a company's development, the different growth/risk profiles will make your business attractive to different investors/lenders. As far as your career goes, you are highly unlikely to form a company that goes on to be traded on a recognized stock exchange. However, if your business grows, especially if you leverage the benefits of your infrastructure, you may find yourself listed on a recognized stock exchange one day.

You are also unlikely to be able to sustain the level of growth that will make you attractive to venture capitalists. Therefore, this source of financing is unlikely to be of interest to you. However, this may not be a bad thing, because you may find that getting involved with this sort of business doesn't fit well with a music career.

You are likely to stay in the area where you want loans and perhaps some private equity. This is not a bad thing: Many businesses remain at this level, especially when the owners want to stay involved and live a certain "non-corporate" lifestyle, and they can make a comfortable living. (Indeed, you may often hear these businesses referred to as "lifestyle" businesses.)

Drawing Up a Business Plan

If you are going to borrow money from anyone or seek an investment, then you will need a business plan.

The point of the business plan is to demonstrate:

- How you intend to run your business

- How the lender/investor is going to make money from their participation in your business

Main Headings in Your Business Plan

The main headings you are likely to see in a business plan include:

- **An executive summary.** This is your opportunity to explain (in less than a page—lenders/investors lose interest quickly) why a lender should lend or an investor should consider investing. The one thing you don't need to do is tell them anything about your business—just focus on the profit they can make!

- **A description of your business.** This is your chance to set out who you are and what you do, and to describe the products you offer and plan to offer.

- **The marketing and sales strategy.** Talk about your fan base and how this group of people can be (and are being) converted into an income stream. You should talk about how you nurture and grow your fan base.

- **The team that is running your business.** Here you need to set out the credentials of the people who are running the business and your business partners. You should also mention your future plans for other people you want to work with to further your business objectives.

- **Your operations—in other words, the details of how you run your business.** Here you should include details of your premises, how your products are produced, and how your products are sold and delivered to your fan base (or customers, as the investor will regard them).

- **Financial forecasts.** As you might expect, this is one of the key aspects of your business plan and is your opportunity to bring all of the strands of your business together to paint a picture of your financial status and projected financial status.

Assumptions

In any business plan, you'll have to make assumptions. It stands to reason—you're looking into the future.

Most investors expect a business plan to look forward five years. The projections about the first two years should be as realistic as possible. It is understood that the following three years will be based on educated guesses, and you have to use certain assumptions.

Whatever assumptions you use, these should be documented and justified. This serves two purposes. First, it allows the potential investor to understand the basis of the projections you are giving him. Second, it is your opportunity to demonstrate your grasp on your business.

If you put in dodgy, unsubstantiated assumptions, you'll make yourself into a laughingstock. For instance, if you're selling CDs to 1,000 fans per year, then some increase may be acceptable. If you suggest that in year four you'll sell 1 million CDs (in other words, sales will increase a thousand-fold by the fourth year), then you'll just look stupid and/or money-grabbing, unless you have some real evidence to back these claims.

The Need to Suffer Pain

Anyone looking to invest in your business will need to know that you are committed. Not only will they need to know, but they will need this demonstrated through your actions. There are two things you can do here.

First, you can demonstrate that you have invested heavily in the business so you will take a substantial loss if it fails. Potential investors will see this, rightly, as a very strong motivator for you. Second, you will need to minimize the amount of earnings you are drawing from the business. If it looks like you need an investment to fund your lifestyle, then the investors will get nervous and walk away.

Costs

One of the advantages of the conventional route in the music business (in other words, signing up with a manager, a publishing company, and a major record label) is that everything is done for you. All you have to do is focus on your music (and the associated duties, such as writing music, recording music, and promoting your music). If you need a present for your husband/wife/girlfriend/boyfriend/son/daughter/mistress/ dog/cat and so on, then you will probably have "people" who will do this for you (at least once you reach a certain level). If you need transportation, then a limousine will be provided. You will find that you can live a very pampered life.

The downside to this pampered lifestyle is that you will be paying a lot of money for it. Not only that, but you will have virtually no control over the costs that are being incurred in your name. As most of the examples in this chapter have demonstrated, when you are on a royalty, all of the expenses are taken from your income, and you get what is left.

This is one of the reasons for the clichéd situation in which a successful musician is living an extravagant lifestyle one day and then is destitute the next.

Much of the money that is deducted from the income generated by a musician, before the musician receives her royalty (if any), is used to meet expenses at various points down the chain.

It may look as if a record label takes a huge chunk of an artist's earnings (and it does); however, the record company will have made a huge investment and will have considerable expenses that need to be met, and these expenses need to be paid from somewhere. The only source of income is the earnings you generate, so the expenses will be met from there. Unfortunately, that is the way of the world. You can rail against the capitalist system all you like, but until someone comes up with a better solution, that's what we're stuck with.

The costs a record company has to meet are significant. I want to look at these in more detail. I want to focus on these costs for two reasons:

- First, so you can understand some of the expenses that a record company may incur to get your music out there, and in particular to get your CD into the stores (and then into your fans' homes).

- Second, if you are going to follow your own path and release your own CDs, then you will have to incur many of these costs, although hopefully you will be more modest in your spending.

Record-Label Expenses

One of the most significant costs a record label will have is its staffing cost.

A&R people need bonuses for luring you, executives need bonuses for seeing your project through, and the chief financial officer needs a bonus because of the work he will have done keeping track of everyone else's bonus. Seriously, people cost a lot of money, so I have separated out this topic in the next section ("The Cost of Hiring Staff").

Before we leave the subject of people costs, let me remind you of one thing. In large, multinational corporations (which many record labels are), executives' bonuses are based on financial results, not on artistic endeavors. Therefore, any executive is going to have his bonus based on how much money he can squeeze out of your product, not on whether your new album (or whatever you are producing) is any good. The only time an executive will genuinely be worried about the quality of your product will be when he assesses whether it will sell (since a product that doesn't sell won't generate any income).

Please don't look at these comments as a damning indictment of the record industry. This is how all corporations work: The music industry is no better and no worse than any other industry (although as you have seen, it does have some particularly archaic practices).

Property Costs

Picture the situation: You're a hot new band, and you have two record labels interested in you. One has its offices in the heart of town. These are the plushest offices you could imagine—the latest designer furniture in the lobby, hand-stitched carpets, and receptionists manicured to within an inch of their lives.

When you get through to the meeting rooms, the tables are inlaid with hand-carved detail, and the chairs are covered in the softest leather you have ever felt. Needless to say, the audio-visual facilities are to die for. The executives who show up to meet you are dressed in smart (but casual) expensive designer suits. Their jewelry (both the men and the women) is discreet, but you know it is about as expensive as you can get.

Now think about another label with its offices about an hour out of town. Unfortunately, you're an hour out of town too, but in the other direction. When you get to the offices, you find that the street on which they are located was recently used as a set in a film about a Victorian strangler.

Inside, the offices are painted white and the carpets have seen better days, showing signs of wear. There are no meeting rooms, so you all congregate in the A&R guy's office, which is a mess, piled high with demos from other acts. The A&R guy apologizes for the mess but doesn't apologize for the state of his Metallica 1997 tour T-shirt.

Okay, which of these two labels impresses you more? Which label says "success?"

You might lie to yourself and say you won't be impressed by the flashy offices. However, when you have been in a position to make a side-by-side comparison, you will always find that the plush office leaves an impression.

Record labels know this and know that they can intimidate artists and their managers with impressive offices—think of it as the building equivalent of power dressing. Accordingly, record labels will always spend money on their premises.

Even if you don't want to have the most impressive office in town, if you are going to follow your own course, you will need some premises, and premises come with a lot of expenses. At a minimum, you are likely to have to incur the following expenses in connection with any property that you use for your business:

- The cost of purchase or renting (including taxes and lawyers' fees)

- Local property taxes

- The cost of amenities, such as water and electricity

- Insurance costs, both for the property itself and against anyone injuring herself while in the property

- Maintenance costs, which may be as low as a door hinge or a coat or two of paint but could get as high as extending or rebuilding part of the building

Computer Costs

Record labels spend a lot of money on their computer systems. There are many elements to these systems, including the computers themselves (both desktop computers and servers), licenses for the software that runs on the computers, cabling and network gizmos, a bomb-proof backup system that cannot fail, staff to run all of this stuff, and training for all of the staff on how to work the computers. This is before a cent has been spent on customized programming for the accounting and royalty-payment systems.

Even with the best will in the world and using free software (such as Linux), you're going to have to spend money installing and running a computer system.

Taxes

Record labels get hit with a range of taxes. These include taxes on the profits that the label makes, employment/social taxes (such as National Insurance Contributions in the UK, which are discussed further in Chapter 7), and sales taxes (such as VAT). Some of these charges get levied on a regular basis (for instance, corporate taxes and employment/social taxes), while others (such as sales taxes) are incurred as part of the daily business of the label.

There's an old cliché that the three certainties in life are birth, death, and taxes. However, this is only partially true. At the time of writing, birth and death are both certain, and although the need to pay taxes is absolute, the amount that will be paid in taxes is far from certain. If you are smart, there's a lot you can do to avoid taxes.

At this point, let me add a few caveats and some other more general warnings. First the caveat: This is a book that offers some ideas about building a successful music career. It is most definitely not a tax-planning manual, and it does not seek to offer any advice on matters of tax. If you are looking for tax advice, then talk to a suitably qualified professional who actively practices in this area.

Second, a more general warning: There is a difference between tax avoidance and tax evasion. Let me look at the position in the UK for a moment, where tax avoidance is legal. However, tax evasion is not. With tax avoidance, you arrange your affairs in a manner that provides the most favorable tax position to you. With tax evasion, you lie and cheat and generally break the law. Similar principles apply in most jurisdictions around the globe.

The line between tax avoidance and tax evasion is a fine one (and can sometimes be quite blurred), so again, I recommend you talk to a suitably qualified professional in the jurisdiction in which you will be generating income. You should also note that there will be consequences if you restructure your affairs to avoid tax. A professional adviser will be able to tell you about the consequences and discuss whether they are significant for you.

So with the warnings out of the way, here are some of the things you can do to avoid taxes (and these are things that companies do in practice):

- **Reduce profits.** This may seem bizarre; however, it is quite logical. With lower profits, there will be less tax. There are several ways to reduce profits; the main one is to spend more money, which you can do by paying shareholders a dividend, paying expenses, or paying staff more. Some corporations will set up an intricate web of intra-company charges, the effect of which is to leave any profit in a jurisdiction that has a very low tax rate.

- **Pay people less.** You may not think that employers need an excuse to pay their staff less. However, given the level of employment-related taxes, employers do have a legitimate interest in minimizing their payroll costs. The reduction in salary can be balanced by paying staff in other ways. For instance, if you reduce someone's wages in the UK and then give them goods to the value of the reduction in their salary (or to a similar value), you can (in certain limited circumstances) avoid employment taxes.

Dividends

I briefly mentioned shareholders. By their nature, corporations have shareholders (people who own the business). Shareholders tend to come in two forms:

- People and institutions (such as banks, insurance contributions, and retirement funds) who own shares in companies

- Other companies, where one company will be a subsidiary of another company

Whatever the nature of the shareholders, they have one thing in common: They want to be paid for owning shares in the company. The way that companies pay their shareholders is by distributing an element of their profits. This distribution usually is called a *dividend*, and the executives of the company determine its amount. (You can guess what the shareholders do to any executives who do not provide a suitable dividend.) Shareholders also expect to see the value of their holding go up, so that when they come to sell their shares, the shares will be worth more than the shareholders paid for them.

If you set up your own business, then you will have shareholders implicitly or explicitly. You will be one of the key shareholders. Although you will probably (at least initially) be saved from the rapacious greed of external shareholders, you will need to extract money from the business (if nothing else, to pay for things such as food and shelter). How you extract the money (for instance, whether you take a salary or a dividend) will have implications for you and your business. I've said it before and I'll say it again: You need to talk to someone about the significance of those implications for your personal situation.

Getting the Product to the Customer

A record label will incur other costs that are directly related to your product. The main costs are manufacturing, distribution, and marketing. If you self-release an album, you will incur these costs too, although you may want to spend less than a record label would, and you are likely to employ other distribution options (such as mail order for your CDs/DVDs) to a greater extent.

A record label will probably be able to get your CD produced for a lower unit cost than you can. This is because a label will put far more business with a pressing plant than you will and so can negotiate much better deals. Also, a label will expect to sell a lot more CDs than you could and so will get many more CDs pressed. Unless these CDs sell, the record company will not generate any income, so the next step is to get the CDs to a place where they can be sold.

The process by which CDs get from the pressing plant into the stores (whether brick-and-mortar or online) is called *distribution*. Distribution always seems such a simple task—you give someone a CD, they sell it—however, there are many factors to be considered. As a first step, a decision needs to be made about the numbers of CDs to be pressed and how many CDs will be sent to each outlet.

Usually, a decision about numbers is driven by the orders received; however, if the label doesn't press enough CDs to meet demand, then it may not be able to get a second order in quickly enough. Conversely, if it presses too many, then it will need to find an outlet to sell its unwanted stock.

Once the numbers have been sorted, the CDs need to be physically transferred. This is partly a logistical exercise and partly a paperwork exercise. For you, the musician, the paperwork is crucial: Each CD that goes into a store constitutes a sale for you. For each sale, you get a royalty. If someone doesn't keep track of the sales, then you won't get what is due to you. The other aspect of distribution is returns. All CDs are 100 percent returnable. Again, it is crucial that proper records are kept, because returned CDs reduce the amount of royalties you will receive.

Advertising

Once your CDs are in the stores (or your track is available for download), then the product needs to sell. If they don't sell, they will be returned.

If you're lucky, some people will buy your CD on the basis of the cover or by tripping over your album on iTunes. However, how often do you walk into a record store and buy a CD by an artist you've never heard of? My hunch is not very often. If you, as a musician, don't buy other musicians' products without hearing them, what expectation can you have that an average punter will go into a record store and buy your music? For this reason, you need a marketing campaign.

Major labels can spend huge amounts on marketing. If TV advertising is involved, it is not unheard of for a label to spend more than 50 percent of the cost of putting out the album on advertising. There are, of course, cheaper options, but these may not be as effective as TV advertising. Also, your audience will largely determine the form of marketing: If you're a pop act, then TV advertising may be a reasonable choice. However, if you're a heavy metal band, then TV advertising may not work, but touring is far more likely to generate interest.

If you're only intending to sell your music directly to your fan base (in other words, you are intending to avoid the retailers, whether brick-and-mortar or online), then your marketing costs can be contained. However, if you are looking for sales from a wider base and you are hoping to sell your album through the retailers, then you will need to do some marketing to ensure that your CDs are not all returned.

The Cost of Hiring Staff

There will come a time when you need people to help you in your endeavor. This is good if you like to brag, because you will then be able to say, "I'll get my people to call your people." However, in all other ways, hiring people is a really tough thing to do.

Although this chapter is about the economic aspects of the music business, please indulge me for a moment as I mention some of the human aspects.

Most people take employment because they need money. That is not to say that they can't or don't enjoy their work, or that they wouldn't do some work if they weren't paid. However, on balance, given the choice between working and not working, many people would choose not to work.

Some people will work for you for free because they want to get close to you as a musician, but on the whole, if someone is going to work for you, then they will expect to get paid. They will use the money you pay them to provide for themselves and their family, and they will make plans for their life on the assumption that you will be a fair employer and the employment relationship will continue.

Their plans may not be big plans—in fact, they are probably going to be very average sorts of plans (perhaps taking the kids to the cinema or going on holiday with the family). There also will be more serious plans, such as paying the mortgage or saving for their retirement.

In return for their service and loyalty, these people will be relying on you to continue to provide a source of income. If this income stops, the effect for your employees and their families could be catastrophic. The impact will be the same regardless of whether the income stops due to your fault.

Before you hire anybody, please ensure you are confident that you will treat that person as fairly as you can, because, quite literally, you will be playing with his life.

Hiring people and keeping them on your payroll is a costly exercise and a logistical nightmare. The rest of this section deals with some of the costs you will incur. These are costs that involve direct expense (for instance, paying your staff); indirect expense (for instance, the time you have to spend each month to process paychecks); and your time, which you could otherwise spend making music.

Employment expenses vary according to territory. For instance, in some jurisdictions you are required to provide a certain level of pension contribution in respect of your employees. However, this is not a requirement in all jurisdictions. If you're looking at hiring people, and you want to know what requirements apply in your jurisdiction, I suggest you talk to an employment lawyer.

As a general rule of thumb, you should expect any employee's work to generate income for your business of at least three times that employee's pay. The reason for this multiple is that salary only constitutes one third of the expense of employing somebody. Let me elaborate with a more complete list of the expenses of employment:

- The largest single expense of hiring someone is likely to be her pay. The amount you will need to pay someone is likely to depend on the skills she brings. For instance, if you are hiring someone to package up your orders and send them out, you will probably be able to pay less than you would if you were hiring an accountant to work as your business manager.

  At the end of the day, wages are generally set by market conditions, so if you work in a high-wage area (for instance, a capital city), you are likely to have to pay higher wages than you would if you set up in a backwoods area. At the bottom end of the wage scale, you may find yourself caught by the minimum wage that applies in some jurisdictions.

- Coupled with wages, you may have to pay employment taxes or social charges. I have already mentioned National Insurance Contributions, which are the UK's equivalent of these costs. They hit both employees and employers, with employers paying up to 13.8 percent of earnings as (Secondary) National Insurance Contributions. You can see that when employer's contributions are added to the 12 percent of earnings that employees pay as (Primary) National Insurance Contributions, this is quite a significant tax.

- In addition to an employee's direct earnings, you usually also have to pay the employee indirectly by way of benefits. The benefits you have to provide will differ according to the custom and law of the marketplace in which you are operating, as well as the seniority of the employee and the level of desperation you have to hire them. However, other benefits you may have to provide could include a car, pension savings, death benefits, and health insurance.

  In addition to the obvious benefits, there are some less obvious benefits that may not have a monetary value for your employee but that will cost you. These include sick leave and holiday vacation.

- Another considerable expense associated with employees is the space within which they work. Even if they only have a workspace that is the size of their desk with a bit of room to get a chair in and out, you will find that employees take up a lot of space. This means you will need premises of some sort. Once you get premises, you get a whole heap of new costs (including maintenance and insurance) as well as a whole heap of time wasted (for instance, getting a maintenance person to deal with the blocked sinks in the restrooms).

- As well as needing a space to work, staff will also need tools. The needed tools will depend on the task they are asked to perform. However, it is likely that the tools will include a desk, a computer, a phone, pens, paper, and so on. When you start adding up these costs (along with the training costs to use the tools) and then multiplying them by a number of staff, you will see your costs rise rapidly.

- You will find there is a lot of administration associated with having staff. In fact, you may even find out why corporations have Human Resources departments. When you get to a certain size, then you are likely to have to pay people to look after the other people you have hired.

  The sort of administration you are likely to come across includes running a payroll for your staff, so you will have to calculate how much to pay people, deduct their tax and social contributions, deduct anything else you are required to deduct (for instance, child support or a court-imposed payment), and then calculate how much you have to pay in social costs. When tax rates change or you give a pay raise, you will find your administration systems will temporarily be thrown into disarray.

  There are many other pieces of administration in which you could get involved. Let me give you one more example of an area that will swallow up time and money: recruitment. You first need to define the task you want undertaken, agree on the role with anyone else who needs to be involved (such as band mates), agree on the salary, and then look for the person to fulfill the role. In this quest, you may well interview a number of people. The whole process can waste days of your time.

- Having people around will lead to other costs, such as theft and damage caused by your staff. You may also be vicariously liable for the actions of your staff. For instance, if a member of your staff working on your business harms someone else, that person may sue you.

- To cover the financial risk related to the injuries staff may suffer and the damage they may cause while working for you, you may want to take out (and indeed, you may be obliged to carry) insurance against these risks. As you would expect, this is a cost you will have to meet as the employer.

- You may also find there are costs if the relationship with any employee goes sour or his performance is simply not up to scratch. If you terminate the employment relationship, you may be obliged to pay a lump-sum termination payment, or you may be sued for damages. Sometimes you will find that the cost of hiring a lawyer to fight claims against you exceeds the cost of damages that are being sought, so it may be easier to simply pay the claimant.

This list is not complete; however, I hope it does go some way toward illustrating the costs of staffing your operation. It should also explain another reason why it is so expensive to run record labels, publishing houses, and the other businesses associated with the music industry.

So What Do I Get Paid?

This has been a pretty long and quite heavy chapter. I would apologize, but the content is necessary if you're going to set up a business.

In the next chapter, I'll move on to look at what you can actually earn and how to spread those earnings over the rest of your life.

7 Your Pay Packet

I'm guessing you probably didn't get into music because you wanted to hear someone talk about being sensible and saving for your pension. However, I'm also guessing that if you've read this far in the book, you are serious about your career, and you're very serious about making a living from your music.

The Cat-Food Years

Unless you die young, there will come a time when your earnings from music will be reduced. This happens for all artists: As they mature, their fan base contracts.

Fan bases contract for a number of reasons:

- Musical tastes change, and as the act becomes less trendy, fans lose interest in music and/or the act, not to mention having other priorities in their lives.

- The act may tour less and undertake less promotion. This is not unreasonable: Most people can spend only a number of years living the nomadic lifestyle of a musician on the road before they burn out. In addition, many musicians also broaden their interests, perhaps pursuing other projects that have arisen as a result of their success.

A declining fan base can, but doesn't have to, lead to a decline in income.

Although a fan base may have declined, the income expectation can become more certain and sustainable (provided the fan base is nurtured). It is not unreasonable to expect that if you have kept a fan for 20 years, that fan is not going to desert you in the short-term, unless you upset him or her, and you may also find that with age, each fan becomes more profitable.

Also, if your fan base is maturing, then your fans' tastes are likely to change. With a younger fan base, particularly a teenage fan base, you will be able to sell a much greater quantity of merchandise. For the more mature fan base, you are likely to sell less, but the merchandise you sell may be of a higher quality, allowing you to charge higher prices and make better profits.

The financial strategy underlying this book is to develop a long-term, sustainable career that will continue to generate income over as long a period as possible. Provided you can sustain your income over a sufficiently long period, you will avoid the cat-food years—those declining years when your career has gone, the money you had has gone, and you are left so impoverished that all you can afford to eat is cat food.

There are many ways you can achieve this longevity. One strategy would be to make your income from the same sources that you do in the earlier part of your career, such as downloads/CDs, merchandising, and live performances. You will still be able to generate income from these sources, but to a lesser extent as you mature.

As you hit the middle stage of your career, you will probably generate less money from direct sources (downloads and live performances), but you should be able to increase the income you make from indirect sources, such as television and film licensing. Then, as you approach retirement, you can look at possibly selling off the rights to your future income in exchange for a lump-sum payment.

Of course, this is only one option. However, it does show how you can have a steady income over your whole career (or at least over a longer period than you can under a conventional music career).

The Income Stream

So will you avoid the cat-food years? Let's take a look at some income streams.

"Conventional" Highly Successful Career Income Stream

Take a look at Figure 7.1. This shows the earnings pattern for many successful, but now forgotten, artists.

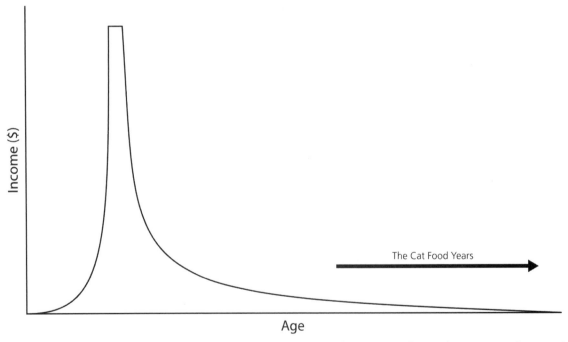

Figure 7.1 The income pattern of an archetypal successful artist. After a few years of struggle, the artist hits the big time, and after the peak, fades into obscurity around the time of his or her 30th birthday.

This graph could show the income for a guitarist in a successful band. Let me explain how his career could play out.

When the band started off, it didn't generate very much income. This is normal for a band when they are paying their dues. However, this band became successful, signed a deal, and started to sell a lot of records. On the back of this success, the band toured and generated some income (primarily from the merchandising). At this point, the members of the band were starting to see quite a healthy income for the first time and were receiving incomes in the high six figures or into seven figures. (They were very successful.)

After a few years of wild parties and a good bit of money, the band split due to musical differences. The drummer joined a cover band, and the bassist decided to become a professional surfer and moved to Australia. The singer joined another band, and that left the guitarist.

The guitarist still had some royalties coming through (mostly from overseas sources) and started to put together a solo project. The solo project was an artistic success but made a poor financial return, and on his 30th birthday, the label dropped the guitarist.

With no other skills and no inclination to do anything else, the guitarist survived on the last few royalty payments that trickled in over the next few years until the income from his musical career finally dwindled.

We have now reached the cat-food years.

"New" Style Income Stream

Now think about the income stream you may be able to generate if you take control of your career following some of the ideas set out in this book. Have a look at Figure 7.2. Here, I have superimposed an income stream that could be generated if you follow your own course over the income stream that our unfortunate guitarist received (which was originally shown in Figure 7.1).

There are a few things to notice about this alternative income stream:

- First, income is generated more quickly by this approach because you begin earning immediately. You don't wait for a record or management deal before you start generating income.

- The income stream builds more slowly. Because you are relying on (assisted) organic growth, the increase in your income will be more controlled. However, see the next bullet.

- The income stream remains at its peak for longer. (Indeed, the peak is more of a plateau.) With a more solid fan base, you will be able to sustain momentum over a longer period.

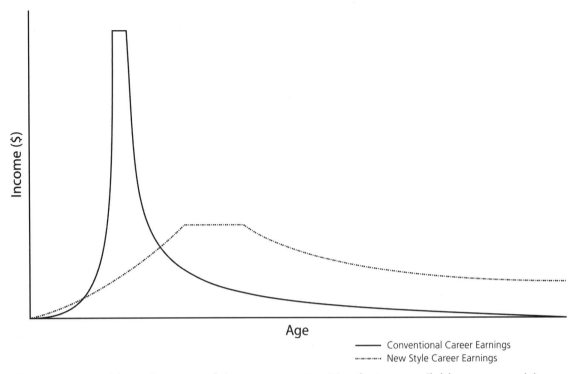

Figure 7.2 By taking advantage of the new opportunities that are available, more musicians can develop a long-term career and live on more modest earnings over a longer period. You should also remember that while very few musicians actually earn mega-bucks (and then end up spending huge amounts of this money very quickly), the more modest level of earnings is achievable for many more musicians. You should also bear in mind that I am calling the earnings "modest" because they are lower than the earnings shown in Figure 7.1, but they are still good earnings and would support a good lifestyle. The scale used on the graph only makes these earnings look lower.

- The income stream then declines at a more measured rate.

- The income stream does not decline to zero—instead, it remains at a reasonable level until around the time that you are ready to retire (and even after that date, it may still provide an income).

What may not be obvious is that under this latter approach, the performer makes more income than under the first approach, because the income is received at a reasonable level for the whole of the musician's career.

How Much Money Do You Need?

Either you are independently wealthy, or you will need money in order to live. Most people have a range of expenses that include food, keeping a roof over their head (including paying for water, electricity, and so on), gear for making music, and taxes (local, national, and including any social contributions). After that, most spending is on what are, in effect, luxury items.

How much money do you need? It's an interesting question, and one I propose not to answer. Instead, let me flip the issue over and give you two alternative approaches to dealing with your income.

- First, live within your means. You know how much money you have earned: Do not spend more than that. This may mean you will need to cut every possible expense. If you own a house, sell it and move somewhere cheaper; if you're renting, quit and move back with your parents; if you're in an expensive location, then move somewhere cheaper. Do everything you can do to stay afloat financially.

- Second, if the amount you *want* to spend exceeds the amount you are earning, then you are not earning enough. You (and you alone) directly control your earnings so, instead of going into debt, go out and earn more money. If that's too difficult, then you need to live within your means (so go back and read bullet point one again).

As a musician, your pay packet is not determined by the amount you earn. Rather, it is determined by how much is left after all of the deductions. We've looked at many other deductions throughout the rest of this book. I now want to look at two very specific deductions that are pertinent to you alone: taxes and pension contributions.

Tax

In most jurisdictions, you will be taxed on your earnings. Unfortunately, this is the nature of society, and there is little you can do about it (except find a smart accountant to show you the loopholes, move to a low-tax jurisdiction, or both).

Each country has its own tax regime that will affect its own citizens and foreign citizens working in the country (such as touring musicians) in different ways. Most countries have tax treaties with other countries (often called *double tax treaties*), whereby foreign nationals can avoid tax on earnings in the foreign country, provided the earnings are taxed in their own country.

Tax is a hideously complicated and dreadfully dull subject, so I don't want to go into the minutiae of double tax treaties or any of the other tax matters. However, I do want to give an indication of how tax can do really bad things to your income.

Tax systems around the world work in many different ways, and tax rates can vary greatly. However, there are a few principles that are fairly global:

- No one wants to pay tax, but people do. If people don't pay tax, then the tax authorities will pursue them and crush them mercilessly.

- Tax for self-employed people (that is, people who are not employed by someone else—as a musician controlling your own career, you will probably be self-employed) is calculated after the deduction of expenses. So, for instance, if your tour earns $1 million, but you have expenses of $900,000, then you will usually be taxed only on $100,000.

- In addition to taxes, there are often social charges at a much more modest level. These are often payable irrespective of earnings or based on a stricter calculation of earnings that ignores some expenses.

These are general principles: You should take detailed tax advice in your own jurisdiction (and also consider taking tax advice in any other jurisdiction where you earn money), because each locality will have its own tax laws. For instance, in the U.S., self-employed people (such as musicians) pay an additional 15 percent self-employment tax above regular federal and state taxes. If you're not expecting this tax hit, it can be quite painful.

As I said, I want to give an example of how tax can eat up your earnings. I'm going to illustrate the loss to your pocket using the UK taxation system, looking at the situation as it applies to self-employed individuals. For this example, I will consider someone who is earning quite a reasonable amount of money: £50,000 (or roughly $85,000) after expenses. This figure may be more than many musicians earn (indeed, it is roughly twice the average earnings throughout the UK); however, I am using it because it will show how the higher tax bands can have a greater effect on earnings (although it does exclude the current UK top rate of tax, 50 percent, which is applicable for taxable earnings over £150,000). I should point out that all figures quoted here are for the 2011/2012 tax year.

In the UK, social contributions are called National Insurance Contributions (often known as NICs). For self-employed people, there are two components—a fixed weekly amount and a percentage based on certain earnings:

- The fixed weekly amount is £2.50 per week (or £130 per year).

- The percentage-based amount is 9 percent of earnings between £7,225 per year and £42,475 per year. So in our example, the individual would pay the maximum amount of £3,172.50 (that is, 9 percent of £35,250, which is the amount of earnings between £7,225 and £42,475).

So in this example, National Insurance Contributions of £3,172.50 are due on earnings of £50,000. National Insurance Contributions cannot be set against tax.

Under the tax system, a basic allowance of £7,475 is given. This means you can earn £7,475 before any tax is paid. So in our example, only £42,525 (in other words, £50,000 − £7,475) is taxable. There are then two tax bands (the starting rate of 10 percent does not apply here):

- The first £35,000 of taxable earnings is taxed at the rate of 20 percent.

- The next £7,525 (the taxable earnings after the £7,475 basic allowance and the £35,000 basic rate band) is then taxed at 40 percent.

Some figures should help to illustrate. Look at Table 7.1.

Table 7.1 The Tax Paid in the UK by an Individual Earning £50,000

Band of Earnings	Tax Rate	Earnings in Band	Amount of Tax
Earnings up to £7,475	0%		£0
First £35,000 of taxable earnings (that is, earnings between £7,475 and £42,475)	20%	£35,000	£7,000
Taxable earnings over £42,475 (that is, earnings between £42,476 and £50,000)	40%	£7,525	£3,010
Total			£10,010

So in this example, the tax amounts to £10,010 (or 20 percent of earnings).

The total deduction from earnings is £13,182.50 (£10,010 tax plus £3172.50 National Insurance Contributions), or 26 percent of earnings.

After deduction of tax and National Insurance Contributions, the take-home pay is £36,181 (or £3,068 per month).

To illustrate the effect of tax, take a look at Figure 7.3, which shows each component of the pay packet.

As I mentioned at the start of this section, this example shows the effect of UK taxes. This book is about how to develop a career in music; because it is not a book about tax, I have not illustrated the tax position for every jurisdiction in which you may work. Non-UK tax laws would obviously paint a different scenario than our UK example, but the overall outcome is the same in either country: You must pay taxes, and they will eat up a significant portion of your income.

Pensions and Retirement Funds

I now want to talk about one expense that you may think is irrelevant: pensions, or as you might want to think of them, retirement funds.

Conventionally, the purpose of a pension (and a retirement fund) is to provide income when you stop working. However, under the model I am advocating in this book, you will hopefully be generating income over a much longer period. Ideally, your music will still be generating income after you retire. Don't get too hung up on any difference between pensions and retirement funds. They are essentially the same thing—a source of income when you retire.

However, instead of thinking of a pension as being just for when you retire, consider it as another income stream that will come online as your earnings decrease. The idea

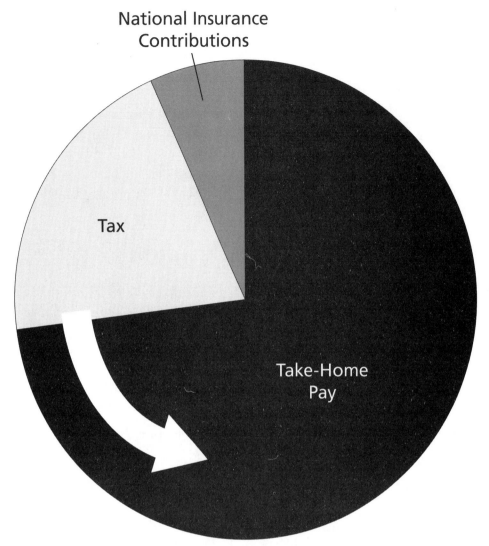

Figure 7.3 The effect of income tax and National Insurance Contributions on earnings. Under current UK legislation, as earnings increase, the tax burden will increase, until 50 percent of income is taxed.

should be that your combined earnings and pension will maintain your income at a certain level when you decide to make the transition into retirement (see Figure 7.4). Then if (or when) the earnings from music cease, you will have another income source.

There is one problem with pensions: They cost a lot. Let me first explain how they work. Once I've done that, I'll look at some of the practical steps you can take.

Betting on Your Life

Pensions are a gamble: nothing more, nothing less. What makes them interesting is that they are a bet on your life!

Perhaps the most secure way to provide a pension for yourself is to buy an annuity. An annuity is another way of saying an income for life. Annuities are sold by financial

Figure 7.4 You can use the income from a pension to ease the financial transition as your earnings from music decline.

institutions, such as insurance companies. The cost of an annuity is determined by many factors, but it is essentially a guess by the financial institution about how long you will live (based on statistics about the population as a whole).

If you live longer than was assumed, then you make a profit. If you don't live longer, then you won't have made a profit. You will only be able to know how long you lived after you have died, so any profit or loss will then be immaterial. However, the key factor about annuities is that they can provide you with security—they protect you against the risk of living longer than you expected.

The risk of living longer than you expected is a serious problem. Suppose your income ends when you are 60, and at that point you have savings of $500,000. You might expect to live for another 20 years. Ignoring the effects of interest and inflation, that would mean you could spend $25,000 a year (that is, $500,000 ÷ 20) or roughly $2,000 per month for the rest of your life. If you then die at the age of 80, your money would be gone.

But what happens if you don't die when you expect to? If you knew you were going to live to be 90, then you could spend $17,000 a year, or $1,390 per month. If you knew you were going to live to be 100, you could spend $12,500 a year, or $1,000 per month.

Unfortunately, we don't know when we are going to die, so there is a tendency to spend less and hold back some capital. However, this can never counter the effect of someone living to an unexpected old age. Take the previous example: What would happen if the person lived to be 110? Although not many people live to be that age, can you be sure that with all of the advances in medicine and technology, you will not live to be that old? Or older?

Because of the uncertainty, annuities have a great use. However, because of the uncertainty, annuities can look very expensive (although to be fair to insurance companies, they take a very small profit on this element of their business).

As a side note, you might think that all this stuff about annuities is dull and you can just live on the interest of your capital. Apart from tax, possibly living to be 120 years old, and fluctuations in interest rates (which could lead to wide swings in your level of income), another factor that makes this a risky strategy is inflation, which will erode the value of your capital. You would therefore need to reinvest some of your interest to ensure that the interest level retains its buying power, whereas an annuity can include inflation protection.

How Much Does an Annuity Cost?

The cost of an annuity varies according to a number of factors, including:

- **Geographic location.** Annuities are calculated in different manners in different jurisdictions.

- **Age.** If you are younger, an annuity may be expected to be paid for a longer period and hence will be more expensive.

- **Pension increases.** You can buy annuities that provide the same amount for every year. However, these annuities mean that the pensioner becomes poorer over time because prices will rise due to inflation. To counter this, you can buy an annuity that increases. The increases can be linked to inflation or can be a fixed percentage. The cost of an annuity will increase if you want pension increases (because the amount the annuity provider will pay out will increase).

- **Dependants.** Many people want to also provide for their spouse/significant other in the event of their death. It is common for an annuity to provide a pension for a spouse/significant other on the death of the original annuitant. Often the dependant's pension will be of a lower level, perhaps two-thirds or one-half of the original pension. A dependant's pension will increase the cost of an annuity.

- **Prevailing market conditions.** The financial institution will invest the money you pay to buy your annuity. If the company thinks it can do better with its investments, then it will charge you less for your annuity. However, if the company thinks the financial markets do not offer much scope for profit, then it will charge you more.

I said annuities are expensive. Let me give you a practical example. These are indicative market figures (in the UK) taken in mid-2011.

For this example, I have taken the following scenario:

- An individual retiring at age 60…

- …with a spouse who is the same age…

- …with the pension increasing in line with UK price inflation, and…

- …on the death of the annuitant, the spouse will receive a pension for the rest of his/her life of 50 percent of the pension that was being paid at the date of death.

Based on these assumptions, a pension will cost more than 34 times the yearly amount that is to be provided. So, if you wanted to provide a pension of £15,000 (roughly $25,000) that would cost £512,300 (more than $850,000).

Once you have pondered the eye-watering expense of pensions, let's move on and look at some of the practical steps you can take to ensure that you secure a modest income in retirement.

How Much Do I Need to Invest?

If you want to provide a reasonable pension for yourself (and perhaps your loved ones) when you retire, then either you can hope you have a very large chunk of money when you retire (which is quite unlikely) or you can start making financial provisions (in other words, saving) now.

Several factors will affect the amount of money that is available to you when you want to buy an annuity:

- The amount you invest

- When you invest

- The returns generated by your investments

Clearly, the amount you invest will have a direct effect on the amount of money available when you come to retire.

The timing of your investment also has a significant effect on your income. The earlier you invest, the longer that investment will have to grow. If you invest $10 on your 20th birthday and $10 on your 40th birthday, by the time you get to your 60th birthday, ignoring any financial disasters, the $10 you invested on your 20th birthday will be worth much more than the $10 you invested on your 40th birthday.

The statement in the last paragraph assumes that your investments always go up. As we know, depending on the nature of the investment, returns can go up and down. Broadly speaking, if you take fewer risks, then you would expect lesser returns, but those returns are more likely to be certain. However, if you take more risks, then you would expect greater returns, but there is also a much greater risk of your investment performing poorly.

The nature of your investments will vary depending on your attitude to risk and the returns you are looking for. One thing you should always remember is that any investment returns need to be greater than the rate of inflation to have any real effect. For instance, if inflation stands at 3 percent and your investment returns 2 percent, then you will actually make a loss of 1 percent. However, if the investment returns 5 percent, then you would have achieved a real return of 2 percent.

This is a book about your music career, not about financial investment. However, your investments are important because they have such a direct impact on your living standards, so you should always take proper financial advice before making any investment decision.

Pensions are eye-wateringly expensive, but there is a small bit of silver in this pension cloud. In most jurisdictions, pension contributions can be set against tax.

You should, of course, take advice in your jurisdiction to confirm whether these contributions are allowable for tax purposes, and if so, what conditions apply.

Some People Just Earn Less Than Others

I've thrown a lot of figures at you. I make no apologies for this: The factors affecting your take-home pay and your financial well-being are complicated.

Whatever your personal situation, you need to understand what will affect your earnings and how much money you need to be able to live your life at a reasonable standard. You then need to make some serious decisions about how you make money from music. Those decisions may be uncomfortable because two of the factors you will have to consider are:

- Does the music I am producing have sufficient commercial potential? Remember my example earlier about poets—a highly successful book of poetry may sell around 800 copies in a year. If the poet does really well and makes $3 for each book of poetry sold, that still only works out to $2,400 income, which really isn't enough to live on. Are you just being a musical poet, condemned to live your existence in poverty?

- Am I/are we really good enough? Or is the reason for your lack of income simply that you are rubbish?

If your music has sufficient commercial appeal and you're good, then you stand a fair chance of making a living, provided you cultivate and nurture your fan base.

End of Commercial Boot Camp

That's the end of the commercial stuff. In the next part I'm going to move on and look at how you can pull together all of the various elements to develop a career with forward momentum.

Putting the Theory into Practice

8 Building the Team around You

You might be wondering why it has taken so long for me to get to the chapter about building your team. After all, I have mentioned many of the people who will be in your team in several places throughout the book. Added to that, you have probably already figured that one person who can really help take your career to the next level is a manager.

Let me explain by adding one detail that I have yet to explicitly articulate. So far, I have suggested that you take a businesslike approach to your career in the music industry. However, I am actually going further than that and advocating that you establish your own business. I'm less concerned about whether you decide that the right course for you is to self-release an album or to go with a major record label. Whatever choice you make for how you get your product to your fan base, I am concerned that you treat your business as a business and ensure that it is properly managed.

That doesn't mean you have to become a businessman or businesswoman and turn up for work at 9 a.m. every morning (in a suit with a freshly laundered shirt and your umbrella under your arm) and then leave at 5 p.m. It does mean that you need the right attitude and you need to ensure that if you don't look after the business, then someone else (whom you trust completely) is attending to these details.

Structure of Your Business

There are many ways that you can legally structure your business—for instance, as a sole trader, a partnership, a partnership with limited liability, or a limited liability company. I'm not going to talk about these options here because they are irrelevant to the subject of your career. Another reason why I'm not going to talk about the structure of your business is that the options open to you will differ according to your jurisdiction.

If you are serious about your business, then I recommend you get legal and other professional advice, because there are many other implications that flow from the decisions you make about structure. In particular, there are issues of tax and personal liability. I will talk more about getting professional advice later in this chapter.

For the moment, I want to talk about how you structure your business in terms of the roles and responsibilities that people will play in driving your career forward.

Key Functions That Need to Be Performed

Any business has a range of people who will do different things to help the business. Take a look at any business, and you will probably find most of these people performing the following functions in one way or another (see Figure 8.1):

- The shareholders (or partners) own the business and are responsible for appointing the board.

- The board sets the strategy for the business.

- The management team implements the strategy set by the board, and each member of the board is accountable for his or her own performance.

- The workforce undertakes the work that makes the money for the business.

- Advisers (such as lawyers or business consultants) offer advice to the board and the management as is needed. This advice could be on a range of issues, from legal points to matters of strategy.

- Agents (in the broadest sense—not simply talent/booking agents) are appointed to undertake specific tasks on behalf of the business (for instance, to look after the business's computers).

So how does this apply to you and where do you fit in?

Most importantly, you, the musician, are the workforce. As with any business, it is the workforce who will make the money. The function of the management is to ensure that the product created by the workforce is sold for the best possible price and that the systems for selling the product are as efficient as possible to ensure that profits are maximized.

However, you are also the shareholder of the business—this is your business, after all. You should therefore also be an active member of the board, setting a strategy to propel your career forward.

Separate the Goals to Be Achieved from How You Achieve Your Goals

Before we go too much further in thinking about the team of people, I want to remind you about the range of choices you have.

There are many different things you can do in many different ways. Your focus should be on what you are trying to achieve financially, as well as on the artistic and marketing aspects. For instance, if you are thinking about producing T-shirts, you may have several aims. These could include:

- Making money from the sale of T-shirts

- Getting as many people as possible wearing your T-shirt to raise your profile

Who?   Does What?

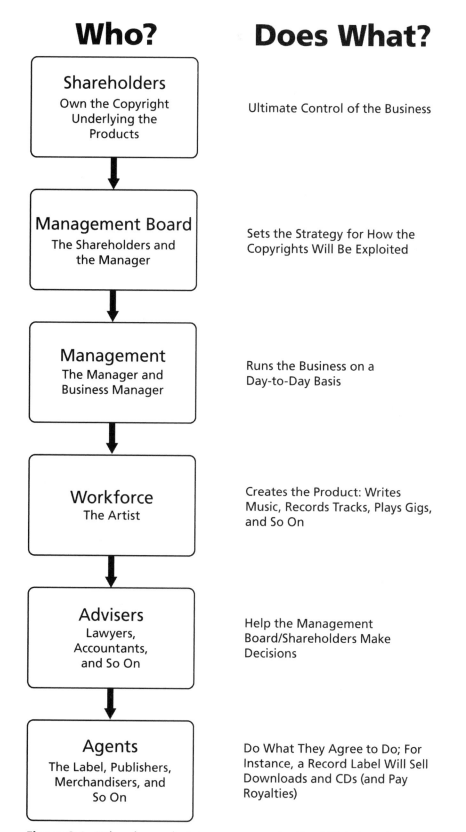

Shareholders
Own the Copyright
Underlying the
Products

Ultimate Control of the Business

Management Board
The Shareholders and
the Manager

Sets the Strategy for How the
Copyrights Will Be Exploited

Management
The Manager and
Business Manager

Runs the Business on a
Day-to-Day Basis

Workforce
The Artist

Creates the Product: Writes
Music, Records Tracks, Plays Gigs,
and So On

Advisers
Lawyers,
Accountants,
and So On

Help the Management
Board/Shareholders Make
Decisions

Agents
The Label, Publishers,
Merchandisers, and
So On

Do What They Agree to Do; For
Instance, a Record Label Will Sell
Downloads and CDs (and Pay
Royalties)

Figure 8.1 Who does what in your organization? This is a simple structure for organizing a business. See Figure 8.2 for an explanation as to how this becomes a practical reality.

There are many ways you could achieve these aims. These options include:

- Ordering some T-shirts printed with your design. (If you like hard work, you can order the stock and printing from different suppliers.) Sell the final product directly to your fan base.

- Using an on-demand service and marketing the T-shirts to your fan base. You may also find that the on-demand service generates a number of sales.

- Ordering some T-shirts and then supplying them to a range of outlets (primarily clothing stores).

- Licensing someone else to produce and sell T-shirts with your logo/branding.

Each of the different options will produce different results in terms of financial return to you and the size of the population that is reached with the product. Some options will realistically only reach your fan base; others are likely to reach lots of people who are not in your fan base.

The options also have differing financial risks from your perspective. As you increase the amount of stock you are holding without having firm orders, you will be increasing your financial risks and increasing the likely costs from storage and other associated expenses.

So, if you are looking for the lowest financial risk and the widest geographical coverage, you may want to consider licensing, although that option may not be the most immediately appealing. However, do remember that just because you have chosen one option, that doesn't close off the other options—for instance, you could license your product and sell a product directly. (You may even be able to sell your licensee's stock and generate more income than would be generated from the license fee alone.)

The key issue in this example is that the goal (for instance, to get as many people as possible wearing your T-shirt) is different from the method by which the goal is achieved (for instance, licensing). And remember, to have a valid career, you don't have to do everything yourself.

The Right People at the Right Time

Any business will need to expand or contract depending on various factors. For instance, if you run a toy shop, then you may need more staff during the Christmas season. By contrast, if you run a seaside hotel, you probably need a lot less staff during the winter period. (Clearly, the staff who aren't wanted in the hotel should go and work at the toy shop.)

As a musician with your own business, you don't necessarily need to have staff (that is, people who you directly employ and for whom you need to deduct tax and social costs from their wages). However, you will probably want a permanent relationship with certain people. For instance, you will want a permanent relationship with your manager—a manager's job should not be seasonal.

Then there are people whose services you will want only on a temporary basis. For instance, if you are going on tour, then you may need to hire a sound engineer for that tour. At the end of the tour, the sound engineer would then effectively cease to be an employee. When you next tour, you might hire the same sound engineer again, but the contract would still last only for the length of the tour.

As well as hiring people directly, you may outsource some of your tasks. In this instance, you pay someone else to do something for you. The benefit to you is that you don't have to find someone to undertake the task and, provided you find a suitable service provider, you will be looked after by people whose business is dedicated to performing that task, so you may be able to expect a higher service than if you undertook the task yourself. An example of this arrangement could be if you use a third party to mail out your CDs.

As you will understand, one of the key challenges to running a business is ensuring you bring in the right people for the business needs, and that appropriate service providers are appointed. This coordination is one of the key tasks that a manager will perform. If you don't have a manager (or someone fulfilling that function), then much of your day will be spent organizing other people.

I now want to look at who the team could be. I then want to think about some of the details of what you could expect from your team members and what they can expect from you (in other words, what you are likely to have to pay them).

One point you should note is that you don't necessarily need a separate person to fulfill each of these functions—you just need to make certain that someone has responsibility for ensuring that all of the necessary tasks are undertaken.

So Who Does What?

It is crucial to the success of your business that everyone knows what they are meant to be doing and understands what constitutes success.

If you hire a manager, then there is no point in you trying to undertake the functions the manager should be performing. Although you shouldn't try to do his job, you should ensure that the manager performs as expected. If performance is not up to standard, then you should end the relationship. Think about a business: If an executive isn't performing, he gets fired. Why should a manager be any different?

So who should be doing what? Take a look at Figure 8.2 for an example of how the parties work together.

The Shareholders and the Board

In legal terms, the shareholders (in the broadest sense) are the people who hold the copyrights underlying the products being marketed. So for instance, if you are a band and you all own the copyright to a sound recording (that is marketed as a CD or a download or may be licensed for use as a cell-phone ring tone), then you would be a shareholder.

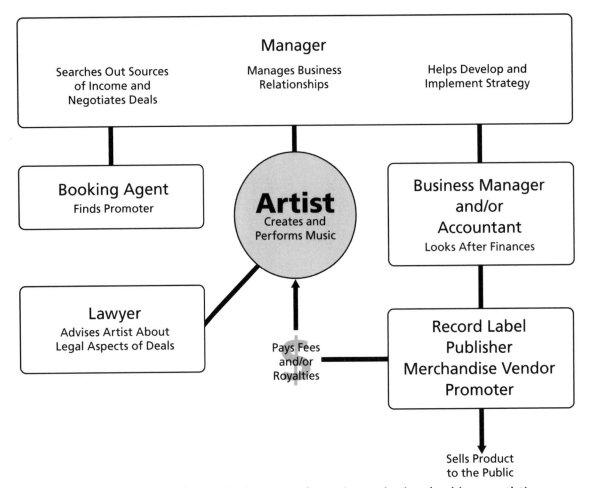

Figure 8.2 The working relationship between the main parties involved in an artist's career.

The board is there to represent the interests of the shareholders and to set the strategy for the business. You probably don't need the formality of many corporate board meetings; however, it is important that there is a forum for strategy to be discussed and agreed upon.

The board meeting should be open to more than just shareholders. For instance, your manager should have a lot to say about your strategy. (If she doesn't, why did you hire her?) You should ensure that she is present whenever strategy is being discussed—first for her input, and second because this is the person whose role it is to ensure that the strategy is implemented successfully.

The Management Team

The management team will implement the strategy set by the board and will be accountable for their performance to the board. There are two key players that you need:

- **A chief executive.** This person is in charge of running your business on a day-to-day basis while you are getting on with making music. This role usually is filled by your manager (sometimes called a *personal manager*).

- **A chief financial officer.** This is the person who looks after the commercial aspects of your business and is often called a *business manager*. This person will ensure that you get paid and that it's the right amount. Many artists do not have a separate business manager—they leave the function to their personal manager.

I will talk more about managers later in this chapter.

The Workforce

The workforce undertakes the work that makes the money for the business. As a musician, you are the workforce. The creation of music is a pure blue-collar occupation. Each day you will be working at the factory; whether your task is writing songs or playing a gig, your role is to manufacture the product that is then sold.

Advisers

You will need several key advisers to assist you in your career.

Perhaps the first adviser you will need is a lawyer. I'm sure you have heard countless tales of young, naïve bands who got ripped off. This tends to happen for two reasons: First, they have little negotiating power, and second, they haven't taken appropriate advice.

Half of this problem is dealt with by finding a lawyer. The other half of the problem is addressed by ensuring that you have as much negotiating power as possible. If you are running your career as a business and have adopted many of the principles set out in this book, then you will have much more negotiating clout than the average musician.

The other advisers you are likely to need early in your career will include:

- An accountant to advise you on finance and tax matters

- A banker to help provide funds to run your business

Picking the Team

I've outlined the various elements of the team. When building your team, you must think about several things.

Does the Team Work Together?

You need to make sure all of the people in your team work together. You need to ensure that everyone gets along—you don't want two advisers working for you who are suing each other. You also need to ensure that everyone understands the extent of their role—you don't want to pay for two people to perform the same task, and equally you don't want any gaps in responsibilities so that two people can say, "It wasn't my fault," when something goes wrong.

Hiring the Right People

You need to make sure you get the right people. Finding the people is hard enough—making sure you've got the right people when you've found them is even harder. When you're looking for people, ask around and get any recommendations. If possible, the first people you should talk to are the people who have been recommended more than once. Don't just look in a directory and hope to pick the right person because you like his name.

When you've got a shortlist, then get references on those people. Talk to their existing clients (and, if possible, former clients) to get a well-rounded picture of these people's business sense.

Finding the Person Who Actually Does the Work

When you are looking to build a team around you, you may not always be hiring a single person. For instance, if you are taking on a manager, then the manager may have associates. Equally, if you hire a lawyer, then you are probably actually hiring a firm of lawyers. This is a good thing. You want to know that there are other people around to support the person who is working for you.

However, you should be cautious. Many firms will put up a salesperson to bring in new business, and then once your account has been won, they let someone far more junior run the account. Again, this may not be a bad thing—the junior person may be very keen, very talented, and able to dedicate all of her waking hours to your business, plus she will have the resources of the bigger firm and more experienced colleagues to call upon.

However, it may be a bad thing: The junior may be an inept fool.

Whenever you are looking to appoint a new team member, ask who will be working for you. Get to meet that person and make sure she is the sort of person you want to work with. If she isn't, but you still like the organization, then ask to meet someone else who may fit better with you.

Errors and Omissions

What happens if someone else gets something wrong?

For instance, what happens if your accountant makes an error in calculating your tax figures, so you submit an incorrect tax return? Nothing, you may think, until your tax authority fines you and audits your books. This is a comparatively minor problem—there could be much bigger problems.

One way to protect yourself against any financial cost is to ensure that your advisers have errors and omissions insurance (often called *E&O insurance*, for obvious reasons). This is insurance to protect their business in case they make mistakes. This is good for you because first, they will have funds to be able to compensate you for their mistakes, and second, their business will not collapse if you raise an errors and omissions claim.

It might seem odd to want to ensure that their business does not go down the tubes. If you find any errors, you may want to take your business elsewhere; however, you probably want to ensure that you can extract yourself in a businesslike manner, rather than losing everything because their business has gone into liquidation.

You can expect professional advisers (such as your accountant and your lawyer) to carry errors and omissions insurance. However, you should confirm this. Some of the other parties you deal with may have some form of insurance, but it is unlikely to be as rigorous as that carried by your advisers.

The Shareholders

I want to look at the shareholders. As I indicated earlier, I am using the term "shareholder" in its broadest sense to mean anyone who owns the copyright that underlies a product that is created and anyone who may earn royalties through having sold/licensed his or her copyright. I am not intending this term to mean only those people who own part of the company if your business is incorporated.

The people who are most likely to be shareholders are:

- The songwriter(s).

- The artist(s)/band members who each own part of the copyright of a sound recording (or visual performance). Clearly, if you have signed with a major record company, you are unlikely to own your sound recordings; however, you will have an interest in the royalties generated from these recordings.

You may have other shareholders—for instance, the person who designed your artwork. To run your business efficiently, you may want to buy out other copyrights (such as the artwork).

The nature of music is such that you will almost never create a product on your own without any involvement from another person. You may write a composition with someone else, or you may perform with other musicians who have equal rights to you. Whenever you are collaborating, it is important that all of the shareholders work together. For instance, if you co-write a song, and your writing partner then seeks to block its release, not only is this frustrating, but it will stop both of you from earning money.

For this reason, it is important that all shareholders have a common understanding of how their assets are going to be exploited (for the benefit of all shareholders). The most straightforward way to establish and document this understanding is through a written agreement between the shareholders. This could take the form of a band agreement or similar document.

Perhaps the hardest challenge you will face with your co-shareholders is recognizing that you can't fire these people. These will be people with whom you will always have some link (like two divorced parents), so think hard before you go into business with someone else.

The Manager

In the conventional way of thinking, you want to find an experienced manager, because these people know the key executives at several record labels and will have credibility with those people. The supposed benefit for you is that the manager can walk into the record label with your demo, and you stand a really good chance of being signed. There's no need to worry that you're a bit of a rough diamond; your manager will be able to help the record company see what they are signing.

There is a lot of truth in this view—or rather, there *was* a lot of truth.

As you might expect, in a changing world, managers are changing, too. Many are getting more entrepreneurial, rather than being pugnacious bruisers. Recognizing major record companies are signing less talent and that due to the increasing number of small labels, they can't have a relationship with everyone, managers are now putting a greater emphasis on artist development.

Instead of approaching record companies with a diamond in the rough, managers are approaching record companies with a polished product (an act with an image, a professionally recorded and produced album, a video, and so on). By taking the development uncertainty and presenting a record company with a product that is ready to be launched, managers are helping recording companies to significantly reduce their risks.

Another reason why the relationship between managers and record companies is now much less significant is that the income artists generate from record companies (as a percentage of total earnings) is now less significant (although you do still need the central product—the music—from which to generate the spinoffs). As we have already seen, there are many more sources of income from which a manager can negotiate deals. This also means that there is much more a manager needs to understand (and, of course, far more for a manager to get wrong).

So that explains something of what managers can do for themselves. What could a manager do to help you?

What Can a Manager Do to Help You?

There are several main areas where a manager can help you. It is easy to suggest that any one of these areas may be more important than the other; however, in practice, when you are looking for a manager, you want someone who can bring all of these strands together (whether on her own or through bringing together a team of people).

Strategy

You may not believe it, but you do need a strategy. You need to understand:

- Where you are going

- How you are going to get there

Strategy in the broadest sense should be discussed and agreed upon at board meetings, and your manager should be there giving his view about the strategies you should be following. However, strategy then needs to be implemented on a day-to-day basis and refined for a particular situation. Your manager should have a firm grasp of this aspect of your business.

Business Administration

You are running a business. Someone should make sure everything that is meant to be happening is in fact happening.

This means you need someone who understands how business works. That person will need to understand how your income from each and every one of your income sources is calculated and when payment can be expected. He will also need to take action if the money is not forthcoming. Once you have been in business for a while, you may have hundreds, if not thousands, of sources, so your manager must have robust systems (computer databases, paper filing, and so on), or else you will lose money.

You may well use a business manager (and the role of the business manager is discussed in a moment). If you are using a business manager, then your manager should ensure that the business manager is on top of her job.

Representation

You need someone to go out and find deals and/or create income for you. Your manager should be the person who finds deals, brings them to you, and negotiates the deal. This may be a deal with a record company; it may be a deal with a publisher; it may be a deal with a CD-pressing plant; it may be a deal with a merchandiser. It doesn't matter who the deal is with. Your concern is that:

- The deal is good for you (both financially and for your reputation).

- You are being represented in the best light. You don't want a manager who makes promises and threats that may be embarrassing to you.

- There are no side deals that benefit your manager but not you. He may have negotiated a good deal for you; however, this counts for little if he should have negotiated a great deal.

Who Should You Get as a Manager?

Artists often have a dilemma when they consider a manager—whether to go with a more experienced or a less experienced manager.

The advantage of a more experienced manager is, well, experience. You can expect this person to know the business and to be competent. However, if a manager is competent and experienced, then she will have other clients, and so the question for you is whether this manager will give you the time you need to help you develop your career (if she will even consider signing you).

You may also find that because the experienced manager already has a perfectly adequate source of income, she may take a rather laidback approach to your career. After all, the manager won't starve if you don't get a deal.

The advantage of a less experienced manager is that she has everything to prove and everything to lose. You can therefore expect this person to work every hour of every day to further your career. The disadvantage is obvious: A less (or zero) experienced manager has less (or zero) experience.

However, don't dismiss a less experienced manager. If she has bucket loads of get-up-and-go and really *can* make things happen, then that person might be just what you need to kick-start your career. If your manager believes in you, then she is likely to be happy to work for a greatly reduced fee while you have minimal earnings. If your manager genuinely has business sense, then she will help you to start earning money. If she doesn't, then you may wish to end the relationship.

Between the two extremes you will find a range of people. My only suggestion in dealing with these people is to beware of anyone whose business and acts are mediocre. Some people can see the good in others; some can see the bad: The manager of mediocre acts can see mediocrity. They will find the mediocrity in you and convince you that it is what you wanted. If you want a career that is, at best, adequate, knock on these people's door. If you want more, then run screaming if you ever find these people.

What Does a Manager Charge?

Each deal will be different, but as a general rule of thumb, a manager will charge 20 percent of your gross earnings (that is, 20 percent of what you earn before any expenses). You may find that there is a commonly accepted figure in your jurisdiction. You shouldn't simply accept any figure, but rather seek to set a figure that is right for you.

Some managers charge less (for instance, 15 percent), and some will try to charge more. If you have huge earning potential, then you may be able to negotiate below the 15 percent figure. However, if your earning potential is that great, you've probably got a very successful career already, and you may feel you don't need to read this book.

Many artists have perished on the rock of not understanding the difference between net and gross. These are two technical terms that you must understand, because the implications are so significant. As a start, gross is usually a big number, and net is a smaller number (hence managers want their fees calculated on gross figures).

Your gross earnings are your earnings before any deductions. Your net earnings are what you are left with after all deductions. (You may even be left with a net loss—even with a gross profit.)

Say you have a tour, and it generates $1 million. In this case, your gross earnings would be $1 million. If your manager takes 20 percent of your gross earnings, then his fee would be $200,000.

Now, say you had costs associated with the tour of $1.1 million. In this case, your net loss would be $100,000. However, it gets worse if your manager is on a gross-earnings deal, because you will have paid him $200,000, giving you a net loss of $300,000 (while your manager still gets paid).

For this reason, many artists do not like their managers getting paid on gross (especially for touring income).

However, the manager's counterargument to this is that many tour expenses can be constrained. Taking this example further, the $1,100,000 spent on the tour may, to a great extent, be directly attributable to the artist's insistence that the whole of the band and the crew stay in five-star hotels and drink the most expensive champagne every night. Perhaps without those extravagant expenses, the tour could have made a profit.

Accordingly, if a manager is going to take a percentage of a non-gross figure, he will probably want to constrain certain expenses—for instance, the manager may limit hotel expenses to a certain figure.

One area to pay careful attention is what the manager's fee is a percentage of. This is something you should ask your lawyer to look at in detail.

Historically, managers' fees have been in the 15 to 20 percent range because the manager is running his own business. The manager has an office to pay for, staff to pay for, and so on. However, if you are expecting a manager to run your office with your business, then it may not be necessary for your manager to have his own separate overhead. This would imply that you may be able to negotiate a lower fee.

You may also find that a manager doesn't want a percentage of gross earnings; instead, he wants a share of the profits. This is much riskier, so it is likely that the share of profits (that is, net profits) will be much higher. A manager may particularly want this kind of deal if he is being more entrepreneurial and developing the act himself. If the manager is taking more risk, then he will expect more reward.

One last thing to think about when deciding on your manager's remuneration is the issue of post-term commission. In other words, how much are you going to continue to pay your manager after his contract has ended? For instance, if the manager negotiates a record deal, then he may expect some payment for this work. However, if the contract ends before the first payment under the deal is made, you may not want to pay (especially if you have a new manager in place who is taking a percentage).

Clearly, this could lead to much unhappiness on all sides, so you may want to think about the point sooner rather than later. Again, this is an area where your lawyer will be able to give you some very useful advice.

The Business Manager

The nature of business managers can vary greatly according to the requirements of the act and local custom.

The identity of the business manager and the manner in which the functions are carried out are irrelevant. For an act running its business on a sound footing, it is important that someone undertakes the functions of the business manager. This someone could be the act's manager, or it could be an accountant. It doesn't matter who, as long as the functions are undertaken.

What Does a Business Manager Do?

The nature of what a business manager does will vary depending on your needs. However, the main functions you can expect a business manager to perform are:

- Monitoring money received and money paid. This may sound simple, but remember that you may have hundreds of sources of income that each need to be individually monitored, verified, and accounted for.

- Agreeing budgets (in other words, agreeing how much money can be spent), which may include budgets for recording, making videos, or tour support.

In some jurisdictions (such as the U.S.), it is quite common for a business manager to also act as a financial adviser and advise about investments. In other jurisdictions, this practice is uncommon. (For instance, in the UK, financial advisers need to be regulated, so it is rare for business managers to perform this function.)

What Does a Business Manager Charge?

There are many different ways that business managers will be paid. The fee structure usually depends on the nature of the relationship.

- Some business managers are paid a salary. You may expect to pay a salary (which may be broadly comparable to what the person could earn if she worked for, say, an accounting firm) if you employ someone directly. One advantage of having a business manager on the payroll is that she may also be able to act in other functions (for instance, she may be able to also work as your tour accountant).

- Some business managers expect to be paid an hourly rate (in other words, you pay $X for each hour the business manager spends working on your account). This is the kind of arrangement you may expect if you hire a firm of accountants to perform the functions of a business manager.

- Other business managers may charge a percentage of (gross) earnings. A typical indicative percentage may be around 10 percent. The business managers who are most likely to look for this sort of fee arrangement are those whose business is being a business manager. These are often accountants who set up their own business-management businesses (as opposed to their own accountancy practices).

One of the most influential factors determining a business manager's fee is the manager's fee. If you are paying your manager 20 percent, then it may not be unreasonable to expect that she will provide (or procure) the services of a business manager. It would certainly be regarded as expensive to pay 30 percent in management fees (20 percent to your manager and 10 percent to your business manager).

Risks in Hiring a Business Manager

There are risks in hiring a business manager, in the same way that there are risks in hiring a manager. One of the biggest risks may be your assumptions. Just because someone holds himself out as a business manager, that does not mean he is an accountant. (It doesn't even mean that the person is competent.)

It isn't necessary for your business manager to be an accountant, nor is it mandatory that your business manager be regulated by an accountancy body. However, if you are considering working with someone who is not regulated, then you should consider the level of risk you are taking with your business. See the "Errors and Omissions" section earlier in this chapter.

Lawyers

You have probably heard countless tales of young artists being ripped off. The simplest way to reduce your risk of being treated shabbily is to find a good lawyer.

A good lawyer will do several things for you:

- Explain what each legal document actually means. You can probably read a contract and understand what each word means. Your lawyer should be able to take that concept forward and explain what the contract (or other document) means in terms of your income (in particular, how much and when) and your obligations (for instance, you may be entering a deal that will take up the next 15 years of your life).

- As well as explaining what each contract means, your lawyer should be able to give you some sense about whether you are entering a good deal or a bad deal. The lawyer will have experience in the area in which the deal is being done (if he doesn't, then run away) and so will be able to tell you about similar deals he has come across.

A lawyer cannot guarantee you will get a good deal. If there is only one deal on the table, and it is a take-it-or-leave-it deal, then all your lawyer will be able to do is warn you about the risks. In this case, the lawyer cannot make the deal financially better, although he may steer you away from disaster.

Which Lawyer Should You Appoint?

As with appointing any professional adviser, you should always look for personal recommendations when appointing a lawyer.

When you do appoint a lawyer, it is particularly important to find one who has experience in the music industry and music-industry practices. Given the long-term nature of deals within the industry, advice from a less than competent lawyer can cause you problems over a very long period. Indeed, poor legal advice may end your career.

Ideally, you should appoint a lawyer you trust and respect and with whom you can develop a long-term, mutually beneficial relationship.

How Much Do Lawyers Charge?

Lawyers' charges depend on the jurisdiction within which the lawyer is operating and the rules of the body that regulates the lawyer (assuming the lawyer is regulated).

In the UK, lawyers are typically paid on an hourly basis, so you will pay an agreed-upon fee for each hour that a lawyer works on your account. Subject to appropriate disclosures and client agreement, fees can be adjusted for other contingencies (essentially success-based criteria); however, this practice is quite unusual in the UK.

In the U.S., hourly rates are still used, but they may be less common in the entertainment industry. Some lawyers are kept on a retainer so the client pays a monthly fee and the lawyer advises as necessary. Other lawyers charge a percentage of the deal on which they are working. A typical percentage may be around 5 percent. A third option that some lawyers adopt is value billing, which is where a fee is charged according to how much value a lawyer feels she has added to a deal. This is likely to be a percentage of any increase to the financial terms of the deal.

However you structure the remuneration, you should have a clear indication of how her fees will be calculated before you instruct the lawyer to start work for you. Ideally, you will have the fee agreed upon up front. If this is not possible, then you should aim to set a limit on the fee that the lawyer cannot exceed without your agreement.

On the subject of lawyers and fees, I would add a word of caution: Always pay your lawyer. Lawyers know how to sue people—there are many lawyers who spend the whole of their professional lives suing people for their clients. If you don't pay your lawyer, she will sue you, and this will be an easy and cheap thing for the lawyer to do. And don't think you can fight lawyers by taking them to court. You are likely to find it very hard to find another lawyer who will help you to take legal action against your lawyer.

Accountants

The main function of accountants is, as the name suggests, to account for things. In other words, they count and make a record of everything.

Your accountant will be able to tell you how much income you have received and how much you have spent. He will also be able to tell you what you have not received that you should have. Many accountants will also advise you on tax-related matters (including VAT/purchase taxes and National Insurance/social charges) and will help you structure your business in a way that is most efficient from a tax perspective.

As with lawyers, you should look to appoint an accountant who has experience in the music industry. There are several (quite legitimate) practices in the industry that may cause confusion for accountants who are not aware of the practices. For instance, it can take a long time to receive your earnings—possibly even years. Accountants without the necessary experience may have difficulty giving you a true understanding of your financial position.

Most accountants will charge an hourly fee. However, as with lawyers, you will find other accountants whose fees can be calculated in other ways.

Bankers

We've already looked at some of the role of banks in the "Sources of Finance" section in Chapter 6.

In short, there are three things you can expect your bank to do:

- Receive money on your behalf (whether in the form of cash, checks, direct credit transfers, or credit cards) and then look after that money for you.

- Pay money on your behalf. (Again, this may be by direct credit transfer, check, or some other form of transfer.)

- Loan money to you. These loans may take several forms, including an overdraft facility or a loan made directly to you.

One other thing you can expect from a bank is for them to shut you down if you don't pay back money you borrow.

You can find banks in your local neighborhood that will provide basic banking facilities. When you are first starting, these banks may be ideal for your purposes. However, you are likely to be treated like any other customer and will probably find that any loan applications are decided according to criteria that are applied by a central loans department. The result of this may be that you are seen as a high risk (and face it, music is a high-risk business), so you will be turned down.

Once you reach a certain level of success and income, you will be able to make use of more specialized banking sections. You should look for a bank with a department that specializes in creative industries. Once you get hooked in with these people, you will find you are treated much more like a regular business customer.

Booking Agents/Promoters

There are several ways to get gigs. When you first start off, you will probably arrange your own gigs and take whatever you can get as a fee. This may be a couple of beers and a small amount of cash to cover gas; it may be less. If you have a manager, then she will spend a large part of her time trying to find gigs for you until you become an established act (when hopefully you have something of a following and so gigs are easier to book).

Booking Agents

As you start to develop a reputation, you may find that you can use the services of a booking agent who will find gigs for you. The main advantages of a booking agent are:

- He will have a range of contacts and so should be able to get you more gigs over a wider geographical area.

- He should be able to get better fees (since he takes a percentage).

- He will free your and your manager's time (as well as cut your phone bills).

For this, the booking agent may take a fee in the range of 10 to 15 percent of the gross figure negotiated for the gig (and often the manager's fee will then be calculated on the gross figure less the agent's fee). Usually, a booking agent will expect exclusivity from his client. This exclusivity may be limited to a geographic region.

Promoters

The role of the promoter is more venue-specific than a booking agent. A promoter is the person who arranges the entertainment at the venue for the night when you are playing. She will hire the venue and sell the tickets. In other words, this is the person who is hiring you and the person who will be responsible for making sure all of your riders are met (which can range from requiring that certain equipment be provided or certain food be made available, to insisting that the dressing rooms are painted with green, pink, and purple stripes).

Some promoters will work with just one venue, others with a range, and some work nationally.

The artist and the booking agent are both dependent on the promoter for their income. The promoter will be reliant on ticket sales and other income that can be generated (for instance, from advertising/sponsorship; concession stands, such as hot dog stalls; the bar; and so on).

At lower levels, the artist's fee will often be a fixed amount. As the artist can negotiate better deals, the fee will usually be a percentage of net receipts (in other words, after the promoter has met as many expenses as she legitimately can). Depending on your clout, your booking agent may be able to negotiate an advance (often called a *guaranteed minimum*) from the promoter. Naturally, this advance will be recouped before you start to receive any share of the net profit.

When you get into the big league, a split of net profits can be in the 80 to 90 percent range (in the artist's favor and before the booking agent and the manager take their shares). However, you can really expect these figures only when you start selling out arenas. Before then, these figures are just a nice aspiration.

Alternatives to Booking Agents and Promoters

You don't need a booking agent or a promoter to put on a gig. However, they can prove useful allies to have on your team because they can provide a large chunk of upfront payment as well as reduce your risks.

If you have your own fan base, then there are other options. The first main option is that you can put on your own gigs. This cuts the cost of the booking agent and the promoter. The downside to this approach is that you are taking the whole risk and assuming responsibility for organizing every detail. (For instance, do you know where to find security people or cleaners for the venue, if these are not provided?)

Another alternative, as noted in Chapter 6, is for you to bring your fan base to the promoter and receive a commission (from the promoter) for all sales you make.

Merchandising

As I illustrated at the start of this chapter, there are many channels you can use to make your merchandising available. Remember, merchandising is much more than just T-shirts—it can cover a range of goods, including clothing (hats, scarves, sweatshirts, hoodies, and anything else you can think of to wear), posters, programs, buttons (badges), stickers, patches, mugs, dolls, and so on.

In essence you have two choices: procure your own merchandise and sell it yourself, or license someone else. If you sell the merchandise yourself, then you need to order and hold this stock (which involves investment). If you license a third party, then your main role is to approve the merchandise and sit back and wait for the royalties.

There are many reasons why you may wish to consider appointing a merchandising firm.

- A compelling reason for appointing a merchandising firm is that they may pay you an advance.

- By appointing a merchandiser, you take yourself out of the whole process, so you don't need to order T-shirts, store them, and market them. That being said, if it is in your financial interest or if there is demand from the fan base, you may still want to sell your own T-shirts.

- Hopefully, even though you will be paid a royalty and will not be taking the full profit, you should be able to generate more income. There are two reasons why your income may increase. First, a firm dedicated to merchandising should be able to get the product to market for a cheaper price than you can. Second, a professional merchandising firm should be able to sell the product at many more outlets.

As a rough (and not particularly helpful) indicator, a merchandiser may pay you anything in the region of 20 to 80 percent of the retail price (less VAT and other sales taxes and credit card charges).

It should go without saying that you need control over copyrights to license other parties to produce your merchandise. For instance, if don't own the copyright to your logo, then it is likely that the copyright owner could expect to generate some income from merchandise licensing.

Record Company

In Chapter 6, I looked at the income you might be able to generate from a record company when you release a CD. Now I want to talk about some of the benefits of working with a record label, beyond the fact that they will pay you. In other words, why would you want a label as part of your team?

As well as having a certain degree of financial clout, a record label is also likely to have certain strengths. These strengths include:

- **Marketing.** The record company will have tried most methods of marketing and is likely to have a very good idea about what will work and what won't. Also, as a regular buyer of advertising, the record company will be able to negotiate the best price. As an act working on your own, there is no way you would be able to negotiate deals as favorable as those a record company can negotiate. Their marketing expertise is also likely to give a significant input into the act's strategy.

- **Funding.** As you have seen, a new act needs financing in a number of areas—for instance, to record an album, to tour, and to live. Rather than borrow money from a bank, the record label can pay an advance against future earnings.

- **Logistics.** Record companies are well experienced at the mechanics of getting CDs pressed (for the cheapest price and at a high quality) and getting CDs distributed through any and all retail outlets. If the record company does handle the logistics, then they will involve wholesalers and distributors, both of whom will take a cut (which increases the record company's expenses and so indirectly reduces your income).

- **Globalization.** Many artists are able to find a level of fame in their own country. However, reaching out to an audience outside of their country can be difficult (although it is getting easier). Many record companies have the infrastructure to help artists in their global ambitions.

Clearly, different record labels are going to have different strengths and differing financial resources. As I've said for several other issues, look at what you're trying to achieve. If your aim is to get your product distributed efficiently, then a label can probably perform that task better than you. If you believe that a large-scale marketing campaign is what you need, then you probably want to find a label. However, if you're after a marketing campaign, you should perhaps ask yourself why your efforts haven't been as successful as you would have hoped before you approach a label (because the label is likely to ask itself this question).

The downsides to doing a deal with a record company are that they will take a lot of the money you earn, and they will want you to assign the copyrights of your recordings to them.

There are some other apparent downsides. For instance, you will sign exclusively with a record label. However, I'm not sure this is such a problem in practice. Most record companies understand the commercial value of collaborations (especially when it helps you reach a wider market) and will not stand in the way of this sort of work (as long as it is going to make them some money).

Do also remember that record companies are commercial organizations with staff and shareholders that need to be paid. If you are intending to enter into any arrangement with a record company, then your product must be commercially viable from their perspective. To be commercially viable from the record company's perspective, an album will need to sell enough copies to provide a large chunk of income for the record company.

If the record company takes the view that your album will not sell sufficient numbers so it can make a profit, then it will not enter into a deal with you.

Publishers

If you are a songwriter, you can publish your own songs and collect all of the royalties that are due by joining the appropriate collection societies around the world. This is feasible; however, if your record is released in more than a few territories (which could be the case if you have a European hit), then it is a tedious task, and the administration will become very long-winded (not least of all because you will need to speak a lot of different foreign languages to join the foreign collection societies).

If you want to streamline this administration, it makes a lot of sense to appoint an expert to undertake this on your behalf. The experts in administering songwriters' rights are the publishers, so you could ask a publisher to administer your songs on your behalf.

Under an administration deal, you would retain the copyright for your songs and for a fee (typically in the region of 10 to 15 percent) the publisher would collect your royalties and remit them back to you. You would not normally expect an advance under this sort of deal.

However, if you go for an administration deal, then the publisher will administer only your catalogue. In addition to the administration, you may want other services from your publisher, such as:

- An advance

- Covers for your songs (in other words, you want your publisher to look for other artists to record your songs)

- TV/film use (in other words, you want your publisher to find ways for your songs to be used in TV and films)

If you want the money or these sorts of services, then you will probably have to enter into a sub-publishing deal or an exclusive publishing arrangement. Both of these are likely to involve you in selling (or long-term licensing) your copyrights.

Under a sub-publishing or an exclusive publishing deal, the publisher may take around 20 to 25 percent of your gross income (but might take more or less, depending on the deal you can cut). You should be aware that the systems in the UK and the U.S. for calculating songwriting royalties differ. However, the end percentage that is paid may be reasonably similar at the end of the day.

For further details of what you could expect from a publishing deal, check out the "Songwriting Royalties" section in Chapter 6.

Putting the Team to Work

So that's the team in place. Let's move on and look at how you can bring all the elements together to propel your career forward.

9 Developing Your Own Career Plan

I hope that by now you've realized that the strategy I am outlining in the book is really quite simple; there are essentially two strands:

- First, find a fan base. When you have the fan base, cherish these people so that you can nurture and grow your fan base.

- Second, collect lots of small (and perhaps less small) pieces of income from lots of different sources. Whatever you do, ensure that you don't miss any small piece of income. If you are running an efficient and low-cost-base business, then all of these small pieces of income will form a significant stream of earnings that can easily get lost if you have disproportionate overheads.

This is a robust and scalable business model that allows for great flexibility—for instance, if you want to sign up with a major record label for part of your career, you can. The principles are also applicable to any musician, irrespective of genre.

The Jigsaw Puzzle of Your Career

Before we look at the issue of scalability of your business, I want to draw out a few points about this chapter. First, let me state a few blunt truths that I hope are self-evident:

- Just because you have produced an album, that does not mean you have a career.

- Just because you are the most talented musician who has ever walked the Earth, that does not mean you will have a career making music.

To have a career, you need to focus on strategy. The success of your career, like a successful military operation, is based on strategy and logistics. Once you have the basics (that is, you can actually create music that people want to listen to), then it's all about what you do and when. The only differentiating factor between those who succeed and those who do not is implementation.

If you cannot implement a strategy to achieve your goals, then you will fail.

This chapter is about putting together all of the pieces that are necessary for a successful career to create a cohesive strategy. To think about it another way, this chapter is about defining your own roadmap to success.

A Question of Scale

The issue of scalability is important, and I've already briefly mentioned the topic in several places.

In many ways, it is very easy to run a one-person business. The difficulty with one-person businesses is that they can only generate so much income—there are only 24 hours in a day, and the person running the business needs to sleep and so on. To generate more income, the business needs to grow.

To a certain extent, anyone working in the music business has scale constraints. For instance, you may find it hard to play more than 365 gigs in a year. (In fact, if you play 200 gigs a year without burning out, then you're doing well.) You cannot play more shows than you are physically able to.

Simply growing your business is not enough: You need to increase the revenue and increase the profitability while reducing the risks that your business is taking. If you can't grow your business, you can always look at ways to make it more profitable. The ways to make a business more profitable are to cut expenses (which you can achieve by a number of means, including cutting staff numbers and using cheaper suppliers) and to increase your prices (see Figure 9.1). These are both quite drastic actions.

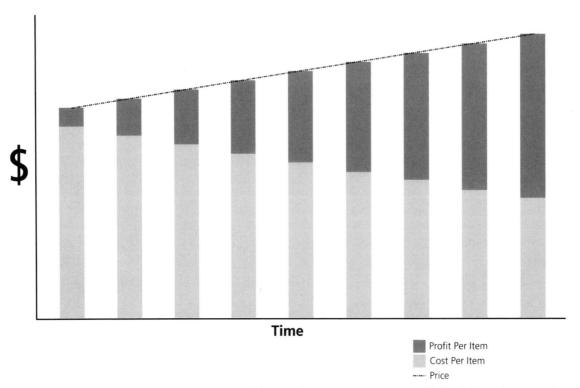

Figure 9.1 By increasing your prices and decreasing your costs, you will find that the combined effect leads to a rapid increase in the profit you generate on each item.

There are several ways to scale up your business. Here are a few examples:

- **Create more (profitable) products.** There is probably a practical limit to the number of songs you can write and therefore the number of tracks/albums/CDs you can release. Also, there is a limit to the amount of music that your fan base will buy. However, you can increase your range of products by producing DVDs and merchandise.

- **Take on staff (who you can pay lower wages) to undertake functions you had previously carried out.** This works if you can then use your free time to create more income. If you take on new staff and don't create more income, then all you have done is increase your costs (and waste profits).

- **Play bigger gigs.** As I have already mentioned, there is probably a limit to the number of gigs you can play, and this limit is probably determined by the physical stresses that gigging will place on all of the musicians' bodies. Therefore, to generate more income from touring, you can play bigger gigs. Bigger gigs are more expensive to stage and hence may increase risk. However, they do offer the potential to generate more revenue. If you feel like grabbing even more money from your fan base, then you can also look at increasing the price of tickets at gigs as another way to increase your income still further!

Figure 9.2 shows how you can significantly increase your profits by scaling up your business. In this figure, the increasing profitability shown in Figure 9.1 is multiplied by increasing sales. The combination allows for profitability to grow by a considerable amount.

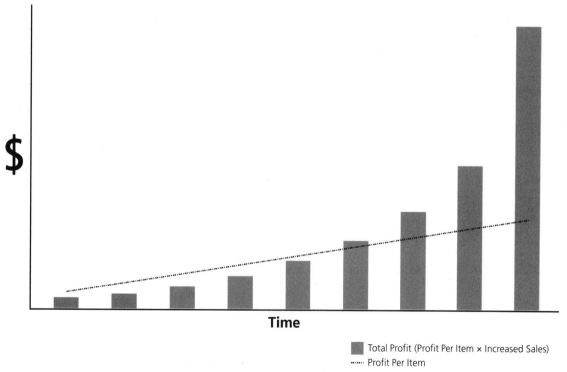

Figure 9.2 When you multiply increasing profitability by increased sales, your profitability can grow rapidly.

However, as you scale up your business (that is, as your business grows because you are more successful), there is danger that you will be less efficient as your costs grow. In particular, you are going to need to build a team around you, and with a group of people, as well as the wage bill, there is an inherent inefficiency. However, that inefficiency can be managed, and you should be able to counteract it with a greatly increased income due to the increased sales (which is the reason why you would have needed to hire people in the first place).

In scaling up your business, as well as retaining the efficiency, you must make sure you continue to exploit the foundations of your business. So make sure you continue to take advantage of the speed with which you can create and release products; the direct link to, and communication with, your fan base; and your low-cost operation. The easiest way to lose these advantages is to get swept up with an entourage and a bunch of hangers-on who will drain the life out of your business and bleed its finances dry.

Reducing Risks and Increasing the Certainty of a Sustained Career

You can generate income without a fan base (for instance, you can license your music for use with TV, video, or film, or you might find a patron to sponsor you). However, it is far riskier to focus your long-term career on a single source (or a limited number of sources of income) than it is to put in the time to build a broad fan base. You can afford to lose one or two fans, although I recommend that you try not to. However, if you only have (say) two sources of income, and you lose both of them, then you're in trouble. Added to which, if you're relying on individuals to give you work, then you're effectively an employee—I'm advocating that you become self-employed and direct your own work.

It may take longer, and it may be slower, to build a career on a solid fan base when compared to the apparent quick buck of getting a recording contract (or getting hired by anyone else). However, when you build your own fan base, you start to get results sooner because you can earn money immediately, rather than having to wait until you have repaid all of your record-company advances. Also, with the more solid foundation, as well as reducing your risks, you are increasing your chances of having a long-term career.

You've probably heard the old saying that it's not about *what* you know, it's *who* you know that matters in the music industry. This is true, but many people misinterpret this idea. Many people think this means that all you need to do is become acquainted with a senior person at a record label (or a well-known producer or something similar), and you will have a career for life.

This couldn't be further from the truth. In reality, the person you need to know is each one of your fans, individually. Once you understand these people and know what they want, then you will produce product that they will buy. Once you have a stream of income flowing from your fans, you have the basis of a career.

Now that I've reinforced the messages of this book, I want to do several things with this chapter:

- Pull together all of the various strands that were discussed in the earlier chapters

- Look at how the elements can then be developed into a strategy

- Talk about how to start implementing this theoretical strategy in practice

In short, this chapter is about your strategy, and you need a strategy for several reasons:

- First, you and your collaborators need to agree upon how you will proceed together.

- Second, if you are going to borrow money or look for an investor, you will need a business plan. Your business strategy will form the basis of a business plan, which you can present to a lender or an investor. Without a coherent business strategy, you will find that no one (apart from family, friends, and fools) will give you any of his money.

The Arc of Your Career

Without wishing to sound like a tearful Hollywood actress, grasping an award and mindlessly blubbering about the wonderful arc of her character, let me talk about the arc of your career.

First, let me explain what I mean by the arc of your career.

When you start out, you will start from nothing. Over time, you will gradually build a fan base until you reach the point at which you can be self-supporting. As you progress further (provided everything goes well), you will reach the point where you are making a good living from your career. If you reach superstar status, this is the point at which you will be thinking about a Rolls-Royce; a Ferrari; properties in London, Paris, New York, and your own private island in the South Pacific; a boat or two; a plane or two; and any other dreams that may come to mind.

From this peak, your career is then likely to decline over time. This happens to all artists and is quite natural. It doesn't mean your career is over; it's simply the case that you are not at the peak earning power. For examples of this, look at Sir Paul McCartney or the Rolling Stones. These two are no longer at the peak of their earning power, but they still have highly lucrative careers.

The arc of your career is the pattern by which your success rises, reaches a peak (which will hopefully be a long peak), and then falls. Your career may not necessarily follow a perfect arc—for instance, you may have several peaks (or several troughs if you are of a less optimistic frame of mind); however, it is not uncommon to follow this general pattern. Perhaps the most unknowable factor is how high the peak will be.

That being said, the idea of going from nothing to being a superstar overnight (a hero from zero) may be appealing. However, it may not be the best course. One of the key advantages of a measured and managed growth is that you can gain hands-on experience about how your business works (and from a performing point of view, you don't do your growing up in public). This knowledge will be invaluable when your business grows, especially when you need to hire other people to help you, because you will know what to expect from the business, as you have already run it yourself.

The reason I am introducing the notion of the arc of your career is that I want to give some context around the strategies I am going to outline. Different business strategies may be appropriate at different points in your career. As well as defining your strategy at certain points, you have to find a way to seamlessly transition from one strategy to another as your business grows. If you can't manage change, then you will find that your career may not evolve in the way you hope.

The points I'm going to identify on the career arc are, by their nature, very generic. Please don't see this as a career map, but rather as an indication of the main stages that your business may pass through.

Figure 9.3 shows a typical arc of a career and highlights the main areas through which your career will pass.

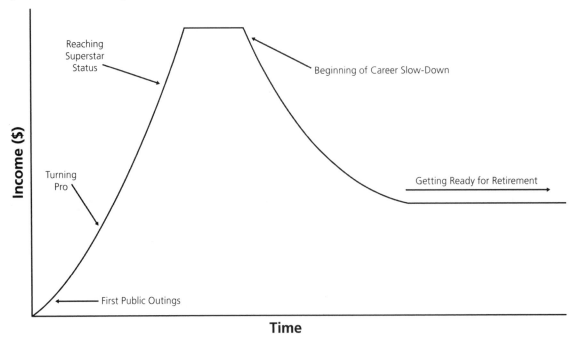

Figure 9.3   A typical career arc.

Preparation for Your Career

When you are starting, the only finances that your business is likely to have on hand are the money in your bank account and any loose change you can find down the back of the sofa.

This lack of money is a good thing: It means you can't go and spend money on stupid things, such as recording your first album in the most expensive recording studio in town. One recommendation I would make (and this is about as far from rock and roll as it is possible to be) is to start saving. It doesn't matter how or where, just start saving. If you're smart, you'll put your money somewhere where you can get interest (ideally tax free). You are going to need investment in your career—this is where your savings will help you.

When you start out, you should have one focus: to create some good music. There's little point in trying to reach out and find a fan base if you don't have any music for them to listen to or if all you've got is a really poor recording of a few turgid songs.

You need to take time to learn your craft and to improve your skills. If you are intending to create an act that will be performing songs you have written, you need to ensure that your songwriting skills are as good as your skills as a musician. Learn as much as you can and, if possible, learn from the experts.

It may seem that this apparent lack of action goes against everything I have said so far in that I'm not saying get out and gig on the day after you first pick up a guitar. However, it is a smarter strategy: If you start before you are ready, then you will just look like a fool in public. As well as losing credibility you never really had, all you will do is land your business in debt. Once you're in debt, your expenses will double: You will have to pay interest on your debts as well as paying living expenses.

That being said, please learn to distinguish between preparation and procrastination.

First Public Outings: Accelerated Learning

When you are confident of your basic skills as a musician, performer, and songwriter—and you have developed your first products—you are ready to take the next step: reaching out and looking for a fan base.

At this stage of your career, you will probably find that you have a lot of time between public outings. This is a good thing—it gives you more opportunity to practice your craft and to create new music. Think of this as being your research and development stage for the next part of your career.

To reach this point, you don't need to be as skilled as you could ever hope to be. You can still have a lot of room to develop. (In fact, if you don't have room to develop, then your career is going to be very short.) You just mustn't be embarrassing or so excruciating that you will lose your audience before they have found you.

Your initial public outings—whether they be virtual outings by putting music on the internet or real outings, such as live performances—should have one purpose: to seek out fans. If you can make any money to offset your costs, that is good. However, you should ensure that your focus is on finding an audience and not on making money.

Soliciting Feedback

One thing you will find when people hear your music is that they will give you their opinions.

Take the time to listen to these opinions, especially the negative comments. If possible, try to ask people about their opinions and find out exactly what it is they like and don't like. Often a comment such as, "You're just rubbish" (which may be phrased in slightly harsher terms), will tend to show that actually people don't like specific songs or don't like your style, not that they think you are a talentless waster who should be deported to Siberia to live out the rest of your natural musical life in the frozen wastelands.

Also, take some time to find what people like. There may only be a few elements that appeal; however, it is important to find what you are doing well so that you can build upon it. I'm not suggesting that you should simply become a populist outfit driven by what you perceive people want. Instead, I am suggesting that you should understand what it is that you do that people like. I am presuming that what you do is credible, so giving your growing fan base more of the stuff they like (without repetition) should be a good thing.

Now, I'm sure we've all seen the graffiti: Just because no one understands you, it doesn't mean you're an artist. Unfortunately, this is true. If no one "gets you," then you're going to have a really hard time forging a career. Artistic freedom may be great; however, absolute freedom also gives you the freedom to fail, absolutely.

(Not) Building a Career on the Web

For many people, it will be much easier to put music on the web than it would be to get out and play live. This is especially so for people who are creating music on their own. If you are looking to build a fan base solely on the internet, then you are going to have a really tough time, not least because there are thousands (if not millions) of people trying to do this, too.

There are several key challenges that you will encounter with this strategy:

- First, you have to draw attention from a lot of people. There are several strategies you can adopt at the start of the process. For instance, you may be able to draw some attention to yourself if you hit every music-related forum and then spend months on Facebook and get people talking about you. However, if you follow this option, you are likely to spend more time on the internet than on making music.

- Once you've drawn attention to yourself, you have to stand out from the crowd. Given the numbers, this is nearly impossible. If you're putting your music out on the internet, then it is going to have to be as good as or better than anything that's around at the moment (including music on the charts). After all, you are in competition with every other artist who has released music that covers your genre.

- There's also a question about your motivation if your only intention is to share your music on the internet. Music is an inherently social activity. If you are looking for a career in music, then it would not be unreasonable to assume that you are trying to communicate with a wide group of people. Why, therefore, would you shy away from opportunities to communicate directly on a face-to-face basis? The best way to communicate on a face-to-face basis is through a live performance, not anonymously through cyberspace.

- If you do create any sort of following on the internet, then it may be hard to capitalize on it. First, the internet creates a very temporary, easy-come-easy-go type of loyalty. Second, the internet is likely to give you a very widely spread fan base (in this context, widespread on a geographical basis). You may have thousands of fans, but if the closest one fan lives to another is 100 miles, then pulling these people together for a gig (or other publicity/revenue-generating exercise) will be nearly impossible.

- As a purely internet-based act, one of the biggest difficulties you will have is that you will have little or nothing to say. If you're not gigging or getting your music out there in any other way, then this greatly reduces the story you can tell your potential fans. Essentially, the only story you will be able to tell is, "Sat in my bedroom today making music." That looks like a sad and tedious existence that is unlikely to draw people to you.

That's the downside of the internet. However, there are many upsides. One of the best uses of the internet is to solicit opinions from your peers, which may be a sensible idea before you start trying to get your music to a wider public. This is where one of the social networks could be useful to you, especially the likes of YouTube, MySpace, and SoundClick (soundclick.com), where there are large music communities.

Although there are stories of people breaking into the mainstream based on their internet offerings, don't misunderstand these sites and see them as a quick way to success. Instead, think of these sites as ways to get some feedback from your peers and perhaps to get one or two initial fans.

Setting Up Your Web Presence

Whatever you do with cyberspace, I suggest that you establish your own website at a comparatively early stage. This may be a very simple affair, or you may want something more sophisticated.

Although you may have little to say, I suggest you establish some form of presence. This will give people a chance to sign up for your mailing list and will also give the search engines an opportunity to start indexing your pages. By the time you move on to the next stage, you will need a fully functioning website and a substantial mailing list.

At this stage, you can afford to experiment with your website. Ideally, it will become a conduit for communication with your fan base and a place to involve fans and show them how much they matter to you. You can do this in simple ways—for instance, you could put up lots of photos of the people who come to your gigs. As well as involving fans in this way, hopefully the site will also encourage others to come along and see what all the fuss is about.

And of course, you should start to establish your presence on the social networks and begin to interact with/nurture your fan base through these conduits.

Live Performances

If you are looking to interact with a real audience, then to a certain extent you will have to take whatever opportunities arise. However, not all opportunities will be suitable. If possible, try to match the forum for your live performance to your potential audience. So for instance, if you're a rock band, then a gig in a bar may be suitable. However, if you're a bubblegum pop act, then you might want to try and arrange some shows at a school. If you're a dance act, it is always going to be difficult to build a following; however, perhaps a series of nightclub appearances would be a suitable place to start building a fan base.

These are the obvious starting points. If you are to stand any chance of working in a creative industry (which the music industry is), then you will have to be creative in finding venues and looking for outlets where you can connect with people.

Any gathering will do; you just have to find a way to set up the gig. For instance, if you are a progressive rock act with a whole bunch of songs about sorcerers and goblins, then maybe the ideal forum for you to try to connect with your fan base would be at a convention for people with an interest in fantasy comics. This could be a very profitable option because you may find that many of these people have never seen live music before (let alone daylight), and so you could find a whole new audience. Added to which, these people are on the whole very loyal (remember, they go to fantasy comic conventions) and so are likely to stay with you as you build your career.

Your first public performances present you with a great opportunity to sell product. At this stage, don't! You will still be growing as an act. Instead, make sure you use all of your public performances as an opportunity to get to know your audience (and get to know their contact details or persuade them to follow you on the social networks). Seek their feedback and find out what they like. As you can align your output with your potential fan base's tastes, you will increase your chances of success.

Releasing a CD

There will be one temptation that you may find irresistible: the desire to release an album, and in particular, the desire to make a CD. You may find this desire is particularly hard to resist if you have recorded some tracks that you have made available on the internet. However, I would still counsel you against releasing an album.

My main reason for cautioning against releasing an album is that it will be bad (and in this context, bad means of poor quality, not good). At this early stage, unless you are a modern-day Mozart, you will not have the talent to put together an album of sufficient quality, although you may have one or two good songs. Everything will be wrong: The songs will be poor, the arrangements will be dubious, the playing will be weak, and the recording will be second rate. You are still growing and still learning—don't record your mistakes for posterity.

If you really, really, really have to release an album from captivity, then please find a producer: You need someone who is prepared to tell you that you are useless. If he tells you that you're good, he's just flattering you to get your money.

Your choice of producer is going to be quite difficult. Unless you are exceptionally lucky, there will be a very limited number of people to choose from, if you can find anyone. Also, you are unlikely to have many contacts to ask for a recommendation. However, although this may be difficult, you do still need a producer.

With the producer in place, hire a studio and record your best son...and only your best song. Get the song mixed and mastered so it is of the highest possible quality.

At this point, do nothing. Wait a week and then listen to the song. This will either be the best thing you have heard or it will be a disappointment. If it is a disappointment, that is good: You will have learned something about the process. Wait at least six months and then repeat the process, and hopefully the six months will give you the opportunity to write some new songs that are better than the one you recorded.

If the song really is the best thing you have ever heard, then create some CDs. Burning a few CDs on your computer will be fine. On the CD label, you want to include the name of the act, the name of the song, and your web address. Anything else is superfluous and will distract from the music. (However, I won't argue if you want to add a copyright notice.)

Now, if, against my suggestions, you have reached the point of releasing a CD, then I assume you have a website, and on that website you have:

- A list of forthcoming gigs

- Links to your presences on the social-media sites

- A way for people to sign up for your mailing list

If not, then you should.

Assuming your website is up and running as intended, give your CDs away. Don't just give the CDs to anyone; give them to people who really dig your music and give them to people who care about music. What you are looking to do is use word of mouth to create a buzz. Don't give the CDs to your mom/dad/uncle/friend who is into origami—give them to people who can act as your ambassadors.

At this point I can sense that you're trying to say to me, "But why only one song? We've got two/three/seven/twenty-five (and so on) great songs!" My reasoning here is simple: If you give away two songs, then you are doubling the chance of disappointing the listener. Give away three songs, and you triple the chance of disappointment.

You will also find that if you give away one song and someone loves it, then that is great. You may have found a new fan. If you give away one song, and someone is so-so about it, then she will probably give you the benefit of the doubt and may turn up at a gig, which gives you an opportunity to really wow that person. However, if you give someone two songs and she likes one but is so-so about the second, that person may see you as only having one good song and may not bother coming to the gig.

Remember, the only reason you would give away a CD is to create buzz that will encourage people to find out more about you. Hopefully, this will help you to get some more names onto your mailing list and followers across the social networks. You are not trying to create something for posterity at the moment, nor are you trying to generate any income from CD sales.

I suggest you hire a studio and a producer for several reasons. First, as I have already explained, I think you will get a better end product and will gain some useful feedback, hopefully learning a lot from an experienced person.

The second reason is that it will test your commitment to your career and test whether you can behave like a professional. If you are not prepared to make a comparatively small investment in your career at this stage (and remember, this will pretty much be your first "major" investment), then you should be hearing alarm bells ringing. Not only will a reluctance to invest in your career graphically illustrate your lack of commitment, it will also demonstrate to potential investors that you don't believe in what you are doing.

Another reason for going into a proper studio with a producer is to check out your ego. You may well have the technology to be able to record at home. However, you may also be too arrogant to make a good recording. Take some time in a studio and with a producer, and show a bit of humility by allowing yourself to change. You will be surprised by the improvement.

Funding

Clearly you will not be generating much, if any, income. If you need a source of income at this stage, I recommend you follow the age-old tradition of getting a job. You don't need a glamorous job—in fact, the less glamorous it is, the easier it will be to turn your back and walk away—you just need a job where you have sufficient flexibility to be able to get out and play gigs and write new material.

The lack of money should also teach you financial discipline. It is crucial that you maintain this discipline when the money starts to come in. Remember, you will be dealing with lots of very small amounts of money. Spending large amounts will rapidly wipe out many months of hard work.

Accelerated Learning

You have seen that in this section (as with the next section), you are going to have to do a lot of new and different things. Essentially, I am advocating a learning-by-doing strategy, or if you prefer, on-the-job training.

You will make a lot of mistakes through this strategy. However, your learning will be far deeper than could be achieved by simply reading a book or theorizing about a strategy. Through this approach, you will find your own path (if you don't, then you won't have a career), and most importantly, you will find what works and what doesn't work for your specific situation.

You've seen that I advocate you limit your activities. For instance, I have suggested that you don't release an album. I have set out my reasoning for the courses I have suggested. One other reason for focusing on what you are doing is to limit the scope of your mistakes. This will help to limit the financial risks you will be taking by making mistakes.

I'm also keen that you don't start with something until you are able to take full advantage of each situation. Staying with the example of an album release, you may happen to release an acceptable-quality album; however, if you don't have the skills to exploit this product and generate income from the release, then you have wasted an opportunity.

In the next section ("Turning Pro"), we will go from accelerated learning to turbo-charged learning.

Turning Pro

The next stage in your career is often seen as the pinnacle for many musicians: turning pro. However, this is really just the beginning. Anyone can turn professional—generating an income, continuing to work as a professional musician, and creating a sustainable career, year after year, are the hard parts.

This stage may come one or two years after you start interacting with the public. It may (and probably will) take longer. It depends how good you are and how hard you work (the really hard work being building up your fan base).

How Do You Know When You're Ready to Turn Professional?

There are certain key indicators that will tell you when you are ready to turn professional.

- **Great songs.** Not good songs or all-right songs, but *great* songs. Not only do you need great songs, but you need lots of them—enough to fill a set and/or an album with some (lots) left over. Having enough truly great songs is a real challenge, and it will probably take years to reach the stage of having enough great songs.

One way to check to see whether you have a lot of really good songs is to count the number of songs you have rejected and thrown off of your set list. The number of songs that you once thought were good enough but that you obviously don't now should greatly outnumber the included songs. If it doesn't, then you are probably not being sufficiently discerning, and you need to get back and write some more. Alternatively, you are just not creating enough new (great) songs.

- **Perfected stagecraft.** By this point you should be able to put on a really good show. You should know how to work an audience, how to structure a set, and how to make sure that there is always a lot of energy on stage. In short, your show should be as good as any professional act that you might go and see.

- **A mailing list with thousands of names.** You should have thousands of followers across the social networks.

- **The ability to hustle.** You will know how to get gigs, and you will have gig dates set for up to a year in advance. More than that, you will know how much you can earn from gigging, and you will have cut your gigging expenses to the bone so you stand a chance of making a profit.

Hopefully, this won't be all you have achieved; however, it is the absolute minimum before you move to become professional.

Making the Transition

The transition to being a professional music maker should be an organic change. You won't wake up one morning with the realization that you are at this point; it will probably be something that comes to you gradually over time.

You will probably initially keep your day job (if you have one) and work as a musician, but then drop the day job when you can afford to. However, I caution against burning all of your bridges and generating your income solely from music until you are convinced that you have enough great songs, your stagecraft is sufficiently developed, and your fan base is sufficiently well established.

That being said, while you keep your day job, you are likely to find excuses not to force yourself to be successful in your music career—there's nothing quite like the prospect of poverty and starvation to force you to go and find work. There are many advantages to having a "proper" job—for example, regular pay. You will find many options for self-sabotage that will keep you doing the sensible thing and staying employed (even if, as I suggested, you took a scummy job so it would be easy to quit and you would be motivated to do so).

There are many other reasons why you may be unwilling to let go of a regular, secure income. For instance, you may have financial responsibilities (such as a mortgage), or you may have family responsibilities. Without wishing to sound harsh, if these are concerns for you, then the unsettled existence of a working musician is probably not a career you should follow. By all means keep music as a hobby—perhaps even a hobby that makes some money—but don't kid yourself that you're going to make it a career.

When you are convinced you want to be a professional musician and you are ready to be, then go for it! There's no need to go wild; you can build your income and career steadily. However, it is imperative that you do start to build your career and stop making excuses for not being successful.

Marketing

If you have read the rest of the book, you will have seen that I am pretty skeptical about marketing as a separate, specific exercise because I feel it has little tangible, measurable value. Instead, I much prefer building a relationship with the fan base.

That being said, you will need to do some marketing at this stage in your career, largely to help you get in touch with the people who will help you build your career. In other words, you need to raise your profile so that people who may hire you for gigs will hear about you, or if you contact these people directly, you will have some materials to support you.

At this stage in your career, you need a fully functioning website. When I say "fully functioning," your website should perform the following functions for you:

- **Tell people a bit about the act.** This doesn't need to be anything too extensive, just enough to be interesting and encourage people to keep looking at the website.

- **Capture interest.** In other words, there should be a way to record the details of anyone who is interested so you can contact them to tell them about upcoming gigs, new products, and so on.

- **Give details of how you can be contacted.** There's nothing worse than someone wanting to book you for a gig but not knowing how to get in touch.

- **Sell product.** I'll talk more about your product range in a moment. (For now, just accept that you need some, but you will need a very limited range.)

- **List all of your gigs.** Also include details of how to get to each venue.

- **Interact with fans.** You don't need to do much to interact with fans—for instance, you don't need to set up a chat forum (provided you're active on the main social networks). However, you do need to demonstrate that the relationship between you—the artist—and your fan base is a two-way thing. You can do this in small ways. To extend an example I've used before, perhaps you could include pictures fans have taken at your gigs.

- **Carry video clips.** These are usually embedded YouTube videos.

Added to this, your website should be capable of being (and should be) picked up by the search engine spiders.

If your website does all of these things, then it will be working both as a marketing tool and as a support for your business.

You may also seek out some press reviews around this time. I'm not convinced that reviews will increase your fan base. However, reviews are useful if you want to include comments on your flyers and other publicity. If a recognized music magazine calls you the next big thing (or some other similar cliché), this will help to add an element of credibility.

Anyone who hires you for a gig can then put this sort of comment on posters advertising the gig. Think of it from the perspective of the person hiring an act for a gig: If there are two acts that look fairly similar, what could sway you to choose one over the other? One influence would be favorable comments by a trustworthy source.

Keep On Keeping On

Although this will be a period of huge change in your life, there are certain things you need to keep doing:

- **The most important thing is to keep learning.** As you progress, you will find what works and what doesn't. You will find new ways to generate income that you can exploit to your advantage. You will also continue to grow as a human being, and this will influence your creative output. In parallel, your fan base will grow (as individuals), and their tastes will change. You need to learn and understand how this affects their relationship with you.

- **The second most important thing is to keep creating new material.** Each new song is a possible new source of income. Once you stop creating new material (and thinking about new ways to exploit that material), your career will start to decline. If it starts to decline at this comparatively early stage in your career, then it won't take long before you have nothing.

- **The one thing you should be cherishing and protecting with your life is your fan base.** These people need to be nurtured so that the numbers will continue to grow. If your fan base doesn't grow, then you stand little chance of growing your income to sustain a successful career.

Generating Income

At this stage in your career, your income becomes serious.

Hopefully by now you will be generating a reasonable income from your live shows. That is not to say you will be generating a profit, just that you're not making too much of a loss. Obviously, your aim should be to generate a profit, and if you are doing so, then I congratulate your hard work and business acumen.

Unless you are performing every day, then you probably need to perform more shows and make more money/fewer losses from each show.

As well as gigging, now that you're a professional musician, it is time to start developing a range of products. If nothing else, you should now be at a stage when you are ready to record your first album, and you should have a sufficiently large fan base to ensure some sales. With any products you may want to create, and irrespective of what stage your career is at, if you don't have people to buy your product, then don't create it. Find an audience and then create a product to sell to these people, not the other way around.

Your first album may be your first really big project. It could therefore be your first really big opportunity to lose a lot of money in one go. Due to the risks involved, your budgeting needs to be very tight. However, against this you must balance the need to create a first-rate product.

You may be tempted to cut costs and record the whole album at home. In the same way that I advocated the involvement of an external studio/producer if you wanted to release a single track, I would advocate external involvement in any album-type project. However, given the costs and your additional development by this stage, I would not suggest this in such strong terms here.

Indeed, you may find that you can combine approaches. For instance, you might make some recordings in your home facility and some in a commercial studio. You could then pass the recordings over to someone else to mix the tracks. In this manner, you can keep the costs to the minimum and produce a professional result. However, I still believe you will achieve the very best product that you can by using a professional producer from the start to the end of the project.

Before you begin a project such as this, it is worth drawing up a budget. As you probably already know, budgets are nearly always exceeded, so make sure you include a contingency for overspends. The minimum contingency you should include is 20 percent of the budget. If you're inexperienced or have had overspends before, then perhaps think about something more realistic, in the 40 to 50 percent range.

When drawing up your budget, try to be realistic about all of the costs involved. For instance, think about how much it is going to cost to get CDs pressed (assuming you will be putting out a CD in addition to downloads). It's pointless to spend all of the money on recording a project and then to run out of money before you can produce the product that will generate income.

Try to balance your projected sales against the costs. It is incredibly hard to estimate how many CDs you are going to sell, and when making this projection, you need to be very wary about over-optimism. Just because you have 50,000 people on your mailing list, that doesn't mean you're going to sell 50,000 CDs. (You probably won't get 50,000 downloads, either.) In reality, you will probably be doing well if you can sell to between 4 and 5 percent of the people on your mailing list. That being said, if you have 50,000 on your mailing list, and you sell a CD priced at $15 to 5 percent of the list (that is, 2,500 people), then you will generate $37,500 income, which is not bad. It should certainly cover the pressing costs and may even cover a chunk of the recording costs.

The two staples of most gigging acts are CDs and T-shirts, so you should think about T-shirts, too. Remember that as well as generating income, a T-shirt will also work as advertising for you, so it is worth taking a lot of time to get the design right.

Once you've got the design, there are many other areas where you can easily make silly decisions:

- Initially, you will have no clue about how many T-shirts will sell.

- Although you will get a better unit price for ordering more T-shirts, you then have the problem of storing your stock.

- When thinking about T-shirts, it's very easy to think about getting shirts in small, medium, large, and extra-large sizes. However, this only increases the stock you have to carry. Perhaps for your first order, you could get shirts in large only. If these are successful, then you can consider getting a wider range of sizes. Alternatively, take orders for other sizes (and print the shirts when you have enough orders to cover your costs).

The way to minimize your losses due to stupidity is to keep your orders for T-shirts to the minimum and to place an order only when your stock has nearly all been sold. Although this may mean that you are not getting the best prices when you buy your stock, it will mean that you will not be left with huge amounts of stock that cannot be sold, and the losses due to theft and so on will be reduced.

The easiest way to sell your CDs and T-shirts will be at gigs. You will have a ready audience who (provided the gig has been good) will be receptive to buying whatever you can sell. If you limit the range of goods on offer, then you will increase the chances of selling the individual items you are offering (because there are few other options).

One advantage to selling at gigs is that you can readily take cash, which means you don't have to deal with credit cards if you don't want to. (In fact, dealing credit cards at a gig could be a pain.) The disadvantage to taking cash is that you have to trust the people who are selling your merchandise—it is very easy to pilfer cash and then claim the products have been stolen.

You can sell your products directly on your website; however, I suggest you don't rush in here, because there are several logistical challenges to overcome:

- First, you need to set up a way to receive credit card payments. This isn't overly difficult; however, it will take some time (especially if you want to set up a merchant account).

- When you can receive payment, then you need to find a way to fulfill the orders. This is unlikely to be more complicated than packing the products and putting them in the mail; however, you will need to ensure that the packaging is suitable, the correct postage is paid, and the packages are picked up for onward delivery. (You may find that with the number of packages, you can't fit everything into your local mailbox.)

- You'll also need to figure out who will send out the orders. Initially, it will probably be you. However, if you're going to be out of town (which hopefully you will be, because hopefully you will be gigging), then who will send out the orders for you? This is another area of risk for you. If you delegate the task and someone gets it wrong (for instance, they send the product to the wrong place or they send a product when a credit card has been declined), then you will start taking a loss on your operation.

None of these issues is insurmountable, and you will find they are much easier to sort out if you have kept a very narrow product range.

Non-Performing Artists

If you are a non-performing artist (for instance, a composer, a "pure" songwriter, or a studio-bound musician) who hasn't created some sort of act that can go out and perform (thereby transforming yourself into, and giving yourself the advantage of, a performing artist), then life will be tough at this stage. Your options to build a fan base will be severely limited, and without a fan base, there will be no one to whom your product can be sold.

Life will also be tougher for the non-performing musician because you will reach the stage at which you feel you want to (and are ready to) release an album much sooner than a conventional performing act that is out gradually building up its fan base. You will find that you pressure yourself to record and release an album: Your logic is likely to follow the argument that if you don't release an album, then what are you doing that could constitute calling yourself a musician, let alone a professional musician?

If you're a non-performing musician who is approaching this stage, and you can't find an outlet for your music, then please try harder. Recording and releasing an album may make you feel good (at least temporarily), but if you don't have a fan base to buy your album, it will ultimately be fairly fruitless.

Building the Business: Opening an Office

You will be ready to move on and start building your business when you are:

- Working as a professional musician. (You probably dispensed with any collaborators who did not share your level of commitment to progress their career.)

- Gigging regularly (or putting on some other form of performance regularly) with the necessary equipment to get to gigs, put on a good show, and so on.

- Selling a limited range of products (and these products sell well).

At this stage in your career, you will be building the foundations so that you can grow from a musician scratching out a hand-to-mouth existence to one making a reasonable living.

Raising Money for Investment

This may be the point in your career at which you need to invest money. If you have been working as a professional musician for a few years, then you are unlikely to have much cash (even if you saved your money as I recommended earlier in this chapter). Most of your money is likely to have been spent meeting the expenses of promoting your act.

There are several sources of finance. The main choices will be bank loans and business partners (such as a manager). I will discuss your relationship with a manager later in this section.

If you borrow money from a bank, then you are opening yourself up to a whole new scale of debt (see Figure 9.4). So far in your career, most of your losses (or potential losses) have been containable and/or limited. For instance, if you take a loss on a gig, it

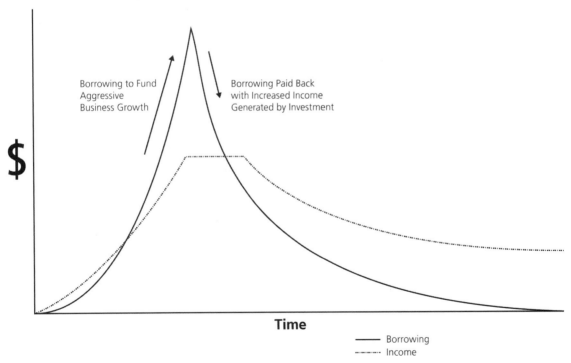

Figure 9.4 To grow your business, you will probably need to borrow money, and this borrowing will be a debt to your business. When you are borrowing to invest to grow your business aggressively, your total level of debt is likely to exceed your income. At this stage in your career, a large proportion of your income will therefore be spent on servicing your debt (that is, paying interest on the money you owe).

is usually a comparatively small loss. Typically, the most you would lose would be the cost of hiring the venue (if you hired it), the cost of promotion, the cost of staffing for the gig, other expenses (such as insurance), and the cost of transportation to the gig.

That is not to say that you couldn't lose a chunk of money with a gig; however, you usually would not expect to lose that much. For instance, if you lost $1,000 on a gig, that may seem like a lot to lose. Typically, if you are looking at a gig with a promoter, then the most you are likely to lose would be your own expenses traveling to, and in connection with, the gig.

Losses of this level are usually an amount you can walk away from. However, it is still possible to get into serious debt just by gigging.

In contrast, if you borrow money, then you are getting a large chunk of cash that has to be repaid. You will borrow money because you need to invest it. Investment is a euphemism for spending with the hope that you will generate income. If you spend money you have borrowed and you don't generate enough income to repay the loan and the interest, then you will owe money to the bank (or whoever has lent you money).

If you owe money to a bank, they will usually be reasonable, initially. However, after a while they will get bored and will stop being patient. At this stage they will ask for the money in an unpleasant manner, usually by making you (personally) bankrupt. You're far more likely to face financial ruin at this stage, when you appear to be becoming successful, than you will when you are at the starving, struggling musician stage.

However, if you don't invest, then you won't be able to grow your career. If you are not willing to invest, then it is probably best that you walk away from your career now.

You are likely to need money to invest in three things:

- People

- Places

- Processes

In short, you are going to invest in the infrastructure of your business. You will need people to run the business for you, a place for those people to work, and processes to get your products to your fan base.

You're likely to find yourself in a bit of a "chicken and egg" situation, wondering whether to sort your infrastructure before you grow your product range. Unfortunately, there is no simple answer here, and you will have to find a pragmatic solution (as I will discuss).

People

Finding the right people to work with you is one of the toughest tasks. However, the joy of finding the right people to work with you and benefit the business is amazing.

The first people you hire are going to have to be very flexible and be prepared to undertake a wide range of tasks. (You certainly don't want people with an overly rigid attitude towards their tasks.) For instance, your first hire's job description could include many of the following tasks:

- Answering the phone

- Chasing up and booking gigs (as well as hustling for gigs)

- Processing orders for merchandise and sending out the products

- Ordering goods for sale

- Acting as webmaster/mistress, as well as moderator on any internet forums and chief reviewer of comments about you on the social-media sites and throughout the rest of the web

- Looking after your paperwork (orders, receipts, and so on)

- Fixing the plumbing and feeding the office cat

In short, your first hire will do all those tiresome but crucially important things that you should be doing but are too busy to do because you're making music. This will be the person who runs your business, so make sure you treat him right!

Places

Your person (or people) will need somewhere to work. If they are flexible enough to take on all of the tasks I have outlined, then they will probably be fairly flexible with their work environment, provided it is warm and dry and there is somewhere to get a cup of coffee. In addition to housing your staff, you will need property to house your stuff (which could include the business's paperwork and your stock).

Buying or renting property is a very expensive business, so if you can (at least initially), borrow space. This may mean you (or more importantly, your staff) have to put up with a slightly less than ideal workspace. For instance, you may find a shed, a garage, or a cheap industrial unit. Whatever you find, make sure it is secure—it will be no fun trying to complete your tax return if all of your records get eaten by mice or shredded during a break-in.

Processes: Getting Your Product to Your Customers

"Process" is one of those nasty management-speak words, so let me turn it into English in the context of this part of the chapter. Your processes are the means by which you get your products to your customers. This is not simply a matter of fulfillment: It also includes getting your stock in the first place, holding the stock, as well as sending out orders after first having made sure that the appropriate payment has been received (and checks cleared, if appropriate).

I mentioned the chicken-and-egg situation about whether processes or products come first. To my mind, processes equate to the egg, and therefore come first. When you first start, your process (such as it will be) will probably be to sell CDs at gigs (as well as encourage the purchase of downloads). However, when you grow, and especially when you want to sell products from your website and you're not there to send out the orders, then you need a solid process in place.

There are probably two ways to get your processes in place. One is to sit down and agree on the processes between all of the shareholders. The second option is to get your office person to sort things out.

I favor the second option. If you trust this person, and she is competent, then she should be perfectly capable of undertaking this sort of task (although you may find your office person gets bored very quickly if this is all she does all day every day).

And by the way, if you don't trust your office person or if she is not competent, then fire that person immediately—remember, that person is looking after your business. For your own peace of mind, you may want to check the processes she has put in place, just to make sure your office person is thinking about the task from the perspective of your fans' experience (rather than trying to make life easy for herself).

When you start thinking about fulfillment, you have three main options:

- Send out the product yourself.

- Use a third party to send out your orders.

- Use an on-demand service.

These three options can be integrated into your processes, and you can, of course, mix and match these options. So for instance, you could start off by getting your office person to send out products, but as you grow, you could outsource this function to a specialized fulfillment service.

When you start scaling up your business—particularly when you start finding new fans who are based overseas (in relation to you)—you may find that an on-demand service offers many advantages to your business. As I have said before, these on-demand services may not generate the biggest profits; however, they do allow you to expand your business while minimizing your business risks, and you can always use them for a very short period of time.

Manager

Many of the challenges associated with people, places, and processes can be readily addressed if you have a manager. Indeed, it would not be unreasonable to expect a manager to supervise these tasks on your behalf and to provide premises (since any manager should already have premises).

However, if your manager is going to help, then you should ensure that he does not charge twice. So for instance, the manager shouldn't charge you for staff he might "lend" you to help run your business but not allow the cost of those people against the fee you pay for management services.

Increasing Income: Increasing Profitability

When you have your infrastructure in place (or at least a basis for your infrastructure to become operational), then you can look to grow the business. To grow the business, you need a healthy, active, and growing fan base, and you need a wide range of products to sell to your fan base. You need both elements (the product and purchaser); one without the other will mean you can't generate income.

Under the previous step, I suggested that you should get your infrastructure sorted before you start to expand your range of products. I stand by this view: You can have all the products in the world, but if you don't have the wherewithal to take money and then get the products out to people who are paying you money, then you will find lots of very unhappy people, and you will spend your life dealing with complaints rather than making music. (And it will be you dealing with the problems, because you won't have hired someone to run your office as I suggested.)

Anyway, let me now slightly qualify that view. It is pointless to have an infrastructure if you don't have anything to sell (or anyone to sell it to). Building an infrastructure will cost you time and money, and as I have already suggested, you may want to borrow money to finance that exercise. Although I have separated the two steps (building your infrastructure and building your products), you should make sure that in practice the two steps are linked so that you can generate some income to repay your investment.

The sensible approach is to build part of the infrastructure and grow the product line. Once that small expansion has been incorporated, you can build your infrastructure a bit more and grow the product line to a greater extent. An example of this step-by-step growth was shown earlier with the illustration of outsourcing order fulfillment.

When you have your products and processes in place, then you can start aggressively scaling up your business. Earlier in your career, it is harder to scale up in a meaningful way. If you have five fans, then you may be able to triple the size of your fan base by gaining another ten people. Fifteen people will not generate sufficient income to sustain a career. When you have a wide range of products and a fan base into the hundreds of thousands, then scale becomes a significant issue.

To really increase your earnings (which, after all, is the point of scaling), you will have to:

- **Earn more money from each fan.** You can do this by offering more products, increasing your prices, or both.

- **Increase the size of the fan base.** To be worthwhile, you need to ensure that this increase is permanent. There's no point in gaining fans and then losing them quickly or alienating your existing fans, because all you will do is create a large number of dissatisfied individuals. That's one of the problems with growing in scale—you can upset many people. When you're small, you can only upset a few people!

- **Take advantage of the size of your fan base.** Anything you do is much more likely to become an "event."

I'll touch on some of these themes through the rest of this section.

Increasing the Product Range

So far I haven't advocated expanding your product range beyond a CD (and downloads) and a T-shirt. Before I go any further and talk about your product range, let me give you some examples of how other businesses make their money. (These are both examples from the UK. Even if the conditions don't apply directly in your market, I am sure you can find a product for which a similar principle does.)

If you purchase a new car in the UK, you can almost always negotiate a discount on the manufacturer's price. It may not be much of a discount (perhaps only 5 percent), but you will be able to get a discount. This isn't because there is a huge profit margin on cars. In fact, the contrary is true—the margins are wafer thin, and having given a discount, there may be no profit for the dealer. Instead, the reason for the discount is that the dealer wants to secure you as a customer.

Once the dealer has secured you as a customer, then it will make money from you in two places: first, by offering financing for the (discounted) car that you will be buying, and second, from the servicing costs. Arranging the financing will give the dealer a lump-sum commission payment (which can compensate for the cost of selling the car as well as provide some profit), and the servicing will provide a stream of income for the dealer over the lifetime of the car.

The other example I want to give you is printers. If you go to a computer store, printers are dirt cheap. However, when you buy an ink/toner cartridge, you need to spend a small fortune. Let me illustrate this: I could buy a Hewlett-Packard LaserJet 1102 today for £75.58 (roughly $125). A print cartridge for the printer (from the same store) will then cost me £61.14 (roughly $100). In other words, every time I want a new toner cartridge, I would have to spend almost as much as I paid for the printer.

So what's the point I am trying to make here? My point is twofold:

- First, don't expect to earn money from those parts of your business that you may see as being your core business. (That is, don't expect that your music will be what sustains your income.)

- Second, don't get too precious about your pricing strategies. You need to bring people in so that you can convert them to becoming fans. In the world of the internet, music is becoming increasingly commoditized, so in the end, you may find that your music (whether as a CD or a download) is sold very cheaply or even given away in certain circumstances, but that you then make your money with gigs and merchandise.

It is very hard for a musician to accept that the activity that defines him (the making of music) can be ascribed a lower value than a transitory piece of merchandising. However, while I share your pain, this is unfortunately the nature of the world today. I don't like saying this, but you're just going to have to get over it and get on with your career.

After that introduction, my thoughts about your product range are quite straightforward: Progressively build your product range. Check back in Part III, when I discussed the range of products you could consider. The challenge in building your product range is to introduce products progressively and to offer the right products.

If you go from offering only a CD and a T-shirt to offering a whole wardrobe, posters, mugs, dolls, and everything else you can think of, then you might look as if you have sold out. You will also find that it takes time to design and order your products (and your product range may more than fill a venue if you're still playing small gigs).

If you have only one T-shirt for sale, then a much more sensible approach is to offer two T-shirts, perhaps in different sizes, and maybe a sweatshirt. When you've got those items and they are selling, then (and only then) think about something else.

Record labels often stipulate a minimum and a maximum number of albums that an artist must produce over a certain timeframe. The minimum number is obvious. The maximum-number restriction is quite sensible. If an artist produces several albums, then it is very hard to market them all. It is much easier to market one album, and then market another a year later. If you are producing albums (or DVDs) or any other product that needs to be highlighted as a specific product, then it makes sense to limit your output.

Also, as a working musician, you are unlikely to be able to produce several albums in a year, given the time it takes to write and record an album.

As you are looking to expand your product range, remember that I included gigs within the scope of products. You should be looking to increase your income from gigs. There are two main ways to do this:

- **Play more gigs.** As an established artist who is looking to grow, you should be playing as many gigs as you are physically able to do. There should be no problems organizing gigs, and you should be increasing the territories in which you are playing.

- **Play bigger gigs.** Larger venues will allow you to make more money, which will come from several sources:

  - The greater number of people coming to see you

  - Enhanced sponsorship opportunities

  - More merchandise sales (as there will be more people at your gigs, and the gigs become more of an event that people want to memorialize with merchandise)

You will also find many other opportunities to generate income from live performances—for instance, support bands will pay to join your tour (or rather, their record labels will pay).

Licensing Deals

I'll talk about the risks associated with running an expanding business later in this section (under the heading "Increased Risks"). Licensing deals can generate income and help you manage the risks in your business. When you have reached this stage in your career, you are likely to be sufficiently interesting for potential licensees to consider a deal with you. You are also likely to have enough clout to negotiate a reasonable deal.

The main advantages of licensing deals are:

- **Risk management.** The licensee will have the cash-flow challenges and will have to make the difficult commercial decisions (such as how much stock to order).

- **Logistics.** The licensee will deal with ordering and fulfillment. If you want to include sales from your website to make life easy for your fan base or generate some commission from referred sales, then you may need to arrange some clever programming, but once that is working, life should be simple.

- **Administrative ease.** At a stroke, all of the paperwork associated with the licensed merchandise will be passed to your licensee.

- **Increased sales.** The licensee should be an expert in selling merchandise and will have an incentive to sell as much product as possible.

- **Advances.** The licensee may be prepared to agree to pay an advance. This may ease cash-flow problems for you in other areas.

There will be additional work in choosing and appointing the licensee that would not arise if you undertake the work yourself (but this is the flip side to removing a lot of hard work you would otherwise be required to undertake). Also, you are likely to have to agree on, and approve, merchandise (which you would do in any case if you were looking after your own merchandising). However, on the whole, the appointment of a licensee can be very beneficial, reducing your costs and risks while increasing your income.

Expanding the Fan Base

If you've been paying attention, you will have picked up on my many references to my skepticism about marketing. This is where things change…

You should still keep nurturing your fan base. (You're really going to need them on the way down.) However, you may find at this stage of your career that advertising can be effective (although it will never be as effective as word-of-mouth recommendations).

Instead of just paying for advertisements in the press, you will have the opportunity to generate far more buzz through your activities—for instance, your gigs will provide an opportunity to gather a lot of press coverage.

If you play a gig to 1,000 people, then no one really cares. (Well, your mother will, and I'm sure you will love it.) If you a play a gig to 10,000 people, that is interesting, and the music press will probably cover the event. However, if you play a gig to 100,000 people, you're going to be making the evening news.

I've said it before, but it is worth repeating: At the stage when you have a range of products to sell, then each new fan is more valuable to you because each one can buy a lot of product. At the stage, when you have only a CD and a T-shirt for sale, the amount of money you can generate from each fan from non-gigging activities is highly limited.

Increased Risks

As you expand your business operations, you are going to be increasing your risks considerably.

When you look at individual items—for instance, the cost to order 1,000 T-shirts—the costs may seem manageable. However, if you look at ordering 1,000 small T-shirts, 1,000 medium T-shirts, 1,000 large T-shirts, 1,000 extra-large T-shirts, 2,000 sweatshirts, 500 hoodies, 5,000 posters, 2,500 baseball caps, 500 mugs, as well as 50,000 CDs, then your cost will increase greatly. However, this is not the only issue to consider:

- First, you will be holding stock. This stock has a value that can be reduced or wiped out if the stock is damaged or stolen. To guard against these risks, you may want to think about insurance (which is yet another cost). If you are using a fulfillment service, you should check who has the risk for your stock. I would guess you would be quite upset is someone else let your assets be stolen and then told you that they're not insured.

- Until the stock is sold, its purchase represents a loss to your business. There will be a timing difference between when you order your stock and when you sell it. You therefore need to ensure that it is available for sale at the very earliest opportunity. You've probably heard businesses talking about their cash-flow problems—this is the situation to which they are referring. In extreme circumstances, buying too much stock without selling it quickly enough can make you technically insolvent.

- With ordering and selling stock, you will have lots of bits of money moving around (and often you will be dealing with a large number of small sums). If you are not on top of the situation, there is a significant risk that some of the sums will not reach your bank account (whether by mistake or by criminal intent).

Superstar Status

You're right; I don't mean superstar.

For the purpose of this section, "superstar status" is a misnomer—by the term, all I mean is that you have reached the peak (or hopefully the long plateau) of your career. This isn't to suggest that your business cannot get better once you've reached this point, just that your income will be at a very good level, and you will be making a good living.

When you reach this status, you won't do many new things, but you are likely to do some of the things you already do somewhat differently. Here are a few pointers:

- You're probably likely to gig less frequently. There are several reasons for this (in no particular order):

  - There will be more opportunities for other forms of publicity and income generation (for instance, from television or offers to write music for films).

  - You will do bigger shows. It is simply not practical to do too many shows. (Generally you can't do mega shows year after year after year in the same city—you can do mega shows for several years, but not indefinitely.)

  - There will be larger geographical distances between shows. Travel and time zones will militate against too many performances.

  - You will probably want more time for yourself, whether to spend with your family, to write new songs, or to get involved with other projects.

  - Your health. By the time you reach this stage, you may be past the very first flush of youth. (In other words, like me, you may be out of your twenties.) Common sense alone may dictate that you slow down (even if only slightly).

- You will probably take a more global approach and will be keen to ensure that you are selling in as many geographical markets as possible.

- To maximize your penetration of global markets, you may well partner with other businesses. In English, this means that you may enter into an agreement with a record label.

- With your increased earning power/fan base, you may want to renegotiate your existing deals. If you don't renegotiate now, you may not get another chance. You will also find that licensees and business partners will seek to maximize their earnings from the business they carry on with you—in short, they will increase their prices to your fans as far as they possibly can.

As I said, these are just a few pointers. How, when, and whether these are practical will depend on a range of situations, and, to be frank, by the time you get to this stage in your career, you need highly specialized advice that will be unique to your situation and is therefore far beyond the scope of this book.

You should not regard this list as only being possible when you reach superstar status. You can do many of them at an earlier stage; however, for some, this is the optimum point to adopt them into strategy.

Managing the Downward Path

At some point your career will move off its plateau. It is probably overdramatic to call this the beginning of your career descent, and it also has all sorts of negative connotations that I do not wish you to associate with a downward trend. However, we must accept that you cannot stay at the very top of your game forever.

It might seem out of place to think about managing the decline of your career, especially if it has yet to start. However, I think it is worth considering, because many of the decisions you make on your way up will have a far greater impact on your way down. For instance, if you sell off all your rights, then you won't have any continuing income from your music. If you get enough money for selling your rights, then you may not care. However, if you don't earn sufficient income, you may spend your retirement years in comparative poverty.

The Start of the Downward Path

There is probably one key characteristic by which you will be able to recognize that the peak/plateau of your career has ended and you have begun the downward path. Your fan base will stop growing—in other words, the number of new people who become fans will be less than the number of people who drift away from you.

Clearly, it is difficult to assess this point because you are unlikely to be able to accurately measure the number of fans you have. However, there are several measures that you can look at:

- The rate of change of your mailing list
- The rate of change of your friends/followers on the social networks
- The rate of change in the traffic that is coming to your website
- The rate of change in the number of products you sell (downloads, CDs, DVDs, merchandise, as well as gig ticket)
- The rate of change of the income of the business

When any of these measures slows or becomes negative, it is likely to be indicative that you're entering the next phase of your career.

You should note that for all of these factors, I suggest you look at the *rate* of growth, not just the growth. The difference is important: If you add one fan, then your fan base is still growing. However, if you only add one fan in a year, then you're probably in trouble. Take a look at Table 9.1, which gives an example set of figures for income.

Table 9.1   An Apparently Healthily Growing Income Stream

Year	Income
Year 1	$1,000,000
Year 2	$1,100,000
Year 3	$1,210,000
Year 4	$1,320,000
Year 5	$1,420,000

These figures look impressive and show year-on-year growth. Now look at Table 9.2, which shows the same figures but has added in the figures for the income growth and the rate of growth. Although income is growing, the rate at which it is growing is starting to fall. This is often an early indicator that the income is going to start falling.

Table 9.2   A Healthy Income, but a Declining Rate of Growth

Year	Income	Income Growth	Rate of Growth
Year 1	$1,000,000	–	–
Year 2	$1,100,000	$100,000	10%
Year 3	$1,210,000	$110,000	10%
Year 4	$1,320,000	$110,000	9%
Year 5	$1,420,000	$100,000	7.5%

As you can see, although the growth is still good when expressed in dollar amounts, in this example between Years 3 and 5 the rate of growth falls by 25%. If this is your business, then this sort of fall is probably indicative that you are entering the mature phase of your career.

Take a look at Figure 9.5, and you will see that I have shown the figures in Table 9.2 graphically. Instead of showing the rate of growth figures, I have shown the change in the rate of growth, because this more clearly illustrates when a career may have started

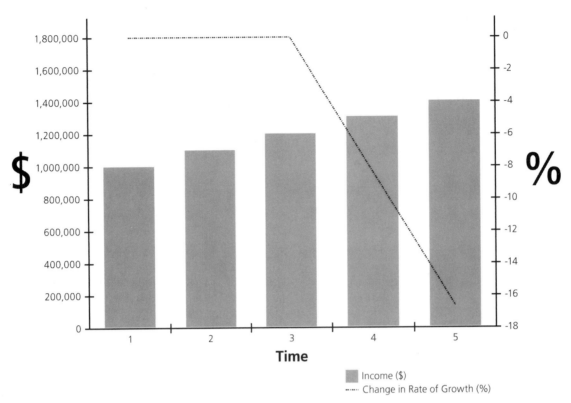

Figure 9.5 Although income is growing, the underlying rate of growth is declining. This is an indication that income may soon start to reduce (especially if expenses are not brought under control).

its downward path, even though the income is increasing (when taken in isolation), which could appear to suggest that everything is fine.

Maintenance Not Growth

When you have reached superstar status, there are a lot of things you can do that cost a lot of money. These massive investments usually can be rewarded with even larger inflows of income. When your income starts slowing, you need to stop spending money (or at least reduce your spending habit); otherwise, you will find yourself taking losses very quickly.

The main expenses you should start cutting and the main costs you should take control of are:

■ **Advertising.** When you are growing your career and at the peak of your career, advertising can be cost effective. However, advertising loses much of its effectiveness when you are on the downhill slope, because you will largely be appealing to an existing fan base (who want direct contact, not flashy public advertising).

Cutting your advertising because you're in a declining market will work as something of a self-fulfilling prophecy, so if you cut all public visibility, you will simply drop off the radar as far as many people are concerned. Therefore, you should aim to maximize your media coverage but minimize your spending.

- **Record-label costs.** If you enter into a deal with a record label, then the label will take a large chunk of the income. This is not unreasonable provided the record label is selling lots of albums for you. However, when sales start to slow, you may find it becomes more efficient to change the nature of your deal or to release your own albums (subject to any deal with the label being negotiable or expiring).

- **People.** Superstars tend to surround themselves with lots of "people." Unless these people have a function that directly contributes to your income, you should end their employment relationship with you.

- **Infrastructure.** While you are growing, it is logical to include some slack in your infrastructure to allow some growth. This is a prudent business practice. When the business is contracting, slack equates to waste, so the efficiency of the infrastructure should be improved.

Publishing Income

You will notice that so far in this chapter, I haven't mentioned one significant source of income: publishing. There are several reasons for this, but the main one is that the time to get a publishing deal (if you are going to get one) will be very dependent on your business and your personal needs.

If you are a death-metal band, then it is unlikely that you would expect many other people to cover your songs, so you may feel that it is not worth the expense of paying someone to search out covers. For this reason, you may want to keep your publishing. That being said, there are probably many opportunities for a death-metal band to have their music synchronized to video, and a publisher may be able to seek out these opportunities.

By the time you reach the end of your career peak, you should have created a reasonably large body of work. When you are on your way down, you need to look for as many opportunities as possible to keep exploiting this music. One of the best ways is through publishing, in terms of both covers and synchronization to various media.

You could find there will be many more opportunities to synchronize your music to video. For instance:

- There will be times when your style/sound fits the time period covered by the video (in the same way that sometimes you need a track from the '60s).

- There will be programs about you, your generation, and your genre.

- There will be times when a particular track is thematically right. (For instance, there are some times when the only track that is right is Elton John's "Sorry Seems to be the Hardest Word.") With a larger catalog, you will have many more chances of hitting these "everyman"-type themes.

When you're past your career peak, the discipline of the early years and the ruthless focus on picking up all of the small amounts of money should come back to you. (Indeed, I hope it never goes away.) These synchronization opportunities may not earn much money when looked at in isolation, but if you add them all together—particularly if you are taking a global approach—you will see that they can generate a healthy income.

Other Sources of Income

As well as looking at publishing, you'll have to find ways to make your assets (that is, your existing recordings) work harder for you. Most of these options are likely to have been followed by any record company (if you signed to one). You should still consider these options if possible:

- Reissue the back catalog at a cut price or with new features (for instance, a remastered version).

- Issue a "Best Of" or other retrospective-type album.

- Include your music on compilation albums.

- Mine the archives for interesting but previously unreleased recordings.

You should be careful not to ignore the other sources of income that are open to you:

- You can still release new albums. However, at this stage in your career, you are likely to sell less than you did at your peak. This doesn't mean you have to make less profit; it just means you have to manage your costs more closely.

- New albums usually create an opportunity to tour. At this stage in your career, you should have a large, loyal following who still want to see you, provided you are making your gigs a real event. Remember that when you reach this stage of your career, your fan base is likely to have aged in the same way that you have. With age, most people get more discerning and will have higher expectations from a gig. They will also be prepared to pay more money, so you will probably find that gigs can become incredibly profitable.

- Unless you have a really strong brand image, merchandise may become less of a significant source of income, but you should still look after this source, because it could continue to generate healthy chunks of income.

And to Conclude

I started this book with the assertion that it has never been so easy to have a career in music, and I stand by that assertion.

However, I'm sure you know countless talented musicians for whom a music career has not happened. Unfortunately, in all but a few cases, the failure is down to the musician—with a strategy and some dedication, he or she could have made a living making music.

The strategy is simple:

- Find people, convert them into fans, and find a way to turn those fans into a source of income.

- Create products that are wanted by your fan base, and keep creating products.

- Continue to nurture and expand your fan base.

It's that straightforward (and also that complicated, since it presupposes you have a musical talent).

The hard bit is implementing the strategy in practice—in other words, making music—but hopefully that's also the most enjoyable part.

Now stop reading and go make some music.

Index

Like the Book?

Let us know on Facebook or Twitter!

facebook.com/courseptr

twitter.com/courseptr

s, events and more!